Crime, Community and Morality

Political leaders and the popular press tell us that society is in the grip of a moral crisis. 'Where have our values gone?' our newspapers scream at us. 'Benefit scroungers', 'greedy bankers', 'intrusive journalists', 'have-a-go rioters', political scandals and criminals of all shapes and sizes are continually cited as evidence that we live in a modern-day Gomorrah. Criminologists have studied this in several ways, including: media representations of crime, mass incarceration, hooliganism and the exercise of power and control through communities.

What criminologists have not studied is the place of *morality* in shaping public debate about understanding crime and how this then shapes crime control strategies. Rather than dismiss statements about community breakdown, 'broken society' and irresponsibility as ideological, self-justificatory rhetoric, what happens when we take these claims seriously? What do they tell us about the causes of crime? How do they shape the crime control agenda? How else might we begin to understand and explain the relationship between crime and society?

Navigating between criminological concerns about control and governance and social theories about culture and identity, this book explores what is meant by crime, community and morality and puts this meaning to the test. Discussion of a new theory of rule-breaking, combined with an analysis of how our justice system is becoming maladapted, makes this essential reading for criminologists around the globe, as well as those general readers interested in the causes of crime.

Simon Green is a Lecturer in Criminology at the University of Hull. He teaches and researches in the areas of restorative justice, crime and politics, criminological theory and reducing reoffending.

Routledge Studies in Crime and Society

1. **Sex Work**
   Labour, mobility and sexual services
   Edited by JaneMaree Maher, Sharon Pickering and Alison Gerard

2. **State Crime and Resistance**
   Edited by Elizabeth Stanley and Jude McCulloch

3. **Collective Morality and Crime in the Americas**
   Christopher Birkbeck

4. **Talking Criminal Justice**
   Language and the just society
   Michael J. Coyle

5. **Women Exiting Prison**
   Critical essays on gender, post-release support and survival
   Bree Carlton and Marie Segrave

6. **Collective Violence, Democracy and Protest Policing**
   David R. Mansley

7. **Prostitution in the Community**
   Attitudes, action and resistance
   Sarah Kingston

8. **Surveillance, Capital and Resistance**
   Michael McCahill and Rachel L. Finn

9. **Crime, Community and Morality**
   Simon Green

In *Crime, Community and Morality*, Simon Green offers a searching and searing critical examination of discourses about moral decline and the loss of community – discourses that have decisively shaped the direction taken by criminal justice and crime control policies in recent decades. In place of this exhausted paradigm, Green offers a nuanced and theoretically rich account of the role that morality and emotions play in our responses to crime and points the way towards a new and different language of crime control that speaks to our post-traditional age. This book is essential reading for criminologists and for all those concerned with the future of criminal justice.

Professor Majid Yar, University of Hull, UK

Over the last few decades, "community decline" (variously defined) has been deployed as a catch-all explanation for crime, immorality, and a fast-diminishing sense of social responsibility. Typically, these accounts either slather the concept of community with a revanchist moral agenda or, worse still, entirely misunderstand how communities function and, thus, how they might serve as a locus of crime control or order maintenance. Simon Green's new book provides an excellent and much-needed corrective to this long history of mischaracterization and confusion. Clear-sighted, crisply written, and theoretically accessible, it drives a coach and horses through existing thinking in this area and, by doing so, kick-starts the debate about how to re-theorize the community–crime link for the twenty-first century.

Professor Keith Hayward, University of Kent, UK

This is a timely and significant text. Green's work is particularly praiseworthy for its scholarly and accessible coverage of the all too often neglected significance of the moral and political debate around community and crime for students of criminology. In particular, this book provides us with a comprehensive synthesis of existing scholarship arising out of the encounters between social science and moral and political philosophy. All in all, it is a pleasing antidote to the all too prevalent narrow, "administrative" conceptions of the contemporary criminological enterprise.

Gordon Hughes, Chair in Criminology, Cardiff University, UK

Crime, Community and Morality

Simon Green

Routledge
Taylor & Francis Group

LONDON AND NEW YORK

First published 2014
by Routledge
2 Park Square, Milton Park, Abingdon, Oxfordshire OX14 4RN

and by Routledge
711 Third Avenue, New York, NY 10017

First issued in paperback 2015

Routledge is an imprint of the Taylor & Francis Group, an informa business

British Library Cataloguing in Publication Data
A catalogue record for this book is available from the British Library

Library of Congress Cataloging-in-Publication Data
Green, Simon (Simon T.)
  Crime, community and morality / Simon Green.
  pages cm. — (Routledge studies in crime and society)
  1. Crime—Sociological aspects. 2. Communities. 3. Crime prevention. I. Title.
  HV6025.G7236 2014
  364—dc23
  2013037528

ISBN13: 978-1-138-12031-0 (pbk)
ISBN13: 978-0-415-62767-2 (hbk)

Typeset in Times New Roman
by Swales & Willis Ltd, Exeter, Devon

For Nicola

Contents

List of illustrations xii
Preface xiii
Acknowledgements xiv

Introduction 1

1 Crime and the community 9

Community decline and the rise of crime 10
Community as agent: community policing and neighbourhood watch 17
Community as locus: offenders in the community 22
Community as beneficiary: crime prevention and community safety 25
A new philosophy of crime control: from taking part to taking
 responsibility 28
The community governance of crime 30
Conclusion: the magic of community 35
References 37

2 Punishment and the community 41

The public spectacle of punishment 42
The rise of the rehabilitative ideal 46
The growth of diversions from custody 48
Tough on crime and populist punitiveness 52
Engendering responsibility for crime control 59
From state to citizen: the case of restorative justice 62
Conclusion: governance, responsibility and *morality 67*
References 69

3 Community, ideology and utopia 74

Communitarianism and the ideas of Amitai Etzioni 75
Devolving justice: from government to governance 78

*Governing through communities: advanced liberalism and
    governmentality 81*
*Assumptions and tensions in communitarian thinking about
    community 86*
The conflation of moral philosophy with moral authoritarianism 89
Conclusion: community as utopian, or dystopian? 94
References 96

4   The politics of moral degeneration   99

From Butskellism to broken Britain: a new political consensus? 100
New Labour: rights, responsibilities and social inclusion 109
*Making sense of the New Labour project: moral conservatism and
    the third way 114*
The values of the Big Society 117
Conclusion: crime, immorality and a time machine 120
References 121

5   Getting a sense of community   126

Defining community 127
Theorising community: tradition and modernity 129
Theorising community: the collapse of stability 135
Community, neighbourhood and crime control 138
Conclusion: the community as crime control? 147
References 148

6   Late-modernity, insecurity and identity   152

Modernity, late-modernity and postmodernity 153
The conditions of late-modernity 156
Disembedding social relations 160
Anthony Giddens, identity and ontological insecurity 164
Ulrich Beck, the risk society and individualisation 166
Zygmunt Bauman, the consumer society and dystopia 169
*Points of divergence and convergence within discourses on
    late-modernity 173*
Late-modernity and communitarianism as irreconcilable 175
Conclusion: a requiem for community? 178
References 179

7 Community, or intimacy? 181

High walls and frightened rabbits: crime, fear and segregation 183
Thin theories of criminality: declining community and rising
 immorality 190
Authenticity and risk-taking: towards a theory of rule-breaking 194
Maladapted justice: the cultural and emotional framing of
 punishment 201
Conclusion: the logic of emotion 207
References 210

Conclusion 214

Index 223

Illustrations

Tables

1.1 Distinguishing local government and community governance: focus orientation and technique   32
1.2 Comparing crime prevention through local (police) government and through community governance: focus, orientation and technique   33

Figures

4.1 Liberty, equality and community in contemporary British political debates   117
7.1 The vicious cycle of communitarianism   189

Box

6.1 The characteristics of late-modernity   174

Preface

What is a Preface for? I'm not entirely sure but I am working on the assumption it's for a short personal statement about the book and why I have written it. I wrote this book because I wanted to demonstrate that immorality and community decline (as aspects of each other) are poor explanations for crime, and trying to rebuild them will not help to reduce crime or improve society. In making this argument, I have tried very hard not to slip into unconscious value judgements. My analysis is not driven by a particular personal ideology or political position. To be honest, I don't have one. I am ambivalent about most political and criminal justice questions, in the sense that I usually find myself caught between two opposite positions and end up frustrated and in the middle. A kind of ideological constipation. This is not to say that I am naïve enough to think research can ever be entirely neutral, but by dint of both my own values and a sense of intellectual endeavour, the argument in this book is not driven by value-judgements but by a careful weighing of coherence and evidence.

In this book, I have tried to avoid three things. One, I have striven to avoid being caught in an endless ideological tug-of-war. This convinces few except those who have already taken a side. Consequently these sorts of debates often feel like preaching to the choir. Two, there is quite a lot of theory in this book and I have tried very hard to avoid using too much jargon, too many neologisms, too many Latin or French phrases. Impenetrable writing is pointless writing. Three, I have tried to avoid being critical without being able to offer something new. So, whilst this book seeks to provide a critique of what I argue is becoming the dominant explanation for the crime problem, it also seeks, in Chapter 7, to provide an alternative. By focusing on rule-breaking, emotions and self-identity, I hope I have at least contributed to a different frame of reference that goes beyond what I see as the dual dangers of criminology. On the one hand, to simply 'buy' into governmental constructions of the crime problem is the equivalent of intellectually flatlining, whilst, on the other hand, to simply 'buy' into a counter-construction is, in fact, just an alternative governmental logic that is not currently represented in the political system. I have read Orwell's (1945) *Animal Farm* and it doesn't end prettily. No one wants to see a pig in charge.

Simon Green
July 2013
Humberside

Acknowledgements

This is my first monograph, so there are quite a lot of people who need to be acknowledged. For the sake of both gravitas and brevity, I shall do my best to refrain from my usual silliness. Sorry.

First, I'd like to thank all of my colleagues, past and present, at the Centre for Criminology and Criminal Justice (CCCJ) at the University of Hull. However, special thanks must go to Helen Johnston, Louise Sturgeon-Adams and Peter Young for being good friends over many years. (Though I think they know they're the lucky ones.) Second, I'd like to thank Keith Hayward, Gordon Hughes, Gerry Johnstone and Majid Yar for reading earlier versions of this book and for not laughing; at least not to my face. Third, thanks to Clive Coleman for encouraging me to do a doctorate and to him, Keith Bottomley, Adrian James and Clive Norris for helping me at the start of my academic life. They may be to blame. Fourth, to Mike McCahill, Iain Brennan and Adam Calverley for not telling me to go away when I knocked on their office doors for a chat. Even when they were clearly in the middle of something. Fifth, to the editorial staff at Routledge for their professionalism and advice along the way, though it's left me with nothing witty to say about them. Sixth, to the editors of the *British Journal of Community Justice*, Palgrave Macmillan and Taylor and Francis for kindly allowing me to use material first published with them in Chapters 3 and 4. Though not much. Honest.

Introduction

Political leaders and the popular press tell us that society is in the grip of a moral crisis. 'Where have our values gone?' our newspapers scream at us. 'Benefit scroungers', 'greedy bankers', 'intrusive journalists', 'have-a-go rioters', political scandals and criminals of all shapes and sizes are continually cited as evidence that we live in a modern-day Gomorrah.

Criminologists have studied the media representations of crime and deviance (Cohen 1987); they have studied the neo-liberal politics that has led to mass incarceration (Wacquant 2009); and they have studied how governments increasingly exercise power and control through communities (Simon 2007). What they have not studied is the place of *morality* in shaping public debate about understanding crime and how this then shapes crime control strategies. Rather than dismiss statements about community breakdown, 'broken society' and irresponsibility as ideological, self-justificatory rhetoric, what happens when we take these claims seriously? What do they tell us about the causes of crime? How do they shape the crime control agenda? How else might we begin to understand and explain the relationship between crime and society?

Navigating between criminological concerns about control and governance, and social theories about culture and identity, this book explores what is meant by crime, community and morality, and puts this meaning to the test. What emerges is a nostalgic urge to return to a previous halcyon age of safety and security (cf. Pearson 1983). But this world no longer exists and trying to recreate it threatens the freedoms, choices and lifestyles that we have come to expect as part of living in an advanced liberal democracy. Instead, this book aims to find a way of embracing the sweaty, emotive, and ultimately intimate, aspects of crime and punishment that give voice to the educative, performative and expressive qualities of both crime and punishment. With this in mind, a new theory of rule-breaking combined with an analysis of how our justice system has become maladapted is discussed. The way forward is to trust in people more, to give them a greater say and greater role in sentencing and punishment and to engage with, not reject, culture, identity and consumer society.

To start thinking about these questions, this book begins by examining the concept of community in relation to crime and crime control. Since the mid-1970s there has been a strong political association between criminality and the breakdown of community and responsibility. The basis of this claim is carefully explored to chart its emergence and to assess its implications for how both criminality and community are understood.

What emerges from this analysis is a convergence of social theory and political values that presents both community decline and rising crime as the consequence of increasing immorality. This convergence centres on the work of American sociologist Amitai Etzioni (1995), who asserted that social problems are caused by an imbalance between rights and responsibilities in society. Etzioni (1995) argued that American society has become overly concerned with individual rights at the expense of collective responsibilities. Crime is seen as one consequent social problem, and Etzioni's (1995) answer to this problem is to rebuild civil society by rebuilding strong communities from which a new moral consensus will emerge.

Etzioni's (1995) ideas found significant support from both the Clinton administration in the USA and the Blair administration in the UK (Driver and Martell 1998). In the UK the birthing of New Labour in the mid-1990s was lent further intellectual credence by sociologist Anthony Giddens (1998), who sought to build a strong intellectual base for the emerging social democracy of New Labour. Key to Giddens' (1998) work was an attempt to link the conditions of contemporary society to New Labour's embryonic social democratic doctrine. Both Etzioni's (1995) and Giddens' (1998) work unashamedly seeks to engage with, and influence the direction of, centre-left politics on both sides of the Atlantic. Similarly, both lend sociological weight to a modernising Labour Party intent on moving beyond its socialist roots to occupy a more secure middle ground that is simultaneously comfortable with market economics and with the role of government in providing a notion of the collective good.

New Labour therefore developed a credo that was sociologically aware of trends towards globalisation, information technologies and individualism and used these trends to justify internal party reform. In response to the threat presented by these trends, New Labour drew on the communitarian philosophies of Etzioni (1995) that aim to rebuild civil society by reinvesting citizens with a sense of their social responsibilities as well as their individual rights. Community is the vehicle by which this new moral investment is to be achieved and crime, as a compelling social and cultural symbol of selfish disinterest in the well-being of others, becomes a natural bedfellow for such a philosophy.

The Blairite mantra of 'no rights without responsibilities' resonates powerfully with communitarianism and is clearly evident in both the 1997 and 2001 Labour Manifestos, which link strong communities to low crime. A moralising tone extolling the virtues of community, family and civic responsibility emerged from Cabinet government and combined with a legislative reform package that attempted to inculcate wider responsibilities across society for crime and its prevention (Gilling 2007). An overhaul of the youth justice system, including the introduction of new civil orders to deal with poor parenting, truancy and anti-social behaviour, are all indicative of the translation of this moralising rhetoric into practice. More recently, the Respect Task Force (2006) and the Casey Report (2008) continue this theme of responsibility, community and crime.

Since the formation of the Coalition government in 2010 these themes have morphed into a new political language and set of policies. However, 'broken Britain' and the 'Big Society' retain the same understanding of the crime problem and continue to cite immorality and irresponsibility in the context of community decline. In particular, a strong sense of individual choice combined with socially conservative values can be witnessed across all governments since 1979. Consequently community, family and responsibility become synonymous with explanations of criminality, and crime control strategies are then understood as ways of rebuilding these social values and institutions.

Moreover, there is significant criminological research that would appear to support this relationship. From the work of the Chicago School of sociology in the 1930s through to the more recent environmental criminology and crime prevention literature, an association between community decline and high crime is well established. Yet there is an important difference between the criminological and the New Labour notion of community decline. The criminological perspective invariably focuses on community decline in terms of deprivation, disadvantage and urban decay. However, despite drawing on the same concepts, the political approach seems more premised on the belief that community is in decline because people have become self-interested and lost their sense of civic obligation. In place of social responsibility, immorality (or at least amorality) rises to create a tsunami of social ills. Divorce, teenage pregnancy, truancy, binge-drinking, obesity, anti-social behaviour, benefit scroungers, corporate greed, tabloid invasions of privacy and all manner of criminality are all seen as compelling examples of this moral turpitude. Thus, the logic of the political values that underscore the relationship between community and crime is that crime is a consequence of moral decline that manifests itself in the decline of community. This is quite unlike the criminological perspective that explains community decline in terms of disadvantage and disorganisation (Hope and Shaw 1988).

This disjunction is arguably the archetype of a much wider criminological dilemma that is rooted in what Young (1997) has called the crisis of aetiology. Up until the 1970s the established criminological wisdom was that high crime could be understood in terms of deprivation and inequality. Yet, with the uncomfortable realisation that both standards of living and rates of crime grew considerably in the post-war period, this explanation increasingly lacked credibility. Coupled with the abject failure to affect the crime rate by bolstering the powers and size of the criminal justice system, there was also a broad political quandary about how the problem of crime should be addressed. What emerged in the run-up to the 1979 election was an increasingly more punitive language of punishment that is often held as being at least partly responsible for Margaret Thatcher's landslide victory. From this point on criminological theories that located the causes of crime in the structure of society and that either explicitly or implicitly called for social policy responses to offending increasingly found themselves out of favour with the direction of both Conservative and New Labour governments.

Thus, whilst a good deal of criminological theory still sought to explore the relationship between social circumstances and crime, these perspectives were increasingly losing ground to those that located the causes of crime in the individual and situational circumstances that explained why a particular crime was committed in a particular place (see, for example, Felson 2002 or Smith and Cornish 2003). This arguably reflects a wider political and ideological shift away from social welfarism and towards neo-liberalism. The politics of the New Right dominated during the Thatcher and Reagan administrations of the 1980s and marked an overt change in the political vogue, away from explanations of crime that were located in social conditions and toward those located in an individual's disposition. Instead of central government having to take political responsibility for the crime rate, it was passed back to the individual offender who had, by dint of personal failing or unhappy circumstance, turned to a life of crime.

This perspective demands that if the causes of crime cannot be saliently explained in terms of inequality and disadvantage, then perhaps they can be explained in terms of individual pathology and situational opportunity. Crime prevention and community safety strategies emerged to address the situational opportunity, whilst a combination of cognitive-behaviour programmes and risk-management strategies emerged to deal with controlling dangerous groups through the use of cognitive behaviour and technological tools to alter behaviour (Feeley and Simon 1992). In this context political rhetoric increasingly turns to proselytising about immorality and irresponsibility, and a growing public punitiveness inevitably emerges in response to a pervasive cultural blueprint of the criminal that is largely based on fear about their predatory and dangerously unstable nature (Garland 2000). This combination of increasing technologies of control and increasing moral outrage typifies contemporary penal and political strategies about crime (Laster and O'Malley 1996).

In this climate, community decline becomes emblematic of the insecurity and immorality that people associate with high crime. Fuelled by a toxic combination of political denunciation and public fears about crime, community assumes a totemic cultural significance as both the explanation for high crime and the logical response to them. If crime is caused by immorality, and community decline is a manifestation of growing immorality, then community must be the active ingredient for combating crime. When viewed in this context community is imbued with both the capacity and responsibility for reducing and controlling crime. As such, the community has been responsibilised (Garland 1996) for crime. This conception of the community's function is underscored by the moral conservatism so evident both in Etzioni's (1995) communitarianism and in New Labour (Hughes 1996) and Coalition (Bochel 2011) rhetoric and policy. This trend further resonates with wider sociological and criminological discourses on governmentality (Garland 1997) and community governance (Crawford 1997, Johnston and Shearing 2003, Hughes 2007).

What becomes apparent is that this community represents a complex intersection of sociological, criminological and political meaning. This is not a neutral conception of community but one vested with ideological and normative meanings that are distinctively different from earlier conceptions of community. The values that drive this particular construction of community have largely ignored the wider social, technological and cultural transformations that were brought about by the onset of modernity and which signalled the beginning-of-the-end for traditional forms of community life. It will be argued that this crucial failing in both the communitarian thinking and the associated political doctrines leads to an ill-advised and ultimately counter-productive pursuit of a homogeneous community life in which people feel safe and crime isn't a major problem. This is a place that conjures nostalgic images of a bygone golden age where no one had to lock their doors and everybody got on. Instead of achieving this utopian imagining, the dissonance between the social conditions that led to the erosion of traditional community in the first place and the politically driven attempt to reinvent it will leave those who are either unable or unwilling to assimilate into this new moral order both disenfranchised and outcast.

It is therefore the contention of this book that a new conception of community is being utilised in relation to crime control. The aim is to explore what is different about this conception of community from others and to explore the political and ideological underpinnings that shape it. The objective is to mount a comprehensive critique of this community, with a view to repudiating and discrediting the very basis on which it rests. In its place a more sociologically and culturally nuanced framework for thinking about and interpreting crime will be presented. Drawing on a combination of Anthony Giddens' (1991) work on modernity and identity and Stephen Lyng's (1990) concept of 'edgework', this book will conclude with a framework for understanding criminality that is based on the search for an authentic identity through which individuals can achieve some sense of existential security in a turbulent and insecure world.

The book therefore operates at the level of political analysis and social theory. The aim is to demonstrate the impact of communitarian thought on contemporary politics, public explanations for criminality and crime control by exploring the statements and published opinion of some of the key political architects of the last forty years: academic research from the worlds of social policy, criminology and political science, and the relevant legislation and policies that have been introduced over this period. The purpose of this exploration is to build a picture of the communitarian influence on politics so that it can then be exposed as an exercise in futility when viewed through a late-modern lens; futile because of its flawed understanding about the nature and causes of crime, and futile because its remedies are consequently unrealisable and potentially counter-productive. In sum, this book aims to locate and critique the prevailing ideological explanation that increasingly underpins both cultural and political understandings of crime. Whilst there are other influences, the contention is that, within the crime control arena, communitarian thinking resonates particularly strongly with recent political rhetoric and policies. This then begins to form a uniting narrative that, regardless of competing perspectives within the system, begins to co-ordinate and co-opt both attitudes and practices about criminality.

What this book is not is an attempt to argue that recent political values have been exclusively shaped by communitarianism, or that its crime control policies are directed with only one purpose. Where I have sought to use community safety and restorative justice as examples of the communitarian agenda, the suggestion is not that these were pioneered or practised by moral authoritarians but that there is a significant confluence between their underpinning logics and that espoused by communitarianism. Hence the popularity of both can be understood in terms of their compatibility with the New Labour and Coalition governments and their wider political perspectives about personal and collective responsibility for crime control. Neither is this book an attempt to develop a normative critique of communitarianism. There is no counter-claim extolling the virtues of some other communitarian model and it does not object to Etzioni's (1995) communitarianism on the grounds that it is ideological. Whilst there is some discussion of the potential dangers inherent in the communitarian and New Labour perspective, these flow out of the sociological critique of its viability, not vice versa.

To this end Chapter 1 begins with an overview of the various ways in which criminological theory has used community to explain offending, before drawing on Nelken's (1985) categorisation of community as agent, locus and beneficiary to explore how community has traditionally been employed within the criminal justice system. This chapter ends with a tentative suggestion that community governance begins to signpost a shift in responsibility for crime control. Chapter 2 continues on a similar track by looking at the relationship between community and punishment. Drawing on public execution and torture, this chapter begins with a consideration of the role of the crowd in the delivery of punishment before charting the various watershed changes in community punishments and how they reflect underpinning political and ideological trends. The purpose of this analysis is to plot the move towards communities becoming involved in the delivery of punishment, and to establish the relationship between political direction and penal reform. This chapter ends by arguing that a new strategy of bifurcation is emerging; one which separates harsh punishment and just deserts from responsibilisation and community governance.

Chapter 3 looks in more detail at the ideas of Etzioni's (1995) communitarianism alongside discussion of strategies of governance, advanced liberalism and the devolution of responsibility for crime control. The chapter then continues with a critique of the communitarian concept of community and the problems associated with the communitarian conflation of moral philosophy with its own agenda. This chapter ends by arguing that communitarianism contains both normative and instrumental logics that contain both assumptions and tensions that are as yet unanswered. Chapter 4 continues by demonstrating the relationship between political values since the mid-1970s and explanations of criminality and associated social policy responses. Arguing that a new political consensus understands crime as a consequence of declining morality, this chapter charts New Labour and Coalition rhetoric and policy about moral degeneration. This then establishes the grounds on which the central argument of this book is premised: that public explanations of and responses to criminality are driven by a sense that community, meaning morality, has declined.

Chapter 5 then considers the meanings and theories of community, before analysing the use of community in research and policy about crime control. The overall conclusion of this chapter demonstrates the problems inherent in the communitarian vision of community revitalisation and sets the ground for Chapter 6, which is concerned with outlining the conditions of late-modernity and their incompatibility with communitarian thinking. This dissonance highlights the problems intrinsic in the communitarian vision and paints this vision as fanciful and misguided; utopian scale that dwarfs even Marx's vision of a communist revolution.

Finally, Chapter 7 attempts to demonstrate the futility of community in understanding crime at all. Beginning with a discussion of Caldeira's (2000) ethnography of São Paolo, the urban experience of fear and segregation is considered in relation to the conditions of high-crime societies (Garland 2000). This is then used to build a critique of explanations of crime rooted in either community decline or immorality. The chapter then presents an alternative framework for thinking about crime and punishment that is based on the search for self-identity, self-actualisation and intimacy. Drawing on an emergent cultural criminology, the chapter concludes that highlighting the cultural meaning attached to criminal acts also suggests that a similar lens might usefully be applied to criminal justice and punishment. In doing so this chapter and the book end by calling into question the very basis on which penal decision making is able to meet the cultural demands of late-modern society.

References

Bochel, H. (2011) Conservative Approaches to Social Policy since 1997, in H. Bochel (ed.) *The Conservative Party and Social Policy*, Bristol: Policy Press.

Caldeira, T.P.R. (2000) *City of Walls: Crime, Segregation and Citizenship in São Paulo*, London: University of California Press.

Casey, L. (2008) *Engaging Communities in Fighting Crime*, Independent Report for Crime and Communities Review, London: Cabinet Office.

Cohen, S. (1987) *Folk Devils and Moral Panics* (2nd rev. edn), London: Wiley-Blackwell.

Crawford, A. (1997) *The Local Governance of Crime, Appeals to Community and Partnership*, Oxford: Clarendon Press.

Driver, S. and Martell, L. (1998) *New Labour: Politics after Thatcherism*, Cambridge: Polity Press.

Etzioni, A. (1995) *The Spirit of Community: Rights, Responsibilities and the Communitarian Agenda*, Hammersmith: Fontana Press.

Feeley, M. and Simon, J. (1992) The New Penology: Notes on the Emerging Strategy of Corrections and Its Implications, *Criminology*, 30 (4): 452–74.

Felson, M. (2002) *Crime and Everyday Life* (3rd edn), London: Sage.

Garland, D. (1996) The Limits of the Sovereign State, *British Journal of Criminology*, 36 (4): 445–71.

Garland, D. (1997) Governmentality and the Problem of Crime: Foucault, Criminology, Sociology, *Theoretical Criminology*, 1 (2): 173–214.

Garland, D. (2000) The Culture of High Crime Societies: Some Preconditions of Recent 'Law and Order' Policies, *British Journal of Criminology*, 40 (3): 347–75.

Giddens, A. (1991) *Modernity and Self Identity: Self and Society in the Late Modern Age*, Cambridge: Polity Press.

Giddens, A. (1998) *The Third Way, the Renewal of Social Democracy*, Cambridge: Polity Press.

Gilling, D. (2007) *Crime Reduction and Community Safety: Labour and the Politics of Local Crime Control*, Cullompton: Willan.

Hope, T. and Shaw, M. (eds) (1988) *Communities and Crime Reduction*, London: HMSO.

Hughes, G. (1996) Communitarianism and Law and Order, *Critical Social Policy*, 16 (4): 17–42.

Hughes, G. (2007) *The Politics of Crime and Community*, Basingstoke: Palgrave Macmillan.

Johnston, L. and Shearing, C. (2003) *The Governance of Security: Explorations in Policing and Justice*, London: Routledge.

Laster, K. and O'Malley, P. (1996) Sensitive New-Age Laws: The Reassertion of Emotionality in Law, *International Journal of the Sociology of Law*, 24 (1): 21–40.

Lyng, S. (1990) Edgework: A Social Psychological Analysis of Voluntary Risk Taking, *The American Journal of Sociology*, 95 (4): 851–86.

Nelken, D. (1985) Community Involvement in Crime Control, *Current Legal Problem*, 38: 239–67.

Pearson, G. (1983) *Hooligan: A History of Respectable Fears*, Basingstoke: Palgrave Macmillan.

Respect Task Force (2006) *Respect Action Plan*, London: Home Office.

Simon, J. (2007) *Governing through Crime: How the War on crime Transformed American Democracy and Created a Culture of Fear*, Oxford: Oxford University Press.

Smith, M.J. and Cornish, D.B. (eds) (2003) *Theory for Practice in Situational Crime Prevention*, Monsey, NY: Criminal Justice Press.

Wacquant, L. (2009) *Punishing the Poor*, London: Duke University Press.

Young, J. (1997) Left Realist Criminology: Radical in Its Analysis, Realist in Its Policy, in M. Maguire, R. Morgan and R. Reiner (eds) *The Oxford Handbook of Criminology* (2nd edn), Oxford: Oxford University Press.

1   Crime and the community

Community has for a long time been closely linked to discussions about crime and criminal justice, yet it has been viewed with a degree of suspicion by many criminologists in recent years who have warned us about the ambiguity of the concept (Hope and Shaw 1988, Lacey and Zedner 1995, Crawford 1997, Shapland 2008). The concept of community is not an easy one to define. It often conceals any one of a number of different ideological as well as descriptive meanings and is often used without an appreciation of these variations. This has never been truer than in the field of criminal justice.

> There is a crucial and central ambiguity in the arguments of many of those who recommend further community involvement in the control of crime. It is left unclear (perhaps deliberately) whether community is being proposed as a means to an end, i.e. as a new resource for tackling the problem of crime, or whether the creation of better community feeling is itself the end which is being pursued.
>
> (Nelken 1985: 239)

Nelken (1985) also goes on to suggest that the call for increasing community involvement conceals the political Right's desire to utilise public support for law and order policies and the Left's aspirations to empower communities as a forum for challenging existing institutions and hierarchies.

Concerns about the political and social meaning of community form a crucial component within this book and the aim of this chapter is to provide an overview of the criminological research about crime and community. The purpose of this is to begin to disentangle the differing interpretations of community and the claims made about its relationship to criminality. However, the primary aim is to provide a comprehensive overview of the growth and development of the concept of community within criminological theory and criminal justice practice. There are two main reasons for this. Firstly, to illustrate the types of ideas and activities that have incorporated a notion of community, and secondly, to distinguish between those ideas and activities that are the concern of this book and those that are not.

In an effort to achieve these goals the chapter is split into three broad sections. The first looks at the relationship between community decline and crime, focusing on social disorganisation, the Chicago School and environmental criminology more generally. The second considers the intersection of community and criminal justice. This is split into three further sections that roughly correspond to Nelken's (1985) categorisation of community as agent, locus and beneficiary. Third, the discussion then begins to look at the mobilising community as offering a distinctive ideological and political approach to crime and criminality that, whilst containing elements of all of the other approaches discussed, is unique insofar as it is primarily focused on devolving responsibility for crime control from the state to its citizenry

Presenting these themes in such neat bundles is potentially dangerous, as it implies a coherency to such strategies as it glosses over the often inconsistent and contradictory perspectives that punctuate both theory and practice. Drawing on Cohen's (1985) work, Crawford (1997) succinctly summarises this danger:

> By reducing history to neat dichotomies, lines of development or 'master' tendencies, there is an inclination to highlight and caricature historical difference and change at the expense of identifying significant continuities.
>
> (Crawford 1997: 15)

As Crawford (1997) states, it would be incorrect to view the somewhat artificial categorisation of trends as definitive break points in the progression of ideas. This is certainly true of the inclusion of community into criminological theory and criminal justice practice. Yet this chapter will conclude by arguing that a new perspective has emerged. Whilst environmental criminology might use community decline to explain criminality and whilst criminal justice policy might deploy community in a range of different fields, mobilising community treats community as both the cause of crime and the means for addressing it. Not just in terms of a passive understanding of community as environment or community as location, but community as a group of people sharing common interests and values, taking responsibility for both the causes of criminality and the means of controlling it. This, it shall be argued, is based on a very particular political and ideological perspective that has gathered momentum since the mid-1990s and which will be both explored and critiqued in detail throughout this book.

Community decline and the rise of crime

Some of the earliest criminological studies that brought the concept of community to the fore argued that high levels of crime could be explained by a corresponding decline in community. Although this observation developed out of research conducted in the United States there has been significant work on the spatial and temporal distributions of crime on both sides of the Atlantic. This section attempts to plot these ideas and to show how they came to the conclusion that there is a correlation between low levels of community organisation and high levels of crime. This approach can be broadly classified as environmental criminology (Brantingham and Brantingham 1981, Bottoms and Wiles 1997).

Alongside this approach is subcultural theory, which attempts to link the spatial clustering of crime to the growth of alternative norms and values that foster criminal and anti-social attitudes and behaviour. Both this and environmental criminology represent the first attempts to explore the relationship between community and crime, and both link what Hope and Shaw (1988) have referred to as community 'disorganisation' and 'disadvantage' to the crime rate.

The focus of this section is necessarily restrictive. The purpose is to show how these early perspectives sought to demonstrate the relationship between community and crime. It is not a review of all the available literature on environmental criminology and subcultural theory. Neither is it an attempt to discuss the merits and variations within these two schools of thought. Some important criticisms will be mentioned, but only when they have implications for the diagnosis of community decline as the cause of high crime. This is a review of community within the field of criminology, not of environmental criminology or subcultural theory.[1]

The origins of environmental criminology can be found in the work of Shaw and McKay (1942), who were members of Chicago University's School of Sociology. Based on a rich source of quantitative and qualitative empirical evidence, they asserted that crime was a result of a breakdown of community life. Using Burgess's (1925) concentric zone theory, they sought to explain why there were distinct concentrations of offenders in certain locations. Burgess's theory posited that the 'zone in transition' that surrounded the city of Chicago's Central Business District (CBD) was typified by a number of social conditions that led to high levels of 'social disorganisation'. Poor housing and the ever-increasing encroachment of the CBD, combined with waves of immigrants moving to the area, meant that the population of this area was constantly in transition. Those who accumulated enough resources sought to leave the 'zone in transition' for the more desirable residential zones further from the city centre. This meant that there was a regular population turnover and the only people who remained in the 'zone in transition' were those who could not afford to leave. Burgess believed that these social conditions weakened family and communal ties that bound people together and this led him to make the claim that such areas suffered from social disorganisation. Burgess and other members of the Chicago School linked this social disorganisation to high crime. Shaw and McKay's studies corroborated Burgess's ideas. Siegel (1995) describes social disorganisation as neighbourhoods in which:

> Residents are trying to leave at the earliest opportunity. Since residents are uninterested in community matters, the common sources of control – the family, school, business, community, social service agencies are weak and disorganised. Personal relationships are strained because neighbours are constantly moving and leaving. Constant resident turnover weakens communication and blocks attempts at solving neighbourhood problems or establishing common goals.

(Siegel 1995: 181)

Social disorganisation thus describes an economically and socially deprived neighbourhood that has at other times been referred to as the slum or the ghetto. This neighbourhood's population is so transitory that social institutions and the associated social cohesion that they bring do not properly develop, leaving the residents in a perpetual state of uneasiness and anxiety (Siegel 1995).[2]

In addition to Burgess's concentric zone theory and social disorganisation, Kornhauser (1978) noted that Shaw and McKay (1942) also believed that criminal values were transmitted in the 'zone in transition'. Based on observations from the life histories of juveniles, Shaw and McKay (1942) felt that disorganised neighbourhoods cultivated criminogenic values that were passed on to juveniles by older boys. It is this notion of shared criminogenic values that differ from the cultural norms of mainstream society that prompted the growth of literature on subcultures.

Shaw and McKay (1942) conclude three things. Firstly, that offenders tend to be concentrated in a particular area; secondly, that the communities in which they reside are typified by high levels of social disorganisation; and thirdly, that criminogenic attitudes flourish in such communities. These conclusions clearly show that a diagnosis has been made. High crime is due to the decline of community life. Yet community decline is understood in terms of poverty and its impact on social cohesion. Hence environmental criminology tends to think about high crime as a consequence of deprived communities and its conditions rather than high crime as a consequence of declining morality.

Before going on to outline how these ideas have proliferated, one important criticism of Shaw and McKay's (1942) work must be mentioned, as it has a bearing on later discussions of the relationship between community decline and high crime. This criticism is of their concept of social disorganisation. It has been suggested that criminality can, in many circumstances, stem from social organisations. Crawford (1998) describes this criticism:

> there is much criminological evidence to suggest that 'organised communities' are criminogenic, such as the Mafia (noticeably absent from Chicago School theory despite its heightened activity caused by the prohibition in Chicago of the 1920s and 1930s), criminal gangs, football hooligans and deviant subcultures.
>
> (Crawford 1998: 129)

In addition, the term 'social disorganisation' has been criticised for being overly deterministic in saying that certain locations lead to criminality and for failing to pay any attention to the distributions of power in society. David Matza (1964) reinforces the criticism by suggesting that social disorganisation can also be understood as diversity. Hence, social disorganisation also assumes an implicit value bias as to what constitutes disorganisation and denies the possibility that alternative legitimate or otherwise types of organisation may exist. Downes and Rock (2003) illustrate this point, distinguishing between the types of intra-social order that can be found in any neighbourhood, regardless of its level of deprivation or criminality, and intra-social disorganisation which compare a neighbourhood to the wider social order across a city or society:

> Social differentiation, a period of excited social change, or uneven develop-ment can exaggerate the instability of those relations, leading to strain and breakdown of local order. In turn, particular worlds can become dislocated, thrown up out of their context and exposed. They can achieve a social and moral independence which some sociologists have chosen to emphasize.
>
> (Downes and Rock 2003: 67)

This hints at the relationship between slum life and the formation of subcul-tures, discussed below. The combination of social disorganisation and subcultural theory suggests that the conditions in which crime and criminality are bred are not ones that lack community per se, but ones in which the breakdown of social institutions and social cohesion prompt the formation of new and sometimes devi-ant communities.

Despite the limitations of social disorganisation, Shaw and McKay's (1942) ideas have prompted a large body of research exploring the validity of their claims and attempting to refine them. In the United States Edwin Sutherland developed his theory of differential association, which sought to explain how criminogenic values were transmitted, whilst in the United Kingdom Mays (1954) and Downes (1966) observed that British youth tended not to have the same reasons for offend-ing as suggested by Shaw and McKay (1942). Similarly, Morris (1957) and later Baldwin and Bottoms (1976) noted that crime in the UK was not only focused in the 'zone in transition' but also tended to be located on housing estates usu-ally found significant distances from the centre of town. In addition, Baldwin and Bottoms (1976) found that offender residences were strongly influenced by council housing location policies, community subcultures and the reputation of an area. Newman's (1973) vision of defensible space has also been of considerable importance in describing the crime-inducing properties of the architectural design of housing estates.

Finally, one further development has been the advancement of the 'broken windows' thesis by Wilson and Kelling (1982). Crawford (1998) describes their work:

> they argue that minor incivilities – such as vandalism, graffiti, rowdy behav-iour, drunkenness and begging – if unchecked and uncontrolled will set in train a series of linked social responses, as a result of which 'decent' and 'nice' neighbourhoods can 'tip' into fearful ghettos of crime.
>
> (Crawford 1998: 130)

Wilson and Kelling (1982) argue that the physical decline of a community leads to the decline of informal social controls and results in higher levels of anti-social and criminal behaviour. This, like all the other environmental perspectives on crime, places the blame for high levels of crime squarely at the feet of community decline. Whilst there may be significant disagreement concerning the spatial distribution of offending and whilst various explanations for criminal behaviour are forwarded, there seems an underlying consensus that the causes of crime are due to community decline. Community decline involves both the degradation of the physical environment and the weakening of the informal social controls that encourage legitimate attitudes and behaviour.

Alongside and overlapping with the broad direction of environmental criminology is subcultural theory. Whilst not so obviously engaged with locality, subcultural theory considers community in relation to the exchange and transmission of norms and values within groups. In many senses it seems at odds to talk about subculture in reference to community, as the authors of subcultural theory have little to say about the concept. However, there are three reasons for its inclusion. Firstly, subcultural theory developed out of a synthesis of the Chicago School's findings on the concentration of offenders in particular localities, the transmission of criminal values and Merton's theory of anomie (1938, 1957). Secondly, subcultural theory has been discussed in reference to the 'disadvantaged' community (Hope and Shaw 1988); and thirdly, subcultural theory gives us an insight into the development of anti-social and criminal values. It also helps to put Crawford's (1998) comments regarding the criminogenic aspects of many organised communities into context.

Two of subcultural theory's most prominent early authors are Cohen (1955) and Cloward and Ohlin (1960). Their work focuses on the evolution of anti-social and criminal values in what Hope and Shaw (1988) have referred to as 'disadvantaged' communities:

> crime would develop as a way of life amongst youth in neighbourhoods where opportunities for personal and economic advancement were blocked. In this view, crime was seen as a reaction by embittered slum youth to a failure to attain qualifications, a good job, a decent income, which are widely valued and seem to be available to people who live elsewhere.
>
> (Hope and Shaw 1988: 3)

It is therefore clear to see that subcultural theory shares the belief prevalent in the Chicago School and in later environmental criminology that high crime rates are typical in areas of community decline. Both are primarily concerned with the relationship between disadvantage and the types of attitudes and behaviour that developed to compensate for blocked access to legitimate goals. In this we can see the influence of the Chicago School's contention that the transmission of criminal values occurs in areas where there are high levels of social disorganisation that lack the necessary social controls to ensure conformist patterns of socialisation. This work draws heavily upon Merton's (1938, 1957) theory of anomie or strain. Merton argues that individuals who do not have legitimate access to culturally desirable goals will adapt in one of four ways (innovation, ritualism, retreatism or rebellion) to compensate for their lack of opportunities. It is from these two perspectives that subcultural theorists draw their conclusion that alternative sets of anti-social values are learned.

In 1955 Albert Cohen published his ideas on how Merton's notion of strain leads to juvenile delinquency in the United States. Cohen was particularly interested in the social 'triggers' that led to adolescent delinquency amongst lower-class males. Whilst he acknowledges that not all lower-class, young males will turn to delinquency, he is interested in explaining why so many of this social group do exhibit anti-social behaviour. Cohen argues that American values are predominantly middle class. These values are primarily disseminated through the media and the education system. Lower-class juveniles are at a natural disadvantage with middle-class boys because of the way they are socialised. As a result they are less able to compete for wealth and status, and in reaction to this circumstance come together with others in similar positions to form delinquent subcultures. These subcultures foster alternative values that are attainable to the young, lower-class males.

In 1960 Cloward and Ohlin progressed their opportunity theory. This developed out of Cohen's (1955) and Merton's (1938, 1957) work and was concerned with explaining why delinquents formed particular types of subculture. Basically, Cloward and Ohlin took Cohen's notion of delinquent subculture and Merton's notion of adaptation and attempted to explore why lower-class, young males formed certain types of subcultures. They suggested that the development of particular subcultures depended upon the opportunities available to youths. Opportunities refer to blocked access to wealth and status and available access to criminal skills and values. In disadvantaged but organised communities, they argued, there would be opportunities to learn from older boys the values and skills necessary to pursue criminal patterns of behaviour. In deprived but disorganised communities, they suggested, violent subcultures would develop. Those juveniles who could not compete with the criminal or violent youths would form retreatist subcultures that would primarily be involved in illegal drug use. These three types of criminal subculture – criminal, violent and retreatist – draw heavily on the work of Edwin Sutherland et al. (1992), who argued that subcultures are transmitted through interactions with others who provide justification and legitimisation for rule-breaking values. His theory of differential association asserts that in socially disorganised slum areas criminal values are more likely to be present and, as a result, individuals are more likely to learn, or differentially associate with, such values (Sutherland et al. 1992).

Of course, there are many criticisms of subcultural theory. For example, there have been significant criticisms of Cohen's assertion that working-class youths will automatically have internalised middle-class values or that they hold anti-middle-class values (Mays 1954, Downes 1966). There have also been criticisms of the assumption that deviancy is confined to the lower classes and of the over-reliance on official statistics. However, the purpose of this section is not to engage in a full-blown discussion of subcultural theory. Instead the aim is to outline those theories and practices that are pertinent to our understanding of community. The relevance of subcultural theory is that it suggests that the environment, its social institutions, its value system and its levels of organisation and deprivation have a significant impact on criminality. These ideas, and those of environmental criminology, have not only identified what they see as the cause of rising crime but also have had significant influence over the direction that should be taken to control rising crime. The next section goes on to look at a variety of criminal justice and crime prevention measures that have developed to control crime by working with, or in, or for the community.

Arising out of these theories are a range of criminal justice and penal strategies that have developed to combat the problem of community decline. In the early 1960s the work of the Chicago School directly led to the 'Chicago Area Project' (CAP) and 'Mobilisation for Youth' (MFY) initiative, which attempted to enhance community organisation and develop community support and self-help. These programmes developed under the Kennedy administration in an era of optimism and social philanthropy and sought to address the issues of inequality and exclusion. Although the success of these schemes is debatable, they did set the scene for a variety of approaches that sought to address the problem of community decline as a method of controlling crime.

It should be made clear that the community and crime control refers primarily to the treatment of the crime problem, not the problem of community decline. Whilst there is sometimes conceptual confusion as to whether the community should be seen as 'means' or 'ends' (Nelken 1985, Crawford 1997), all the approaches discussed below draw on some notion of the community to control crime rather than rebuild community.

For the purposes of this discussion three broad categories identified by Nelken (1985) will be used to consider attempts to engage with the community as a method of crime control. Nelken (1985) has referred to the community as agent, locus and beneficiary of crime control initiatives. He summarises this as:

> To capture these distinctions in a phrase, we may distinguish control of crime *by* the community, control of crime *in* the community and control of crime *for* the community
>
> (Nelken 1985: 241; emphasis in original)

To represent control of crime 'by' the community, an overview of community policing and neighbourhood watch will be provided. To represent control of crime 'in' the community there will be discussion of the context in which community sentences and community 'payback'[3] engage with the community; and to represent control of crime 'for' the community there will be an overview of crime prevention and community safety.

These three approaches encapsulate the main types of activity that have sought to engage the community. Further, they also represent the types of activity that have attracted the most academic scrutiny. It would, however, be wrong to suggest that these are the only types of community-orientated activity that have been discussed. For example, community courts, community prisons and community justice centres have also received some attention in recent years. Community courts either refers to the existing system of lay magistrates and local courts or it promotes the continued devolution of such a system. Community prisons attracted more attention in the wake of the Woolf Report (Woolf and Tumim 1991), which arose out of severe prison disturbances in the late 1980s. Woolf argued for a system of community prisons that locates prisoners as near as possible to their family and friends and that encourages greater interaction between the local community and the prison. Although this summary does a disservice to the wider-ranging and, in many senses, radical proposals in the Woolf Report, the notion of community prisons has never really taken off.

More recently the idea of community justice centres has emerged across some parts of England and Wales. Initially borrowed from a scheme set up in New York (see Berman and Mansky 2005), the first community justice centre was in North Liverpool has and they have more recently been rolled out in eleven other local authority areas across England and Wales. Within these centres the idea of community courts has been revitalised and increasingly includes consultation with members of the public about local problems and priorities. This mirrors the community policing model in many ways and the community justice centres attempt to bring together various agencies and practices that listen, involve and respond to community needs. Whilst these community justice centres represent an important stage in the development of community-based criminal justice strategies, it is first worth outlining the development of seemingly disparate activities that invoke the community in one form or another.

Community as agent: community policing and neighbourhood watch

The first of Nelken's (1985) types of community involvement is the community as agent, or crime control 'by' the community. Nelken argues that this type of involvement aims to give communities:

> a greater role or say in the control of the criminal behaviour which affects them. Police liaison committees or neighbourhood justice centres are each, in their own way, examples of such efforts.
>
> (Nelken 1985: 241)

Although Nelken refers to police liaison committees and neighbourhood justice centres, the focus here will be on the concept of community policing, which commonly enshrines aspects of both community liaison and neighbourhood watch. This is because community policing is intended to involve the community and be responsive to its needs. This corresponds with Nelken's above definition of the community as 'agent'. Community policing attempts to consult with the community in a number of ways to help establish what local residents see as the key problems of the area they live in and what response they would see as most effective and desirable in dealing with these problems. Further, community policing often incorporates a strong emphasis on neighbourhood watch schemes as a method of encouraging the community to take responsibility for local crime and anti-social behaviour. There is also a strong element that attempts to reconnect policing with wider community institutions and groups as a process for improving the supply of intelligence and revitalising community structures as a means of controlling crime. This approach clearly has its roots in the environmental and subcultural assertion that high levels of crime are due to community decline. In general, community policing uses this diagnosis to justify and legitimate its renewed interaction with the wider community.

Before going on to describe the activities of community policing, a brief outline of the circumstances from which community policing developed will be undertaken. This provides a contextual backdrop from which to understand why policing has tried to strengthen its relationship with the public.

The 1970s and early 1980s witnessed some of the most enforcement-orientated policing in the twentieth century. Yet there was no reduction in recorded crime rates and the main consequence of the new 'para-military' style of policing was to alienate the public. This alienation was largely facilitated by the increased use of rapid-response units to deal with specific incidents. Furthermore, new technologies and the necessity of vehicle patrols caused a significant reduction in the traditional beat patrol function. This approach resulted in the development of specialised task forces and increased police stop-and-search activities that were indiscriminate and insensitive in their execution:

> The patrol officer in his air-conditioned and heated car no longer got out of the police vehicle to do preventive patrol or to learn more about the community being policed. The insulation of the police from the public to control corruption and to respond rapidly to their calls had served primarily to insulate the police from the public they were to serve. No longer did the public have confidence that the police were handling, or could handle, their problems, and many, particularly minority groups, felt alienated from the police.
>
> (Reiss 1992: 53)

The media focus upon police misconduct and malpractice during the early 1980s further reinforced distrust and resentment of heavy-handed police practices. The crisis came to a head in 1981 as a result of the disastrous Swamp '81 operation in Brixton. The resultant rioting prompted a report by Lord Scarman (1981) into contemporary policing practices and began the process of self-evaluation within the police service.

Community policing developed out of a period of intense turmoil within the police service. The Brixton riots were the climax of the public animosity towards policing practices at that time. The Scarman Report (1981) heavily influenced the ideas of the Metropolitan Police Commissioner, Sir Kenneth Newman, who sought to place renewed emphasis on preventive police work by stimulating greater public involvement and multi-agency strategies for maintaining social control.

Community policing begins from an assertion that the police are an agency of local government and the community and their authority is derived from the legal powers that the community grants them. As the focus of community policing is order maintenance, not crime control, two competing approaches have developed. The first is based upon attempts to revitalise the 'spirit' of the community in urban society and the second is to expand what has come to be known as 'outreach' facilities. These largely include:

> opening small neighbourhood substations, conducting surveys to identify local problems, organising meetings and crime prevention seminars, publishing newsletters, helping form Neighbourhood Watch groups, establishing advisory panels to inform police commanders, organising youth activities, conducting drug education projects and media campaigns, patrolling on horses and bicycles, and working with municipal agencies to enforce health and safety regulations.
>
> (Skogan 1994: 167–8)

The debate revolves around whether or not it is conceivable that traditional geo-local communities can be reinvented, given the increasingly anonymous and socially mobile nature of contemporary society. Those who do not believe this is possible opt for the second approach, which is dedicated to providing traditional policing functions in new ways. These 'new ways' include assigning patrol officers to specific sectors for prolonged periods of time with a clear, visible role in the community. This is usually complemented by attempts to make the police more accessible by opening police stations in high crime areas.

Community policing also endorses a multi-agency approach to crime, including institutions such as: local authorities, architects, business, social services, voluntary agencies, the probation service, tenant associations, the courts and the crown prosecution service. Within this conglomeration of agencies the brief is to incorporate as many community groups as possible so that social problems that are typically associated with high crime can be tackled. Community policing therefore incorporates a strong problem-solving approach to tackling crime. Rosenbaum (1988) summarises the fundamentals of community policing:

> an emphasis on improving the number and quality of police-citizen contacts, a broader definition of 'legitimate' police work, decentralisation of the police bureaucracy, and a greater emphasis on proactive problem-solving strategies.
>
> (Rosenbaum 1988: 334)

Of course, community policing is not without its critics. There are many issues, such as resistance from the occupational culture of the police (McConville and Shepherd 1992) and tensions in multi-agency partnerships (Sampson et al. 1988), that have attracted comment. However, for the purposes of this review I want to briefly outline those criticisms that relate to difficulties with the community.

One particular problem that has always plagued the effective pursuit of community policing targets has been the inability to involve the local community. Grinc (1994) suggests that this problem occurs for three reasons. Firstly, the community is unaware of the aims and goals of community policing. Secondly, people do not want to work more closely with the police; and thirdly, the failure of community policing projects to maintain a long-term commitment to helping the community breeds scepticism in the community. This is not likely to attract community involvement. This general lack of involvement is further confounded by the unequal involvement of those groups who do participate:

> there is no guarantee that someone acting as a representative of a particular group is necessarily always truly representative of his or her constituency: those who are active in community politics – sometimes known as 'committee-seekers' and 'committee-joiners', or even disparagingly as 'busy-bodies' – are by their very nature unrepresentative of the larger body of people who prefer to leave politics to other people most of the time.
>
> (Sampson et al. 1988: 489)

As such, it is a fairly common complaint that these groups are made up of middle-class, middle-aged, white, pro-police individuals with very little working knowledge of the police service. As a result, the needs of minority groups and the underprivileged tend to be under-represented and the police tend to dominate proceedings.

A further criticism is that community policing has often failed to be effective because of the 'disorganised' nature of the communities targeted. It is generally considered that the best areas for testing community policing strategies are the poorer urban areas. These areas are typified by poverty, high crime, unemployment and weak educational systems where there are few community organisations or little community infrastructure for the police to liaise with. Buerger (1994) suggests that the reason why community policing has met with only limited success is because it is often targeted on neighbourhoods where crime and deprivation are too entrenched for the police to make much meaningful difference. Buerger (1994) draws on Wilson and Kelling's (1982) notion of communities at the 'tipping point' to argue that community policing is most effective when the slightest change can have a sizeable impact on a neighbourhood.

Thus, it would seem that Buerger (1994) is suggesting that one of the main reasons for failed community programmes is that they are directed at the wrong types of community. This would then require a serious rethinking of how to overcome the problem of the unresponsive and disinterested community and whether or not such communities are even appropriate targets for community policing. The implication of this argument is that it is not community policing per se, but community policing in certain conditions that can be effective. In other words, not all communities will necessarily benefit, or benefit equally, from community policing strategies.

This brief, but necessary, synopsis demonstrates how community policing encourages individuals to participate in aspects of criminal justice. Whilst the primary activities are consultative and attendance based, there is a clear emphasis on the need for members of the community to give up their free time and contribute to the well-being and safety of their community. This coincides with Nelken's (1985) vision of the community as 'agent'. Further, community policing attempts to address two things. Firstly, there is a focused effort to repair the damage done to relations between the police and various groups in society. Secondly, there is a definite aim to address the problem of community decline outlined earlier. This demonstrates that the community policing model at least tacitly endorses the notion that community decline is linked to high crime. More recently Johnston and Shearing (2003) have sought to update discussions of community policing by locating them within Foucault's (1982) notion of governmentality. Within this perspective they consider the shift of responsibility for crime control and prevention from a unified police service to a broad range of statutory, voluntary and community organisations. As such, more recent models of community policing increasingly involve a much wider range of groups in the policing of society.

Alongside and usually part of many community policing initiatives are neighbourhood watch schemes. Introduced in the early 1980s, neighbourhood watch sought to actively include local residents in crime-prevention activities by getting them to take an active interest in their security and safety. Initially conceived as part of community policing strategies, neighbourhood watch attempts to engender awareness of personal and domestic security, combined with attempts to enhance local neighbourhood surveillance, and thus provide the 'capable guardians' (Cohen and Felson 1979) required to provide the informal social controls that help maintain public order and tranquillity.

The type of activity involved in neighbourhood watch varies considerably according to the type of scheme established and the commitment of both its members and the local community police officer. Membership might mean as little as putting a sticker in your window or as much as taking on important co-ordinator responsibilities. The intensity of activity and size of scheme vary dramatically from place to place. However, neighbourhood watch can at least claim to be successful insofar as it has attracted a great deal of interest and many thousands of schemes have been started. Nevertheless, concerns have been raised regarding the levels of activity in many neighbourhood watch schemes and the difficulty of establishing schemes in high crime areas (Laycock and Tilley 1995). However, the purpose here is not to assess the success or failure of neighbourhood watch but to point out its undeniable purpose of involving community members in crime-prevention activity.

This is very much in keeping with Nelken's (1985) notion of the community as agent. Yet Lacey and Zedner (1995) have argued that neighbourhood watch schemes endorse neo-liberal sentiments that have little to do with community and everything to do with the politics of self-interest. Given that neighbourhood watch developed in the early years of Thatcher's New Right administration and that it preceded the current communitarian vogue, it is perhaps not that surprising that neighbourhood watch has been described as:

> engaged in promoting individual responsibility for the protection of private property rather than in fostering communal activity.
>
> (Lacey and Zedner 1995: 310)

Lacey and Zedner (1995) argue that neighbourhood watch encourages individuals to be cautious and suspicious of others. Nelken (1985) reinforces this message:

> Initiatives which attempt to build up local activities, such as neighbourhood watch schemes, often appeal explicitly to individual self interest.
>
> (Nelken 1985: 257)

Neighbourhood watch is thus an ideologically infused activity. Built on the back of self-interest, it is premised on the principle of reciprocity (Gouldner 1975), whereby people feel they should take in interest in their neighbours' security because they are the beneficiaries of a similar interest themselves. Thus the community begins to play a more overt part in the surveillance of its neighbourhood and more explicit relationships between the police and the neighbourhood are built. This facilitates both the supply of intelligence to the police and an enhanced social control function in the neighbourhood watch area. Yet, in the context of this discussion neighbourhood watch is a good example of the community as agent. In this example the community moves beyond a passive consultation to a more overt activity. It is not simply providing the police with information, it is being mobilised to take on some crime control functions itself.

Community as locus: offenders in the community

Nelken (1985) describes the community as locus:

> It does *not* necessarily involve ordinary members of the community in any aspect of crime control, but represents rather a concern to keep offenders and others out of residential institutions if at all possible. Halfway Houses, probation hostels, diversion schemes, various forms of supervision on licence and community care programmes of temporary foster-care all illustrate this long-standing but recently much escalated effort to avoid residential care or control.
>
> (Nelken 1985: 241–2; emphasis in original)

This illustrates that using the community as the location for crime control does not require the participation of members of that community, and neither does it concern itself with addressing community decline. In fact, the criteria for using the community as a medium for sanctioning offenders has often had little to do with theoretical observations about the causes of crime and far more to do with the pragmatic concerns of prison overcrowding. There are other factors that have contributed to the expansion of diversions from custody and care of offenders in the community. These include: the stigmatising impact of a custodial sentence; the perception of prisons as 'crime schools', the failure of prison to effectively rehabilitate the majority of its inmates. Before going on to discuss the exact relationship between these approaches and the community, a summary of those measures that use the community as location will be undertaken.

Community sentences started with the introduction of probation in the early twentieth century (Green 2008). At the end of 2005 there were nearly 225,000 people under supervision by the Probation Service (Home Office 2006). Since the Criminal Justice Act 2003 the range of sentences that the Probation Service has been responsible for has been brought together into one generic sentence called the community order, under which the Court decides from a possible twelve specific conditions of the sentence. The exact blend of requirements attached to a community order is often informed by a pre-sentence report which is prepared by the Probation Service at the request of the Court to provide background information about the circumstances of the offence and the level of risk the offender poses to the public.[4] A community order can be made up of a wide range of requirements which include unpaid work (now called 'Community Payback', previously best known as community service) where the offender undertakes a set number of hours of work for the benefit of the community. A comparatively new, yet increasingly influential, option is to put offenders on a programme where the offender attends classes designed to unpick and correct the psychological shortcomings that have led them into offending behaviour. Offenders can still be sentenced to one-to-one supervision with a probation officer but can also be instructed to undertake drug or alcohol treatment; have restrictions imposed on their movement (e.g. curfews or bans from certain public places or activities); or be instructed to take education or basic skills training. The exact amount and type of activity will be decided by a range of factors taken into account by the Court that will typically include type of offence, severity of offence, offending history and risk posed to the public.

Within this broad field of activity it is, arguably, community service that is the best exemplar of the type of work undertaken by offenders in the community:

> The work is provided by an approved agency and is organised and supervised by the probation service. It may consist, for example, of outdoor conservation projects, construction of adventure playgrounds, or decorating houses and flats for elderly and disabled people.
>
> (Cavadino and Dignan 1997: 224)

Since the end of 2008, what was once called community service is now known as community payback.[5] This enables members of the community to vote on what sorts of unpaid work they would like offenders to do. This usually is a choice between removing graffiti, clearing up litter and so on. Interestingly, this has also gone hand in hand with making offenders doing unpaid work wear orange jump suits so that they can be visibly seen doing their payback to the community.

As well as community sentences, there are other types of sentences that use the community as location. Without going into detail, these include: the suspended sentence, the fine, the compensation order, the reparation order, the sex offender order, the child curfew order, the anti-social behaviour order and the parenting order. Each of these sentences leaves the offender at liberty in the community. In addition to these sentences there are also several other forms of criminal justice activity that use the community as location. These are: probation hostels, halfway houses and after-care for prisoners released on licence.

Hopefully, this demonstrates the wide range of criminal justice activities that use the community as location. Within this context there is virtually no involvement with the community. None of these sentences requires the community's participation and they do not derive from the belief that community decline leads to high crime. The only real conception or utilisation of community within this approach is as a geographical location. As stated earlier, the criteria for developing measures that use the community as location have more to do with the pragmatic concerns of managing criminal justice and the ideological preferences of political parties. The exception to this would seem to be the very recent introduction of community payback, with its online voting system that allows members of the public to nominate the types of activity that offenders should be directed towards. This innovation can, arguably, be better understood as a divergence from the traditional role of the community as locus in sentencing, though it could also be seen as a compelling example of the moral authoritarian communitarianism of Etzioni (1995) and New Labour and is therefore better understood as part of the more recent repositioning of the Labour Party and its subsequent moralising approach to crime. This theme is returned to in detail in Chapters 3 and 4.

Whilst it is clear that community sentences are based in the community, they generally do not involve the community in anything other than the sense that the punishment takes place in the community rather than in the custodial setting. Yet community sentences incorporate a conception of community that is distinctive and widespread throughout the criminal justice system. To ignore community as 'location' would be to ignore an important part of the picture. By locating the offender in the community rather than in the artificial and stigmatising environment of the prison, the hope is that through reparative work the offender will develop a 'stake in conformity' (Toby 1957, Hirschi 1969). This echoes the environmental and subcultural theorists' assertion that the weakening of the institutions of social control is linked to high offending. In this case the relationship is reversed to suggest that by strengthening the offender's links to the social order they are less likely to offend. The community therefore provides a forum from which the offender can take a place in society. Adam Crawford (1998) describes the process by which individuals are rehabilitated by taking a 'stake in conformity':

> The assumption behind this approach is that those who are provided with opportunities will be more likely to obtain meaningful roles in society, as a result of which they will develop a sense of fulfilment and usefulness that will translate into a greater sense of affiliation to the social order in which they find themselves.
>
> (Crawford 1998: 107)

It would be foolhardy to overstate this aspect of community sentencing or to suggest that this is a major justification for pursuing sentencing in the community. Yet there seems to be an implicit assumption that the community can provide a positive environment that will be more likely than the prison to instil social conformity. What we can draw from this is limited, but it would seem that within this there is a notion of what community represents that goes beyond just seeing it as a geographical reference point.

Community as beneficiary: crime prevention and community safety

The third and final type of community involvement is community as 'beneficiary'. Nelken (1985) refers to this as crime control 'for' the community:

> Control *for* the community is again a different proposition. The idea here is to give greater recognition to the victims of crime, both as individuals and members of the community at large . . . Those who argue for more control *for* the community see crime as a social and environmental problem which impairs the quality of life of communities and individuals who compose them.
>
> (Nelken 1985: 242; emphasis in original)

Nelken (1985) cites examples of this type of approach as community service, compensation and restitution orders. However, these types of activity have already been classified as 'locus'. This is not accidental. Whilst there is within the justifications for such sentences a reparative aim that can be construed as 'for' the community's benefit, these aims have been systematically sidelined and marginalised in favour of a punishment- and treatment-led agenda. Nelken, writing in 1985, pre-empts the late-1980s and 1990s focus on punishment in the community. Instead, the focus shall be upon crime prevention and community safety. This type of activity is primarily concerned with addressing the problem of crime by altering and improving either the local environment of an area or the social relations within an area. This corresponds with Nelken's above statement as to what constitutes community as 'beneficiary'.

Although this section is titled 'Crime prevention and community safety', the focus is primarily on crime prevention. Of course, crime prevention usually forms a central plank of most community safety strategies. Community safety has been included for this reason, and because it is becoming an increasingly important forum for partnership work on crime prevention and urban regeneration. To exclude it would be to ignore an important sphere of activity that incorporates both the community and crime control.

Defining crime prevention is not a straightforward task. Distinguishing it from community safety is even less easy. Without getting too involved with cumbersome debates regarding definition, the problem revolves around issues of what activity constitutes crime prevention, where it starts and where it finishes. Adam Crawford (1998) points to some of these problems and poses the questions:

> should crime prevention be restricted to measures, the intended outcomes of which relate only *directly* to the reduction of criminal events? Or should it be

sufficiently encompassing to include activity which may impact directly on 'quality of life' issues, such as the 'fear of crime', but which may have only an *indirect* impact on crime? This tension between a narrow and broad definition is reflected in most of the conceptual and practical debates about what crime prevention is.

(Crawford 1998: 8; emphasis in original)

Crawford goes on to distinguish between crime prevention and community safety by looking at the types of activity typically associated with both. He argues that crime prevention can generally be understood as representing the more narrow definition of activity that is directly concerned with the reduction of crime. Community safety, on the other hand, represents a far broader range of activities:

Through reference to the term 'safety' it encompasses not just crime, narrowly defined, but also the much wider physical and social impact of crime and the anxieties to which it gives rise.

(Crawford 1998: 9)

Crawford suggests that community safety is becoming more popular as it provides conceptual space to deal with a raft of social problems other than crime and locates these problems in particular localities in a way that crime prevention does not. Further, Crawford argues that community safety, by virtue of its more holistic remit, requires and encourages a partnership approach to tackling problems. Crawford's definition provides a useful way to distinguish between the two terms. However, there is a fundamental similarity between both these approaches and it is this similarity that often leads the two to be grouped together. Both crime prevention and community safety are concerned with addressing the problem of community decline. This they do by attempting to improve or regenerate environmental and social conditions.

Once more, the focus is on community decline as an explanation for high crime. Whilst there is a clear endorsement of this perspective, it would be a misrepresentation to suggest that crime prevention and those aspects of community safety that address criminality derive exclusively from the earlier work of environmental criminologists. There are a number of crime prevention theories that have been used to explain and direct crime prevention activities. These include: routine activity theory (Cohen and Felson 1979), lifestyle theory (Hindelang et al. 1978) and rational choice theory (Cornish and Clarke 1986). In general these theories share a concern with the environmental and social conditions that are conducive to criminality. Crime prevention attempts to remove the conditions that provide criminal opportunities.[6]

Hope and Shaw (1988) point to the distinction between situational and social crime prevention and their respective focus on reducing opportunity by altering the physical environment or integration policies designed to promote respect and moral values (Clarke 1981). This not only gives an indication of the difference between the two but also points to some typical interventions associated with both.

Hope and Shaw (1988) go on to say that, whilst situational crime prevention has flourished, most social crime prevention measures have ignored the 'community dimension'. Instead they suggest that social crime prevention has focused on individual explanations of criminality. This distinction between social and situational is also obvious in Crawford's (1998) work. He clearly differentiates between situational and environmental strategies and social and communal strategies.

There is so much more that can be discussed in relation to crime prevention and community safety. Discussion of the virtues of the 'bubbling-up' approach over the 'top-down' method of crime prevention could also be incorporated, as could the importance and problems of multi-agency partnerships. However, the aim of this literature review has been to describe those theories and practices that engage the notion of community. Crime prevention and community safety represent another dominant approach to controlling crime, namely the improvement and regeneration of environmental and social conditions.

There are a host of criticisms and concerns that can be levelled at both situational and social crime prevention. For example, situational crime prevention has been criticised for its temporary nature (crime is displaced elsewhere), its intrusive nature (through surveillance), its treatment of the symptom rather than the cause (the social causes of crime) and its socially divisive aspects (excluding those considered a threat) (Crawford 1998). Whilst by no means exhaustive, this list gives a hint of the types of criticisms levelled at situational crime prevention. However, in keeping with the rest of this chapter the focus is necessarily limited to those criticisms that relate to the understanding of and expectations on community. In the context of crime prevention these problems emerge in the literature on social rather than situational crime prevention.

These criticisms are primarily levelled at the implicit theoretical and ideological assumptions about community contained within social crime prevention. Whilst these concerns will be discussed in full later, they are worth briefly mentioning here. Summarising Crawford's (1998) comments, criticism can be made of the assumption that high crime occurs where there is a lack of informal social control. Research (Hope and Foster 1992, Foster 1995) suggests that informal control mechanisms are not always lacking in high crime areas and can act as security and support against crime. For instance, Walklate's (1998) research in Salford has demonstrated that whilst an inner-city council estate may have high crime rates, this doesn't preclude either a sense of community or informal social controls about who and what can and cannot be targeted for crime. Next, parachuting interventions into communities that bolster and regenerate formal and informal community structures as a means of combating crime often ignore the fact that communities may not be able to sustain the social cohesion of the type perceived as beneficial.

The imposition of such efforts by external agencies denies and removes the necessity for communities to take responsibility and provide their own solutions to community decline. There has also been criticism that both situational and social crime prevention ignores the breakdown of geographically defined notions of community and the corresponding growth of communities of interest that do not adhere to any particular locality. Finally, the types of community solidarity usually assumed to reduce crime are not typical of low-crime, middle-class suburban areas. As Bottoms and Wiles (1996) have noted, these types of communities are usually both disorganised and orderly. They do not rely on communal forms of social control and are likely to resort to the formal agencies of control to resolve disputes.

Crime prevention and community safety are designed, in part, to address the problem of community decline by reinventing or regenerating both the environmental and social cohesion assumed typical of low crime communities. Crime prevention and community safety often incorporates a high degree of community activity and, as such, could easily have been discussed under the community as 'agent' heading. Local charities, churches, youth groups and residents' associations are often represented in crime prevention and community safety initiatives. Yet crime prevention can be discussed under the heading of community as 'beneficiary' because, although community participation is common, often essential, it does not represent the purpose of crime prevention. The community's participation is a means to an end, and that end is crime prevention.

This aim is complemented by a range of situational interventions geared towards reducing the opportunities for offending. Of course these types of initiatives do not operate in isolation from the other types of activity, and convergence and cooperation between community sentences, community policing and crime prevention is not uncommon. For example, although it is by no means a prerequisite, crime prevention often incorporates a community-orientated, problem-solving approach to policing. Yet, regardless of the particular concoction of measures, what appears to remain consistent is that the role of the community in these types of measures is primarily to support the statutory agencies in their responsibility to prevent or respond to crime. The contention of this thesis is that this role is changing as new influences and ideologies come to bear on political thinking. Rather than the community simply providing the context and need, it is now increasingly being asked to provide the policing and punishment of crime itself.

A new philosophy of crime control: from taking part to taking responsibility

Community policing, community sentences and crime prevention provide the basis from which various types of criminal activity can be understood to interact with community. What becomes apparent is that each of these interactions takes a somewhat different form and Nelken's (1985) summary of by, in and for the community is a useful way of considering the variations within criminal justice strategies that make some claim to involve and represent the community. Yet, writing in the mid-1980s Nelken (1985) predates a number of important shifts in the way that community is conceptualised within the crime control arena. These shifts began to emerge in the mid-1990s and can be seen as connected to the emergence of Amitai Etzioni's (1995, 1997) communitiarianism in the United States and its influence on the Labour Party in the United Kingdom. Etzioni's (1995) ideas about community and morality will be discussed and critiqued at length in later chapters, but in terms of the influence of his ideas on crime control his influence has been to cement in the collective mind of New Labour the incontrovertible association of high crime with community decline and to provide an ideological underpinning which has at its core a belief that high crime can be understood in terms of moral and community breakdown.

It would, however, be an exaggeration to suggest that Etzioni's (1995) communitarianism is solely responsible for New Labour's approach to crime; rather, sits comfortably alongside Blair (1998) and Giddens' (1998) third way politics. This third way places importance on globalisation, information and individualism (Blair 1998) as important new dimensions of social and political conditions. Hence, Etzioni's (1995) communitarianism sits well alongside the establishment of the New Labour project and, whilst there are elements of this project that do not sit well alongside communitarianism, within the field of law and order Etzioni's (1995) ideas have resonated powerfully and many academic commentators have articulated the close relationship between Etzioni's (1995) ideas and New Labour's approach to crime and anti-social behaviour.

Etzioni's (1995, 1997) communitarianism has been described as a type of moral conservatism (Nellis 2000). This conservatism has heavily influenced the New Labour approach to crime control, both in terms of the rhetoric of rights and responsibilities and in terms of criminal justice policies enshrined in the Crime and Disorder Act (1998) and the Respect Action Plan (Respect Task Force 2006). Etzioni believes that American society has developed an unhealthy preoccupation with individual rights and liberties at the expense of responsibilities. This leads Etzioni to advocate a regeneration of community life that is concerned with balancing individual freedoms with responsibilities:

> If there is no civil order we risk a police state. We must aim for a moral dialogue and agreement on what is right. We cannot leave everything to the state. We must take responsibility in our families and communities.
>
> (Interview with Amitai Etzioni in New Statesman 1995b: 21)

The influence of Etzioni's conception of communitarianism has not been insignificant. In both the United States, under Clinton, and in the UK, under Blair, communitarian approaches can be seen. With regard to criminal justice Nellis (2000) says:

> New Labour in general, and the Crime and Disorder Act in particular was undoubtedly influenced by the mid-1990s debate on communitarianism.
>
> (Nellis 2000: 73)

Many of the rhetorical and ideological statements made by Prime Minister Tony Blair seem to draw on communitarian thinking. Whether it be his comments on parenting or his notion of a 'third way', there is clear and consistent echo of communitarian concerns:

> Tony Blair has embraced the idea of community. He believes that between unbridled market forces and the dead hand of bureaucratic socialism there is a middle way. He has talked about working together, solidarity, partnership and a belief in society.
>
> (New Statesman 1995a: 20)

This establishes that the communitarian ideology has at least had some influence on current political rhetoric and thinking. Within criminal justice the concerns of communitarianism are being reiterated with increasing vigour. Blair's mantra of 'no rights without responsibilities' and the moralising statements of government ministers about family, parenting, anti-social behaviour and civic duty are finding their ways into the policies and practices of the criminal justice system and penal decision making. These themes are largely continued by David Cameron and the Coalition government and are returned to in more detail in Chapter 4.

The community governance of crime

Before becoming embroiled in describing the community governance of crime it is first necessary to clarify terminology. Crawford (1997) refers to the local governance of crime, whilst others (Edwards and Benyon 2000, Edwards and Hughes 2002) refer to the community governance of crime. Whether in fact there is any substantive difference between local and community governance is unclear but, as will be demonstrated, both of these terms address the same phenomena and draw on similar, if not the same, explanations. Therefore, rather than confuse the issue by using them interchangeably, the community governance of crime will be used in all circumstances except when quoting directly from Crawford's (1997) work.

According to Crawford (1997), there has been an increasing shift away from the state as the sole provider of social order and social welfare since the early 1980s. Whereas the modern state once had sole responsibility for addressing social and economic problems, responsibility for finding solutions to these problems is now becoming more diffuse. Increasingly, communities and society have to shoulder at least some of the burden for sorting out problems that were historically the remit of the state to resolve. In other words, along with a range of other social problems, crime is no longer the sole remit of the state. Alongside the state a range of other public, private, voluntary and community agencies are suddenly expected to shoulder some of the burden for crime and criminality. It is this shift which is at the very heart of community governance. Community governance is therefore a shift from a system of sovereign authority to one of collective responsibility (Garland 1996, Edwards and Hughes 2002, Hughes 2002). Yet, on its own, this information does little to help inform us about the central features of this form of governance, how it manifests itself in practice or why this shift took place. By exploring these questions the aim is to uncover the different features and explanations for this fundamental shift towards devolution.

Crawford (1997) goes on to explain that the shift towards community governance draws on three concepts that inform 'governmental strategies' (p. 25).

These are: 'prevention', 'community', and 'partnership'. He argues that a range of policy developments and criminological explanations have led to a diverse and fragmented debate about criminal justice that challenges some traditional criminal justice processes whilst perpetuating others. This fluid kaleidoscope of themes means that:

> We are left with a complex interplay between the logics of new discourses and the practices of old institutions, so that the former are transformed and mutated beyond their surface logic, immediate appearance or intended outcomes. Consequently, appeals to 'community', 'prevention', and 'partnership' can neither be understood as having fully transformed the shape of criminal justice according to their own self-proclaimed image, nor can they be said to constitute a smoke screen behind which the same old practices are occurring.
>
> (Crawford 1997: 61)

This highlights the emerging status of community governance and the complex and often contradictory nature of its development. Attributing characteristics to community governance is therefore no straightforward task. The central feature of community governance is the shift in the arena of responsibility for crime control. Yet it has come to be associated with particular practices, specific forms of prevention, community and partnership.

Crawford's (1997) 'prevention' is usually thought of under the heading of community safety. 'Community' is the locus and orientation of such preventative activity and 'partnership' the organisational mechanism for progressing community initiatives. As such, all three are interconnected and it is as a package that they form the contemporary landscape of the community governance of crime. According to Crawford (1998), community safety can be distinguished from crime prevention in terms of its scope and focus. Whereas crime prevention tends to operate in the narrow and specialised field of opportunity reduction (Clarke 1995), community safety approaches the problem of crime from a much wider perspective. Rather than seek to introduce interventions solely designed to affect crime or criminality, community safety operates from a position that endorses the view that crime is part of a range of related social problems. As such, community safety asserts that crime can be dealt with only by addressing other social problems within a particular area. Crawford (1998) goes on to say that proponents of community safety therefore disavow a deterministic, monocausal explanation of crime, opting instead for a more holistic approach that seeks to understand crime and criminality in the context of localised problems and conditions.

As has already been said, the most obvious manifestation of community governance is community safety. Edwards and Benyon (2000) attempt to outline the features of community governance in relation to its crime prevention characteristics. In the first place they compare local government to community governance and highlight the fundamental differences in Table 1.1.

Table 1.1 Distinguishing local government and community governance: focus orientation and technique

	Focus	*Orientation*	*Technique*
Local government	Delivery of services addressing social problems regarded as monistic and discrete	Unilateral interventions by single agencies	Rigid dependence on hierarchical/ bureaucratic or (quasi-)market mechanisms
Community governance	Managing problems of citizen 'well-being' regarded as multi-faceted and interdependent	Multilateral interventions by public-private partnerships that recruit active citizen participation.	Flexible deployment of bureaucratic, (quasi-)market and networking mechanisms

Source: Adapted from Edwards and Benyon (2000: 38)

Table 1.1 neatly summarises what Edwards and Benyon (2000) describe as a shift from local government to community governance. This shift in focus represents a move towards considering social problems or circumstances as a set of context-specific and interdependent issues that must be addressed according to the needs of a particular locality. Similarly the shift in orientation and technique represents a move towards a more flexible and holistic approach to managing these social problems. In other words this representation of community governance mirrors Crawford's (1997) earlier characterisation. This convergence begins to shape an emerging model for community safety; one in which responsibility for addressing crime rates is located in a multi-agency partnership approach that draws on a range of statutory, voluntary and community agencies. These then address a range of localised social and economic problems in a more holistic fashion, focusing not only on addressing crime and criminality but on a range of other related issues that contribute to the well-being of a particular area.

According to Hughes (2002), this represents a fundamental paradigm shift from crime prevention to community safety. It is this shift that, arguably, reflects a wider socio-political change in terms of who and what is responsible for crime control. No longer is crime control the sole or predominant remit of the state and its associated criminal justice agencies, but also of a range of different stakeholder groups, including other social agencies addressing a diverse set of interests including wider social welfare agencies (e.g. housing, health, education, regeneration) and local community action groups interested in developing local infrastructures and addressing local needs. It is therefore an approach that is located in the community and involving community members that seeks to address crime via a range of interrelated social and economic conditions. Edwards and Benyon (2000) go on to show how this community governance model is more directly applied to preventing crime (Table 1.2).

Table 1.2 Comparing crime prevention through local (police) government and through community governance: focus, orientation and technique

	Focus	Orientation	Technique
Crime prevention through local (police) government	Individual criminals and their crimes	Police operations independent of other (potential) crime control and prevention agencies	Law enforcement, including: routine uniformed patrolling, rapid response to calls for assistance, and investment in detection
Crime prevention through community governance	Problems of 'community safety', in the form of a range of crime events and anti-social acts, in turn conditioned by other dimensions of citizen 'well-being'	Multi-agency partnerships, including the police, local authorities, probation services and local populations	Strategic crime prevention, including networking and co-ordination of partners' preventative efforts, and other initiatives for neighbourhood regeneration

Source: Adapted from Edwards and Benyon (2000: 39)

Table 1.2 therefore provides a clear indication of this shift in relation to crime prevention initiatives. The focus becomes one of partnership, where the police and local authority become facilitators in attempts to prevent offending.

The aim of this overview has been to demonstrate one practical way in which aspects of criminal justice or crime control have been relocated outside of the state apparatus. It is not to say that the state or its agencies no longer play a significant part in this process but that it is no longer their sole responsibility. Instead, the success of such strategies is in part measured by the effective inclusion and consultation with a range of other agencies. The mobilisation of community members thus plays a crucial part in developing strategies for addressing the criminogenic needs of an area.

The historical and political reasons behind this shift can be found in the late 1980s and early 1990s and are, in their earliest inception, enshrined in two watershed documents. As previously mentioned, the first of these was the Scarman Report of 1981. Following the race riots in Brixton, South London, Lord Scarman was commissioned to prepare the report looking at the underlying reasons for these racial tensions. In the context of devolving justice, the Scarman report highlighted that the insensitive and heavy-handed policing strategies of the Metropolitan Police played a significant part in the creation of racial tensions and the correlated creation of local crime problems. Stemming from this analysis, Scarman suggested that the police needed to alter their attitude towards policing ethnic minority groups (in this case, and in particular, African-Caribbean people). Instead of the highly reactive, 'paramilitary' policing (Jefferson 1990, Jones and Newburn 1996) of the 1970s and early 1980s that has often been described as policing *against* the community (Bowling and Foster 2002), Scarman argued that the police needed to adopt a strategy that worked *with* the community. To this end the Police and Criminal Evidence Act (PACE) of 1984 enacted a statutory responsibility on police authorities to liaise with local communities about their concerns and fears of crime:

> If, as I believe to be essential, a relationship of mutual trust and respect is to be fostered between local communities and the police, both sides will have to be prepared to give and take and to work positively to establish and maintain such a relationship.
>
> (Scarman 1981: 152)

The purpose of this liaison, or consultation, was to help the police respond to the needs of the community and develop crime prevention strategies to meet such needs. It is here that the British inception of what has come to be called community policing (Fielding 1996) or problem-orientated policing (Goldstein 1979) has its origins:

> It is therefore vital to note then that much of the impetus for community-based 'solutions' were crucially linked to and inscribed in a broader racialised discourse about managing the 'race and crime' debate in which black communities throughout the 1980s were often pathologised and 'othered'.
>
> (Hughes 2002: 25)

Clearly then, the Scarman Report (1981) played a significant role in the shift towards increased community participation and police responsivity to the needs and concerns of the community. This by no means suggests that this process was then immediately realised or that it has become fully endorsed by the police service, but that the principle of community consultation and the commmunity's implicit participation emerged from the racial tensions between police and the black community in the early 1980s.

The second watershed document that is often cited as crucial in the move towards increased partnership and community-based cooperation is the Morgan Report (Home Office 1991). Although the report was effectively shelved by the Conservative government of the day it nevertheless marked an increasing drive towards community safety strategies (Edwards and Hughes 2002). The report advocated increased employment and training programmes along with community-building projects that provided the practical justification for a host of regeneration projects during the 1990s. Further, and perhaps most significantly, it informed the Labour Party's law and order policy that eventually culminated in the Crime and Disorder Act 1998. For the first time, the Act placed a statutory responsibility on local authorities to become involved in the prevention of crime and anti-social behaviour:

i   Without prejudice to any other obligation imposed on it, it shall be the duty of
    each authority to which this section applies to exercise its various functions

with due regard to the likely effect of the exercise of those functions on, and the need to do all that it reasonably can to prevent crime and disorder in its area

ii This section applies to a local authority, a joint authority, a police authority, a National Park authority and the Broads Authority.

(Crime and Disorder Act 1998, section 17)

Thus, from the early 1980s through to the late 1990s a somewhat fitful momentum towards the growing incorporation of the principles of partnership, community consultation and community safety can be witnessed. This trend continued with the publication of both the Casey Report (2008) and the Home Office (2008) Green Paper on policing. Both of these documents pay rhetorical homage to the notion of engaging and involving communities in crime control strategies and are littered with policy recommendations that further seek to establish the responsibility of a wide range of organisations and groups for crime prevention and control. This strongly suggests a continued commitment from the Brown government to the Blairite concern with community as the vehicle for addressing crime control and suggests that there will be further legislation that reinforces the shift in responsibility outlined above by Edwards and Benyon (2000).

Crime and its consequences were no longer the responsibility of a select few criminal justice agencies, but of all the public bodies responsible for a particular region. Most importantly, the responsibility could be properly discharged only by taking account of the concerns of the citizenry and addressing them correspondingly. The control and prevention of crime was therefore established as the concern of all. The devolution of responsibility within this sphere is clear to see. Whilst there are of course continuing issues regarding the nature of meaningful or equal partnership (Sampson et al. 1988, Graham and Bennett 1995, Hughes 2007), the principle has been established: local criminal justice policy must both engage with, and involve, the community.

Conclusion: the magic of community

The purpose of this opening chapter has been to review the variety of ways in which both criminological theory and criminal justice practice have drawn upon the concept of community to understand criminality and develop crime control strategies. It has not been an attempt to meticulously map out the intricacies of particular theories or crime control strategies. These theories and strategies are useful in highlighting the various ways in which community has been utilised in either an explanatory or an instrumental fashion in the fields of criminology and criminal justice.

Having considered ecological or environmental criminology, what becomes apparent is that there is a broad school of criminological thought that sees high crime in terms of community decline. This notion of community decline is rooted in urban deprivation and poverty that leads to the development of slum neighbourhoods from which their inhabitants flee at the first possible opportunity. These conditions of urban deprivation led to policy initiatives during the 1960s and 1970s that sought to reduce these criminogenic inequalities. Yet Young (1997) has argued that since this time there has been an aetiological crisis in which explanations of crime that were rooted in poverty and inequality have fallen into disrepute as quality of life indicators have risen, without any noticeable impact on rising crime rates. Hence, poverty as an explanation for criminality has fallen out of favour, though community decline as an explanation for criminality has not. This suggests that a different notion of community decline is at work and in need of exploration.

If poverty and deprivation can no longer explain community decline something else must. At this point in steps Etzioni's (1995) communitarianism, which presents crime and anti-social behaviour as a consequence of the permissive society that emerged out of the emancipatory politics of the 1960s and 1970s. Too many rights and not enough responsibilities becomes the explanation. Society has become too individualised. People have stopped caring about each other. Social cohesion and morality are in decline and the solution must therefore be to rebuild social cohesion and through it rebuild a moral consensus which will lead to a reduction in criminality.

This message resonated with the Clinton and Blair administrations on either side of the Atlantic. Both were in search of a political doctrine that side-stepped old-fashioned and increasingly unpopular notions of redistributive welfare which also allowed them to occupy a central position in the political spectrum. From these concerns sprung a new politics that drew heavily on Etzioni's (1995) communitarian logic and which furnished Clinton and Blair with the rhetoric and policies that allowed them to attack the greedy, self-interested depravities of the New Right whilst also maintaining a politics that was clearly distinguishable from that of their political rivals. In the United Kingdom, third way politics was birthed and community was to become one of New Labour's mantras in the field of crime and criminal justice.

Thus the magical power of community is to gloss over these important changes; a sleight-of-hand that offered an antidote to the excesses of the Reagan–Thatcher years without ever really needing to make it clear what it was offering instead.

Yet, what has become apparent in this chapter is that community has been drawn upon in different ways and these different ways often convey different meanings and understandings of community. This perhaps begins to explain the abundance and popularity of the concept. Depending on who is using the word and in what context, it can carry different meanings that appeal to a broad spectrum of political positions and organisational agendas. Perhaps Wirth's (1964) observation about the wild abandon with which the term is used is its greatest asset. Invoking community invites notions of the common good, of collective action and togetherness. This potentially unites people, or at the very least doesn't put them off. As Bauman (2000) has argued, the term 'community' conjures images of belonging that resonate powerfully across society. Yet the flip side of this conjuring is that it also masks much of what is actually meant by those invoking community. How will the community be involved? Who is being referred to when they talk about community? What sort of community is being advocated? This chapter has hopefully begun to highlight the ambiguity surrounding these questions by demonstrating the variety of ways in which the term has been deployed.

This chapter concludes by tentatively beginning the process of distinguishing a shift from the community taking part in crime control to the community taking responsibility for it. Whilst this is by no means a total conversion, and whilst community safety is still dominated by the police and local authorities (Hughes 2007), the Crime and Disorder Act 1998 provides an early indicator of the communitarian underpinnings to the New Labour project in general, and its crime control agenda in particular. Chapter 2 explores this in more detail by examining the relationship between these ideas and the development of community punishment and penal policy more generally.

Notes

1 For more detailed reading on environmental criminology refer to Bottoms and Wiles (1997) and for an overview of the literature on subcultural theory read Tierney (1996) or Downes and Rock (2003).
2 Which strongly resonates with the late-modern conditions of insecurity and uncertainty that are so fundamental to the analysis of Chapters 6 and 7.
3 This is a rebranding of community service orders.
4 See Wasik (2008) for a good summary of these sentencing options.
5 Community service orders were relabelled as community punishment orders between 2000 and 2003, when they were once again relabelled as unpaid work under the auspices of the community order introduced in the Criminal Justice Act 2003.
6 For a more detailed overview of these perspectives see Pease (1997) or Crawford (1998).

References

Baldwin, J. and Bottoms, A.E. (1976) *The Urban Criminal*, London: Tavistock.

Bauman, Z. (2000) *Liquid Modernity*, Cambridge: Polity Press.

Berman, G. and Mansky, A. (2005) Community Justice Centres: A US–UK Exchange, *British Journal of Community Justice*, 3 (3): 5–14.

Blair, T. (1998) *The Third Way, New Politics for the New Century*, London: Fabian Society (pamphlet 588).

Bottoms, A.E. and Wiles, P. (1996) Understanding Crime Prevention in Late Modern Societies, in T. Bennett (ed.) *Preventing Crime and Disorder: Targeting Strategies and Responsibilities*, Cambridge: Institute of Criminology.

Bottoms, A.E. and Wiles, P. (1997) Environmental Criminology, in M. Maguire, R. Morgan and R. Reiner (eds) *The Oxford Handbook of Criminology*, Oxford: Clarendon Press.

Bowling, B. and Foster, J. (2002) Policing and the Police, in M. Maguire, R. Morgan and R. Reiner (eds) *The Oxford Handbook of Criminology* (3rd edn), Oxford: Oxford University Press.

Brantingham, P.J. and Brantingham, P.L. (1981) *Environmental Criminology*, Beverley Hills, CA: Sage Publications.

Buerger, M.E. (1994) A Tale of Two Targets: Limitations of Community Anticrime Actions, *Crime and Delinquency*, 40 (3): 411–36.

Burgess, E.W. (1925/1967) The Growth of the City: An Introduction to a Research Project, in R.E. Park, E.W. Burgess and R.D. McKenzie (eds) *The City*, Chicago: University of Chicago Press.

Casey, L. (2008) *Engaging Communities in Fighting Crime*, Independent Report for Crime and Communities Review, London: Cabinet Office.

Cavadino, M. and Dignan, J. (1997) *The Penal System, An Introduction*, London: Sage Publications.

Clarke, R.V. (1981) *The Prospects for Controlling Crime*, Research Bulletin No. 12, London: Home Office Research and Planning Unit.

Clarke, R.V. (1995) Situational Crime Prevention, in M. Tonry and D.P. Farrington (eds) *Building a Safer Society*, Chicago: University of Chicago Press.

Cloward, R.A. and Ohlin, L.E. (1960) *Delinquency and Opportunity: A Theory of Delinquent Gangs*, New York: Free Press.

Cohen, A. (1955) *Delinquent Boys*, Glencoe: Free Press.

Cohen, L.E. and Felson, M. (1979) Social Change and Crime Rate Trends: A Routine Activity Approach, *American Sociological Review*, 44: 588–608.

Cohen, S. (1985) *Visions of Social Control*, Polity Press.

Cornish, D.B. and Clarke, R.V. (eds) (1986) *The Reasoning Criminal: Rational Choice Perspectives on Offending*, New York: Springer-Verlag.

Crawford, A. (1997) *The Local Governance of Crime: Appeals to Community and Partnership*, Oxford: Clarendon Press.

Crawford, A. (1998) *Crime Prevention and Community Safety*, London: Longman.

Downes, D. (1966) *The Delinquent Solution: A Study in Subcultural Theory*, London: Routledge and Kegan Paul.

Downes, D. and Rock, P. (2003) *Understanding Deviance* (4th edn), Oxford: Oxford University Press.

Edwards, A. and Benyon, J. (2000) Community Governance, Crime Control and Local Diversity, *Crime Prevention and Community Safety: An International Journal*, 2 (3): 35–55.

Edwards, A. and Hughes, G. (2002) Introduction: The Community Governance of Crime Control, in G. Hughes and A. Edwards (eds) *Crime Control and Community: The New Politics of Public Safety*, Collumpton: Willan.

Etzioni, A. (1995) *The Spirit of Community*, London: Fontana Press.

Etzioni, A. (1997) *The New Golden Rule: Community and Morality in a Democratic Society*, London: Profile.

Fielding, N. (1996) Enforcement, Service and Community Models of Policing, in W. Saulsbury, J. Mott and T. Newburn (eds) *Themes in Contemporary Policing*, London: Independent Committee of Enquiry into the Role and Responsibilities of the Police.

Foster, J. (1995) Informal Social Control and Community Crime Prevention, *British Journal of Criminology*, 35 (4): 563–83.

Foucault, M. (1982) The Subject and Power, in H.L. Dreyfus and P. Rabinow (eds) *Michel Foucault Second Edition*, Chicago: Chicago University Press.

Garland, D. (1996) The Limits of the Sovereign State, *British Journal of Criminology*, 36 (4): 445–71.

Giddens, A. (1998) *The Third Way, the Renewal of Social Democracy*, Cambridge: Polity Press.

Goldstein, H. (1979) Improving Policing: A Problem Orientated Approach, *Crime and Delinquency*, 25: 236–58.

Gouldner, A.W. (1975) *For Sociology: Renewal and Critique in Sociology Today*, Harmondsworth: Penguin.

Graham, J. and Bennett, T. (1995) *Crime Prevention Strategies in Europe and North America*, New York: Criminal Justice Press.

Green, S. (2008) The National Probation Service, in Y. Jewkes (ed.) *A Dictionary of Punishment and Corrections*, Cullompton: Willan.

Grinc, R.M. (1994) 'Angels in Marble': Problems in Stimulating Community Involvement in Community Policing, *Crime and Delinquency*, 40: 437–68.

Hindelang, M.J., Gottfredson, M.R. and Garofalo, J. (1978) *Victims of Personal Crime, An Empirical Foundation for a Theory of Personal Victimisation*, Cambridge, MA: Ballinger.

Hirschi, T. (1969) *Causes of Delinquency*, Berkeley: University of California Press.

Home Office (1991) *Safer Communities: The Local Delivery of Crime Prevention Through the Partnership Approach*, London: Home Office (The Morgan Report).

Home Office (2006) *Offender Management Caseload Statistics*, Statistical Bulletin 18/06, London: Home Office.

Home Office (2008) *From the Neighbourhood to the National: Policing Our Communities Together*, Green Paper, CM 7448, London: Home Office.

Hope, T. and Foster, J. (1992) Conflicting Forces: Changing the Dynamics of Crime and Community on a 'Problem Estate', *British Journal of Criminology*, 32 (4): 488–504.

Hope, T. and Shaw, M. (eds) (1988) *Communities and Crime Reduction*, London: HMSO.

Hughes, G. (2002) Plotting the Rise of Community Safety: Critical Reflections on Crime Prevention and Community Safety, in G. Hughes and A. Edwards (eds) *Crime Control and Community: The New Politics of Public Safety*, Collumpton: Willan.

Hughes, G. (2007) *The Politics of Crime and Community*, Basingstoke: Palgrave Macmillan.

Jefferson, T. (1990) *The Case Against Paramilitary Policing*, Milton Keynes: Open University Press.

Johnston, L. and Shearing, C. (2003) *The Governance of Security: Explorations in Policing and Justice*, London: Routledge.

Jones, T. and Newburn, T. (1996) *Policing and Disaffected Communities: A Review of the Literature, a Report to the Standing Advisory Committee on Human Rights*, London: Policy Studies Institute.

Kornhauser, R. (1978) *Social Sources of Delinquency*, Chicago: University of Chicago Press.

Lacey, N. and Zedner, L. (1995) Discourse of Community in Criminal Justice, *Journal of Law and Society*, 22 (3): 301–25.

Laycock, L. and Tilley, N. (1995) *Policing and Neighbourhood Watch: Strategic Issues*, Crime Detection and Prevention Series Paper 60, London: Home Office.

Matza, D. (1964) *Delinquency and Drift*, London: John Wiley.

Mays, J.B. (1954) *Growing up in the City*, Liverpool: University Press.

McConville, C. and Shepherd, D. (1992) *Watching Police, Watching Communities*, London: Routledge.

Merton, R.K. (1938) Social Structure and Anomie, *American Sociological Review*, 3: 672–82.

Merton, R.K. (1957) Priorities in Scientific Discovery: A Chapter in the Sociology of Science, *American Sociological Review*: 22, 219–29.

Morris, T. (1957) *The Criminal Area*, London: Routledge and Kegan Paul.

Nellis, M. (2000) Creating Community Justice, in S. Ballintyne, K. Pease and S. Mclaren (eds) *Key Issues in Crime Reduction and Community Safety*, London: IPPR.

Nelken, D. (1985) Community Involvement in Crime Control, *Current Legal Problem*, 38: 239–67.

Newman, O. (1973) *Defensible Space*, London: Architectural Press.

New Statesman (1995a) *Tough on Crime*, 3 March.

New Statesman (1995b) *Friendly Society*, 10 March.

Pease, K. (1997) Crime Prevention, in M. Maguire, R. Morgan and R. Reiner (eds) *The Oxford Handbook of Criminology*, Oxford: Clarendon Press.

Reiss, A.J. (1992) Police Organisation in the 20th Century, in M. Tonry and N. Morris *Modern Policing, Crime and Justice: A Review of the Research*, Crime and Justice Series, 15, Chicago: University of Chicago Press.

Respect Task Force (2006) *Respect Action Plan*, London: Home Office.

Rosenbaum, D.P. (1988) Community Crime Prevention: A Review and Synthesis of the Literature, *Justice Quarterly*, 5: 323–95.

Sampson, A., Stubbs, P., Smith, D., Pearson, G. and Blagg, H. (1988) Crime Localities and the Multi-agency Approach, *British Journal of Criminology*, 28 (4): 478–93.

Scarman, Lord (1981) *The Brixton Disorders 10–12 April 1981: Report on the Inquiry by the Rt. Hon. The Lord Scarman, OBE*: London: HMSO.

Shapland, J. (2008) Contested Ideas of Community and Justice, in J. Shapland (ed.) *Justice, Community and Civil Society: A Contested Terrain*, Cullompton: Willan.

Shaw, C. and McKay, H. (1942) *Juvenile Delinquency and Urban Areas*, Chicago: University of Chicago Press.

Siegel, L.J. (1995) *Criminology: Theories, Patterns and Typologies*, Minneapolis/St Paul: West Publishing Company.

Skogan, W.G. (1994) The Impact of Community Policing on Neighbourhood Residents: A Cross-Site Analysis, in D.P. Rosenbaum (ed.) *The Challenge of Community Policing: Testing the Promise*, Thousand Oaks, CA: Sage Publications.

Sutherland, E.H., Cressey, D.R. and Luckenbill, D.F. (1992) *Principles of Criminology* (11th edn), Dix Hills, NY: General Hall.

Tierney, J. (1996) *Criminology: Theory and Context*, London: Prentice Hall.

Toby, J. (1957) Social Disorganization and Stake in Conformity: Complementary Factors in the Predatory Behaviour of Hoodlums, *Journal of Criminal Law, Criminology and Police Science*, 48: 12–17.

Walklate, S. (1998) Crime and Community: Fear or Trust? *British Journal of Sociology*, 49 (4): 550–69.

Wasik, M. (2008) The Legal Framework, in S. Green, S. Feasey and E. Lancaster (eds) *Addressing Offending Behaviour*, Cullompton: Willan.

Wilson, J.Q. and Kelling, G. (1982) Broken Windows, *Atlantic Monthly* (March): 29–38.

Wirth, L. (1964) *On Cities and Social Life*, London: University of Chicago Press.

Woolf, H. and Tumim, S. (1991) *Report into the Prison Disturbances, April 1990*, Cmd 1456, London: HMSO.

Young, J. (1997) Left Realist Criminology: Radical in Its Analysis, Realist in its Policy, in M. Maguire, R. Morgan and R. Reiner (eds) *The Oxford Handbook of Criminology* (2nd edn), Oxford: Oxford University Press.

2 Punishment and the community

This chapter is designed to plot the development of penal policy in England and Wales. The aim is to explain these developments with reference to the political and penal conditions that help to explain their emergence. The purpose of this is to plot the various ways in which the community has been involved in punishment. Whereas the previous chapter focused on theories of crime and their relationship to criminal justice, this chapter is focused upon the penal system and therefore more explicitly concerned with the progression of penal policy and legislation. As with Chapter 1, the aim is to plot the emergence and characteristics of a political and ideological perspective within the penal system that is distinctively different from previous invocations of community. This will then provide the platform for Chapters 3 and 4, in which the relationship between politics and community will be more carefully mapped out in an effort to demonstrate the influence of this perspective on both political rhetoric and crime control policy.

This chapter will be split into six main parts. The first provides a brief synopsis of pre-penitentiary forms of corporal and capital punishment. This is discussed because parallels can be drawn between the public humiliation and shaming aspects of this form of punishment and the present-day focus on strategies of responsibilisation. The second section will focus on the direction of policy up to the early 1960s and deals primarily with the rise of the rehabilitative ideal. The third section will examine the diversionary policies that developed during the 1960s, 1970s and early 1980s. The fourth section will outline the shift in the late 1980s towards a punitive political consensus, whilst the fifth section will outline recent attempts to devolve attitudes and responsibilities for criminal justice and public order to the wider community. The sixth section discusses restorative justice as a case study example of the shifting onus of responsibility for crime control.

These sections are intended to reflect broad changes in the direction of criminal justice policy. The first section outlines the types of punishment that were administered before the advent of the penitentiary, when corporal and capital sentences were conducted in the community. This provides an interesting introduction to the development of criminal justice policy in the twentieth century and describes pre-modern forms of public shaming. Both the fundamental reasoning behind this type of punishment and the reasons for its decline will be outlined.

This material will be returned to in Chapter 7. Section two outlines the development of policy from 1900 up until the early 1960s. This period of time is typified by a largely linear method of punishment focusing on the prison system to provide the ultimate medium for punishment, deterrence and rehabilitation. The third section begins in the 1960s with what Jock Young (1997) has referred to as 'a crisis of aetiology' combined with a fiscal crisis in the penal system. Attempts to combat the causes of crime by improving social and economic circumstances had apparently failed and the prison population expanded at a frightening rate. In response to this sharp rise a proliferation of policies offering alternatives to custody developed. The 1970s and 1980s saw the development of a two-tier system of punishment, described by Anthony Bottoms (1977) as a 'strategy of bifurcation'. This strategy offers harsh, custodial punishment for those crimes deemed most awful by society yet offers a multitude of non-custodial alternative punishments for lesser crimes. The fourth section begins in the late 1980s when a reconceptualisation of the 'philosophy' of punishment was witnessed. The rehabilitative ideal further declined and policy moved towards a 'just deserts' model. The re-emphasis on punishment, incarceration and protecting the public were the products of this shift in direction. The fifth section concludes with a discussion of the 1998 Crime and Disorder Act and the underlying ideologies that informed the Labour administration's rhetoric of criminal justice. The sixth and final section seeks to explore restorative justice as a manifestation of these ideological predilections.

The purpose of this exploration into the development of policy is to show how current strategies of responsibilisation have been incorporated within the criminal justice framework and the process by which such appeals have been justified. This will then provide a platform to go on in Chapters 3 and 4 to assess both the ideological underpinnings of current criminal justice policy and the concerns and ambiguities raised by the application of such policies.

The public spectacle of punishment

Until the late eighteenth century much punishment revolved around the administration of physical pain upon the offender. It is these forms of punishment that are of interest here. Not because of their brutality, or because of their eventual abolition, but because the offenders were punished in public. The reasons for this spectacle and the reasons for its decline will be discussed below. The relevance of this discussion is that it represents a point in time when punishment required the involvement of the wider community. This involvement, though in many ways different, echoes contemporary calls for the community to take on more responsibility for crime control (Garland 1996). This material will be returned to in Chapter 7 to help assess strategies of responsibilisation and the underlying ideological assumptions that are used to justify the community's inclusion in the criminal justice system.

Up to the end of the eighteenth century prison was only ever used for offenders in a minority of cases for a minority of offences:

At the Old Bailey, the major criminal court for London and Middlesex, imprisonments accounted for no more than 2.3 percent of the judges' sentences in the years 1770 to 1774.

(Ignatieff 1978: 15)

At this time there were a range of other sentences that could be used for serious offences. These included banishment, hanging, whipping and the pillory. Of particular interest here are those sentences that involve a degree of public participation, such as hanging, whipping, the pillory, branding and the stocks. As such, this discussion will be limited to these forms of punishment and torture. Similarly, no great discussion of the types of offences that would be punishable by these sentences will be undertaken. Suffice it to say that these sentences were commonplace and delivered frequently. For example, by the late eighteenth century, over 200 crimes were punishable by death (Ignatieff 1978). The criminal law was referred to as 'the Bloody Code'.

Hanging and whipping are self-explanatory forms of punishment that everyone will be familiar with. The pillory is a less well-known sanction and therefore requires some brief description:

Offenders who aroused a high degree of public indignation, such as shopkeepers found using false weights, persons convicted of hoarding or speculating in the grain trade, or persons convicted of homosexual assault, were locked in head stocks in a marketplace or in front of a jail and sentenced to endure an hour of the crowds' abuse.

(Ignatieff 1978: 21)

It is clear from this that the pillory did involve some form of social dynamic with the crowd, or wider community. The same is also true for hanging and whipping:

Like hanging, whipping was a public ritual inflicted by a parish officer or court official for the edification of the populace. Hence it was considered important to stage the ritual at a time and place sure of attracting attention.

(Ignatieff 1978: 20)

This clearly identifies the important role of the public in the delivery of such sentences. Not only was the public's involvement important for the punishment of the offender but it was also important for the moral education of the community.

There are many explanations and justifications for the use of such punishments. By and large these are not remarkably different from the explanations used to justify contemporary sanctions. Whilst the rehabilitative ideal may have been broadly missing and the underlying principles of proportionality and the rule of law absent, notions of retribution, deterrence and repentance were fundamental to the delivery of such sentences. Foucault (1977) also argues that public torture also acted as a symbol of the monarch's power. However, what is remarkably different is the public spectacle of these punishments.

Why were the public witnesses to such punishments? How did people make sense of and understand the grizzly spectacle of human suffering (Gatrell 1994, McGowen 2000)?[1] Why did such practices stop? These questions will now be considered in terms of the social and cultural developments that explain these changes. As Ignatieff (1978) states above, there are clearly two components to the public's involvement. Firstly, it provides an opportunity to vent their anger upon particular offenders who may have committed particularly reprehensible crimes, and secondly, it teaches the consequences of criminal behaviour. The visible, certain and graphic nature of these forms of punishment was designed to leave an abiding memory of the punishment, aimed at deterring others from similar courses of action:

> Not only must people know, they must see with their own eyes. Because they must be made to be afraid; but also because they must be the witnesses, the guarantors, of the punishment, and because they must to a certain extent take part in it.
>
> (Foucault 1977: 58)

The public therefore fulfils a vital role in the spectacle and symbol of all forms of public torture. They are at once both 'benefactors' of the educational component of the torture and 'instruments' of the monarch's displeasure, their own anger often vital to the legitimacy of the event:

> All such ritual punishments depended for their effectiveness as a ceremonial of deterrence on the crowd's tacit support of the authorities' sentence.
>
> (Ignatieff 1978: 21)

> The people also had a right to take part. The condemned man, carried in procession, exhibited, humiliated, with the horror of his crime recalled in innumerable ways, was offered to the insults, sometimes to the attacks of the spectators. The vengeance of the people was called upon to become an unobtrusive part of the vengeance of the sovereign.
>
> (Foucault 1977: 58–9)

Of course, it was not always the case that the public's anger remained directed against the criminal. There are numerous instances when the crowd's sympathies shift from the accused to the authorities presiding over the sentence. According to both Foucault (1977) and Ignatieff (1978) these shifts in sympathies derive from a number of sources. In the case of non-capital sentences such as the use of the pillory, if the offender was well liked or if the community felt he had been mistreated by the authorities the crowd would often express its solidarity with the accused and focus its aggressions on the local magistrate:

> Such was the case when Daniel Isaac Eaton, the aged and distinguished radical printer, was sentenced to an hour's pillory in Newgate in 1813. Much to

the government's chagrin, Eaton's head was garlanded with flowers and he was brought refreshments during his ordeal, while the police and magistrates in attendance were reviled and abused.

(Ignatieff 1978: 21)

This clearly undermines the intended purpose of the sentence and demonstrates the implicit power that the community could bring to bear on the manner in which a sentence was delivered. No longer is the experience shameful and humiliating, but mild, and even gratifying. Similar experiences have been witnessed for capital crimes. Whilst the inevitability of the sentence usually remains unchanged, if the crowd feels that the offender's 'last rights' have been violated or if the offender is particularly eloquent in protestations of his innocence the crowd's loyalties may shift. If the torture appears particularly brutal or if the offender shows great courage in his ordeal, again the crowd may shift its sympathies.

This is important because it gives us some interesting clues regarding the types of relationships that existed between the condemned and the wider community. For the crowd to make an informed decision regarding its loyalties in the above-mentioned Daniel Isaac Eaton case, it must have had prior knowledge of the convicted and been aware of his crime and social circumstances. This suggests a high level of community cohesion and social stability where the extended family and communal life-style facilitate detailed and comprehensive relations in a locality. The crowd's hostility towards the condemned in more typical cases also reinforces a notion of community outrage and mutual feeling. This view would seem to be supported by a whole tradition of sociological thought that focuses upon the high levels of community solidarity typical of pre-industrial society (Tonnies 1887, Durkheim 1893). This theme will be returned to in Chapter 5.

If the above explains the reasons for the public's participation in rituals of torture, how then can we explain why the practice stopped? To begin with it needs to be noticed that the late eighteenth and early nineteenth centuries were far from stable times. The Industrial Revolution and all the social, political and economic upheaval that came with that inevitably had implications for criminal justice. Although capital and corporal punishment continued to be practised well into the nineteenth century it became increasingly less severe and was slowly moved behind the prison walls, away from the public gaze:

By the end of the eighteenth and the beginning of the nineteenth century, the gloomy festival of punishment was dying out, though here and there it flickered momentarily into life.

(Foucault 1977: 8)

Therefore, the simplest way to explain the decline of the spectacle of punishment is to 'blame' it on the reformatory ideals of the nineteenth century. This would not be unfair, and the work of social reformers like Beccaria, John Howard and Elizabeth Fry should not be underestimated. However, it is not my intention to detail the growth and expansion of the penitentiary or to plot the impact of industrialisation on criminal justice policy. These factors are undoubtedly relevant and connected. Instead I want to briefly point to the impact of public torture and execution on the crowd and on its perception of the state authority.

Foucault (1977) cites one reason for the abolition of public torture and execution as:

> this rite that 'concluded the crime' was suspected of being in some undesirable way linked with it. It was as if the punishment was thought to equal, if not exceed, in savagery the crime itself, to accustom the spectators to a ferocity from which one wished to divert them, to show them the frequency of crime, to make the executioner resemble a criminal, judges murderers, to reverse roles at the last moment, to make the tortured criminal an object of pity or admiration.
>
> (Foucault 1977: 9)

What Foucault (1977) is essentially saying is that the public spectacle of punishment brutalised not only the accused but also the watching audience. Further, it made violence and pain the instruments of the state and acquainted all with their uses and techniques. This had the effect of threatening the legitimacy of the authorities, who began to look like the criminals they sought to make examples of. This was complemented by a rhetoric of penal reform that sought to demonstrate the brutal and degrading aspects of public torture and punishment. This point should not be overstated and is only a very partial explanation for the abolition of public forms of punishment. However, it remains important because it illustrates the influence that sentencing can have on the public's attitudes both towards the guilty and towards the state.

This section sits less comfortably in this chapter than others and therefore needs to conclude with a moment of explanation. There are two reasons for its inclusion. The first is that it represents a point in time when criminal justice practice relied on a degree of public involvement. The second is that the role of emotions and mob mentality in the delivery of justice and punishment is returned to in Chapter 7, where more recent attempts to re-emotionalise justice are discussed.

The rise of the rehabilitative ideal

Whilst it is clearly debatable whether rehabilitation in prison ever really works, this period in time represents what is typically referred to as the 'traditional' model of criminal justice. Determining when rehabilitation became a significant sentencing aim is difficult. It is clear that activists Howard and Fry believed in the importance of reforming characters as well as systems, though they never demonstrated how the penitentiary would actually achieve this (Ignatieff 1978). However, from the early twentieth century (1907) the modern probation service came into existence. It is from this point that aims to guide the offender to a law-abiding life-style became enshrined within the system. Thus the rise of the rehabilitative ideal has its roots in the early twentieth-century Christian efforts to lead offenders away from criminogenic 'temptations'.

It was during this time that the institution of the prison was considered to be an effective and appropriate method for dealing with serious offenders. This attitude is reflected in criminal justice policy during these years. This is not to suggest that there were not changes to the penal system during this time or that alternatives were not developed, but that the use of custodial sentences was overwhelmingly used to punish offenders. In comparison to today's standards, the prison population was small and the problem of crime was thought to be contained. The deterrent effect of the prison was accepted as effective and, as a result, the development of alternatives was considered secondary.

However, it did become noticeable that there was a class of criminals who were perceived as a problem. Whilst the prison system seemed to be effective for the majority there developed a group of habitual offenders that the system did not appear to deter. This is perhaps the earliest indication that prison did not work for everyone and in 1895 the Gladstone Report (Report on the Departmental Committee on Prisons 1895) endorsed the search for alternatives to incarceration to deal with this group of career criminals. In an effort to address this problem scientific treatment for the rehabilitation of offenders on an individual level was introduced.

Although prison remained the primary method of crime control, the Borstal system was developed for young adults and the role of the probation service continued to expand. In 1907 the Probation of Offenders Act officially introduced the concept of probation as an alternative to custody. The aim of probation was to supervise the moral rehabilitation of the offender and to prevent crime. The use of probation grew steadily and the National Association of Probation Officers (NAPO) was established in 1912. The 1925 Criminal Justice Act made it mandatory for each Petty Sessional Division to have a probation officer attached to it.

It was not until the 1948 Criminal Justice Act that the role of probation was extended to include up to twelve months of after-care. The focus slowly shifted onto the rehabilitation of offenders as all types of corporal punishment were abolished. The Act introduced attendance centres as an alternative to custody for petty offenders, who could give up their free time to partake in rehabilitative activities. Similarly, detention centres were developed for juveniles who were perceived as needing a milder form of correction than was offered by the Borstal system, yet something more severe than probation. In addition to these reforms the Act greatly expanded the use of the fine as a further diversionary, non-custodial measure:

> An even more important reform was brought about by the Criminal Justice Act 1948, which greatly extended the range of indictable offences that were punishable by fines, regardless of the court of conviction. This paved the way for the spectacular post-war increase in the use of the fine.
>
> (Cavadino and Dignan 1997: 209)

In general, the 1948 Act increased the role of probation, expanded and formalised the role of alternatives to custody, introduced a more comprehensive form of juvenile detention and abandoned the punitive prison model. Within this context the rehabilitation of offenders and the protection of juveniles from the criminal influences of prison became far more important.

This period of penal history highlights the shift in focus from the Victorian model of the 'punitive penitentiary' to the rehabilitative model of the modern prison system. Whilst alternatives to custody were introduced, such notions were still in their infancy and the monolithic institution of the prison remained the central fact in the punishment of offenders. This does not mean that prison was the only, or even primary, form of sanctioning offenders. The fine was used and the death penalty still existed. However, the prison came to represent the eventual consequence of offending behaviour. Yet the precedent for alternatives to custody had been set and their proliferation is the fundamental feature of new directions in criminal justice policy during the 1960s, 1970s and early 1980s

The growth of diversions from custody

The 1960s witnessed a dramatic rise in recorded crime and numbers of convicted offenders, resulting in a dramatic rise in the prison population. The number of offenders serving time in penal institutions rose from 20,000 in the mid-1950s to 27,000 in 1960 and a staggering 35,000 in 1967 (Vass 1990). This unprecedented growth placed a great strain upon the penal system. The problem of overcrowding and poor conditions led to a general concern about the ability of the prison system to accommodate the rising crime rate. This concern was further exacerbated by the economic burden that accompanied such an increase.

Both the political and philosophical consequences of this new crime phenomenon are not to be underestimated. At a political level the rising crime rate was blamed upon the newly established state welfare system for undermining individual responsibility and creating a dependent population that was bereft of social values and moral fibre. It is in this classical liberal political philosophy that the origins of the New Right can be found:

> The moral fibre of our people has been weakened. The state which does for its citizens what they can do for themselves is an evil state; and a state which removes all choice and responsibility from its people and makes them broiler hens will create the irresponsible society. No-one cares, no-one saves, no-one bothers – why should they when the state spends all its energies taking money from the energetic, successful and thrifty to give to the idle, the failures and the feckless.
>
> (Boyson 1971: 5)

In the rapidly changing face of British society the rising crime level was decisively linked to the negative effects of the welfare system on those with a propensity for moral weakness and sloth. The effect was to lend popularity to the policies of the New Right movement that advocated the importance of individual responsibility and choice. This can clearly be linked to the Thatcherite approach to combating crime in the 1980s. As well as this political concern, the rising prison population also called into doubt the effectiveness and appropriateness of the rehabilitative model of criminal justice. The resultant panic led to a plethora of legislative reform intended to manage this crisis in criminal justice.

In 1962 the Morison Report (Home Office 1962) was published, with the intention of reassuring the public that the Probation Service was capable of dealing with this new crime problem, and the 1967 Criminal Justice Act increased the powers of the Probation Service. This Act included the extension of after-care responsibilities and introduced parole, placing responsibility for it onto the Probation Service. The 1967 Act also introduced the suspended sentence, intended for offenders sentenced to a maximum of two years' imprisonment.[2] The suspended sentence was seen as a very effective measure for combating the size of the prison population but, once introduced, was largely unsuccessful. This was due to the failure to provide proper guidelines for its use. Despite the intention that the suspended sentence should be used only on those offenders who would otherwise receive a custodial sentence, it was in reality perceived by magistrates as an effective deterrent threat for those who would normally not receive a prison term (Bottoms 1981). Rather than diverting offenders away from prison, the suspended sentence was applied to those who would normally receive some other form of non-custodial sentence. Home Office research (Oatham and Simon 1972) showed that between 40 and 50 per cent of those given the suspended sentence would not normally have received a prison sentence. Further, failure to comply with the conditions of the suspended sentence often led to the incarceration of offenders who would not have otherwise received a custodial sentence.

The Advisory Council on the Penal System (1970) examined the negative effects of incarceration and concluded that custodial sentences did not appear to have an effective deterrent capacity and that prison life was degrading and expensive. Therefore the use of community sanctions could provide an effective alternative that limited the stigmatising effect of the criminal label and provided a more progressive method of rehabilitation. The Criminal Justice Act 1972 incorporated many of the recommendations made by this Committee and instituted the community service order and day training centres. Community service orders proved to be a very popular alternative to probation and by the mid-1970s they were in wide use. Essentially, community service orders required offenders to complete between 40 and 240 hours of unpaid supervised work over a one-year period. The popularity of this order is attributed to:

> concern about the rising prison population in the 1960s coupled with attacks on rehabilitative treatment.
>
> (Worrall 1997: 91)

In response to these concerns, diversions from incarceration were being used far more frequently and the acceptability of keeping offenders out of prison was largely endorsed. In addition to these innovations, the Criminal Justice Act 1972 also introduced the compensation order without the victim having to apply for one. This was significant, as it incorporated more fully the philosophy of reparation and restoration within the criminal justice framework and also asserted the rights of the victim within the sentencing process.

Thus, by the late 1970s there was a pervasive body of legislation that sought to provide alternatives to custody and an effective measure for combating the rising prison population and the associated cost to the state. However, this proliferation of alternatives was coupled with a growing disillusionment with the rehabilitative process:

> At the same time as diversion from custody became a probation service 'ideal' the 'rehabilitative ideal' which had lain behind both the 'missionary ideal' and the 'scientific diagnostic ideal', was in trouble. Probation had been in existence for some sixty years or more but had not proved conclusively its effectiveness in terms of rehabilitation.
>
> (Mair 1997: 1200)

The continuing crisis of the rehabilitative model led to the 'nothing works' ideology attributed to Martinson (1974). Although this phrase is much misused and misquoted it has come to mean a crisis of faith in the ability of our institutions and agencies to either reduce crime or rehabilitate offenders. On the back of such disillusionment the Conservative Party under Margaret Thatcher swept to victory in the 1979 General Election. Thatcher's success is often linked to her hard-line 'law and order' rhetoric that promised to redress the 'nothing works' principle by coming down hard on the offending population. The expectation for reform and consolidation was massive and it was under these conditions that the Criminal Justice Act 1982 was conceived.

One of the main innovations of the Criminal Justice Act 1982 was to reintroduce the notion of the 'short, sharp shock' for juvenile offenders. To do this the regimes in Detention Centres were made far more punitive, involving more menial labour and harsher tasks. At the same time Detention Centre sentences were reduced and the Borstal system was transformed into the new youth custody order. The result of this transformation was that the comparative number of juveniles given youth custody orders (sent to 'Borstal') increased dramatically, whereas Detention Centres were used less and less and eventually abolished under the 1988 Criminal Justice Act.

In addition to these changes, the 1982 Act also gave the courts the power to award compensation in its own right rather than in tandem with another form of punishment. Further, if a fine and compensation were considered appropriate, yet the offender could not afford both, preference was given to the compensation order. The ability of courts to impose a limited form of curfew on juveniles in the form of 'night restrictions' as part of a supervision order was also introduced.

Overall, the 1982 Criminal Justice Act put into legislation and formalised many of the informal innovations developed in the late 1970s and early 1980s:

> The 1982 Criminal Justice Act gave statutory enactment to many of these trends: passing power to make care orders institutional or home based from

social workers to magistrates; imposing criteria for making first custodial sentences and any custodial sentences on offenders under the age of 21; making all youth and juvenile custodial sentences determinate; legislating conditions for probation orders.

(Hudson 1993: 45)

One of the hallmarks of the Thatcher regime was a progressive move towards centralisation, and in this respect the 1982 Act was no exception. One of its fundamental aims was to consolidate a number of accepted practices under the mantle of central government, thereby increasing and clarifying the role of the Probation Service and the courts.

Continuing in this trend, the 1984 Statement of National Objectives and Priorities (SNOP) (Home Office 1984) sought to prioritise the various roles of the Probation Service. The central focus on diverting offenders from custody remained, but the SNOP introduced renewed intervention from the Home Office. The underlying aim of the SNOP was to make the Probation Service more accountable, financially responsible and managerial in its approach.

This section ends with the 1988 Criminal Justice Act. This Act is perhaps most conspicuous by its absence from any literature concerning sentencing policy or the development of alternatives to custody, although it did abolish Detention Centres, amalgamating them with youth custody centres to become youth offender institutions. Detention in one of these centres was for people aged over 15.

In general terms this period witnessed the proliferation of alternatives to custody and the enhancement of the role of the Probation Service within the criminal justice system. These changes were largely introduced in response to a rapidly rising prison population and the associated economic and political costs. Bottoms' (1977) strategy of bifurcation is clearly in evidence as a dual system of criminal justice develops:

Bifurcation refers to the dual-edged approach to the problem of offending: differentiating between 'ordinary' or 'run of the mill' offenders with whom less severe measures can be taken on the one hand, and on the other hand 'exceptional', 'very serious' or 'dangerous' offenders who can be made subject to much tougher measures. In this way a bifurcated policy allows government to get tough and soft simultaneously.

(Pitts 1988: 29)

To summarise, the 1970s and 1980s witnessed a dramatic rise in the number of community-based sanctions and a dramatic decline in the rehabilitative ideal. The end result was not what was hoped for. Crime continued to increase, as did the prison population. The extension of the criminal justice system into the community had begun, and with apparently no effect. Concerns were expressed about the 'net-widening' of state sanctions into previously untouched areas of private life (Foucault 1977, Cohen 1979, 1983, 1985, Scull 1984) and the decarceration debate gained momentum.

By the end of the 1980s a plethora of penal reform measures had failed to effectively combat the rise in crime. Despite the emphasis attached to alternatives to custody and the increasingly centralised and interventionist policies of the Home Office, the crisis had not been resolved. The only noticeable effect was the incorporation of more individuals and environments within the criminal justice system. What was to be done?

Tough on crime and populist punitiveness

Populist punitiveness refers to an underlying ethos of punishment and deterrence combined with a political attempt to use this approach to assuage a population perceived as punitive. This does not mean that the policies of the 1990s have managed to reduce crime or the prison population, but that the discussion has changed from one concerned with controlling the crime problem to one concerned with what 'works' politically. Given that none of the policies developed since the 1960s managed to have a significant impact upon the rate of crime, legislative reform has become increasingly severe. If policies cannot affect the rate of crime, the task becomes one of political management (Garland 1996). The government has to be seen to be strong on law and order whilst simultaneously extricating itself from blame in regard to rising crime. The only pragmatic solution to this conundrum was to shift the responsibility for crime onto social structures such as the family and the community. This was coupled with the 'back to basics' ideology of the Major administration that sought to incorporate a moral agenda into the political mainstream. In this way the government could show its commitment to law and order by introducing tougher penalties on criminals whilst diverting blame for the inevitable failure of these policies on the amorality of society. This in turn facilitated the encroachment of central government into more areas of private life, thus expanding the jurisdiction of the criminal justice system. It is within this context that we can understand the process by which 'appeals to community' have been assimilated into contemporary criminal justice policies.

Although the above outline may appear unduly cynical, and notwithstanding the fact that individual politicians were surely acting with the best of intentions, the late 1980s and 1990s witnessed a renewed focus upon punishment and the 'just deserts' model of penal policy. Despite the policies of the 1970s and 1980s failing to effectively reduce the criminal population, the government continued with its policy of community sanctions and alternatives to custody. Against a backdrop of rising public concern and media pressure the government felt compelled to take steps to allay the public fear of crime. Instead of taking a pace backwards to reevaluate the direction of criminal justice, policy the government charged ahead with a package of policies that reinforced what Bottoms (1995) has referred to as 'populist punitiveness'. The increasingly punishment-orientated focus of criminal justice policy permeated into diversions from custody and further undermined the rehabilitative ideal. In the light of government-fuelled punitiveness, a general consensus developed between the two major political parties that pursuing any policy other than one of 'just deserts' would be politically damaging:

A populist sentencing policy soon came to be thought politically advantageous for both major parties, with Howard leading the way and challenging the opposition to disagree, at peril of being called 'soft on crime'.

(Ashworth 1997: 1096)

This approach to criminal justice policy effectively stifled any debate that did not concern itself with severity and public protection and the two main political parties engaged in a game of one-upmanship. This unspoken consensus continued unchecked until the demise of the Conservative administration in May 1997.

The Green Paper *Punishment, Custody and the Community* (Home Office 1988a) was the first indication of this renewed emphasis on punishment. This document was primarily concerned with alleviating prison overcrowding by increasing the role of community sanctions. What is noticeably different about this Green Paper is the emphasis on community sanctions being seen as a punishment and not a 'soft option':

Community service should be rigorous and demanding, otherwise the sentencers and the general public will not accept it as punishment. The need for frequent and punctual reporting is part of the discipline imposed by the order. The work to be done should be useful and of benefit to the community; there is no reparation if the work itself is pointless. Ideally, the public should be able to see the results of the work and, in the process, the offender's self-discipline and motivation should be improved.

(Home Office 1988a, para. 2.5)

The Government believes there is scope for reducing the use of imprisonment by introducing a form of punishment which leaves the offender in the community but has components which embody the three elements identified in Part I, punishment by some deprivation of liberty, action to reduce the risk of offending and recompense to the victim and the public.

(Home Office, 1988a para.3.8)

These two extracts clearly illustrate the emphasis on community punishment and also the concern that such punishments needed to be seen as effective and punitive by both the sentencers and the wider community. This would suggest that one of the aims of the government was to create a public perception of severity. The Green Paper also proposed a number of further restrictions on the liberty of offenders in the community. These included: introducing curfew powers, the extension of tracking offenders in the community by introducing electronic tagging, intermittent or weekend imprisonment and the court insistence that individuals perform certain activities in their free time (e.g. attending football matches or other sporting events). The other major inclusion within this Green Paper was a clear emphasis upon the economics of punishment. The paper made it very clear that financial considerations were paramount to the effective running of community sanctions:

It costs about £1000 to keep an offender in prison for four weeks. The cost of punishment in the community should not exceed the cost of imprisonment, which is a more severe sentence.

(Home Office 1988a, para.3.37)

Following on from these policy initiatives a circular to Chief Probation Officers, *Tackling Offenders: An Action Plan* (Home Office 1988b), consolidated and developed many of the concepts outlined in the Green Paper. This document called upon probation officers to devise tough new community-based punishments that the courts would deem acceptable sentences for juveniles who would otherwise be in danger of receiving custodial sentences. This document was complemented by the government's National Standards for Community Service Orders (Home Office 1989), which emphasised:

the need to make such orders consistently tough and demanding so as to commend themselves to sentencers and command the support of the public.

(Brownlee 1998: 16)

In addition, this document introduced the notion of partnership approaches into the Probation Service. The suggestion was that utilising charities and other local organisations could lead to the implementation of some diversionary schemes.

In response to the 1988 Green Paper the government produced the White Paper *Crime, Justice and Protecting the Public* (Home Office 1990a). This paper marks the culmination of the philosophies and practices that had been developing under the Conservative government during the 1980s. The prime focus of this document was: 'a new and more coherent statutory framework for sentencing' in order to promote 'a more consistent approach to sentencing, so that convicted criminals get their "just desserts" [*sic*]' (Home Office 1990a, paras. 1.5–1.6). This indicates the importance placed upon the retributive theory of justice and centres on the removal of individual liberties as the underlying principle of sentencing. The only exception to this was that it continued to advocate a dual system of punishment, separating offenders guilty of violent or sexual offences from the rest. The focus on 'tougher' forms of community punishment remained and the White Paper asserted the government's legitimate interest in sentencing practices and placed statutory restrictions on the use of custody. In an effort to increase the punitive element of community sanctions the White Paper also introduced the combined order of community service and probation. Furthermore, the White Paper reiterated the need for partnership between the different agencies of the criminal justice system as a method for increased efficiency and cost-effectiveness.

These proposals were accompanied by another Green Paper, *Supervision and Punishment in the Community: A Framework for Action* (Home Office 1990b). The main thrust of this document was intended to prepare the Probation Service for its new roles and responsibilities. As such this included clarifying the role of the Probation Service, assessing the need for organisational change, funding criteria, training and the involvement of private and voluntary sectors. This paper conferred upon the Probation Service an extension of the National Standards to include not only community service orders but also report writing, probation orders, supervision orders, any new orders, the management of hostels and supervision before and after release from custody.

The 1991 Criminal Justice Act was the legislative expression of these changes. As such, it represents the consolidation and clarification of a new philosophy of justice. With this Act the government's intention was to outline the most important facets of its approach to criminal justice. Anne Worrall (1997) draws upon the work of Sanders and Senior (1994) who identify six key principles within the Act that dictate the direction of policy. The first of these principles is that sentencing: 'should reflect the severity of the offence committed and custody should be reserved for only the most serious offences' (Sanders and Senior 1994: 124). This essentially dictates that the courts must primarily look to the seriousness of the offence for guidance in deciding the appropriate penalty. The second principle asserts: 'A sharper distinction should be drawn between property offences and offences against the person' (Sanders and Senior 1994: 124). This is largely self-explanatory and indicates the government's desire to see violent and sexual crimes dealt with most harshly. The third principle is: 'Community sentences stand in their own right and should not be seen as alternatives to custody' (Sanders and Senior 1994: 125). This principle reaffirms the notion that non-custodial sentences should not be seen as a soft option and are an appropriate punishment in their own right. The fourth principle is: 'Young people should be dealt with in a way that takes account of their maturity and stage of development' (Sanders and Senior 1994: 125). In an attempt to fulfil this commitment the government replaced the Juvenile Court (which dealt with those between 10 and 16 years of age) with the Youth Court (to deal with those between 11 and 17 years of age). The fifth principle is: 'The intention of the court should be properly reflected in the way that a prison sentence is served' (Sanders and Senior 1994: 125). The Act therefore abolished the parole system and replaced it with an early release scheme. This meant that the automatic remission process that released prisoners after two-thirds of their sentence was served or a discretionary release after one-third of their sentence was served was abandoned, in place of provisions that all prisoners must serve at least half their sentence in custody. The sixth and final principle is: 'The whole criminal justice system should be administered efficiently and without discrimination' (Sanders and Senior 1994: 126). This essentially asserts that the criminal justice system should be cost-effective and not discriminate on the basis of race, age or gender.

In an attempt to ensure that these principles were effectively implemented within the criminal justice system the Act introduced many of the changes outlined in the White Paper (Home Office 1990a). The Act introduced the unit fine, which was intended to ensure that fines took account of the offender's ability to pay, and also replaced Social Inquiry Reports (SIRs) with Pre-Sentence reports (PSRs). The main distinction between these two reports was that PSRs no longer allowed the Probation Service to include social and personal information that was not specifically related to the offence committed and removed the ability of the Probation Service to make sentencing recommendations.

The 1991 Act also introduced the 'combination order', which allowed courts to pass down sentences that included both community service and probation. The use of probation as a sentence in its own right rather than as an alternative to a sentence was also introduced. In addition, curfew orders were introduced for offenders over 16 years of age. This order stipulated that the offender must remain in a specific area (usually the offender's home) for between 2 and 12 hours every day for up to six months. For particularly troublesome offenders the use of electronic tags was endorsed to monitor their activities.

The 1991 Criminal Justice Act was hailed as one of the most far-reaching and important pieces of legislation in the post-war period. Its clear intention was to provide a framework for criminal justice that would effectively reduce the prison population by strengthening community punishments to provide an effective alternative to custody. The Act:

> represented the culmination of Thatcherite criminal justice policy and was surprisingly radical in its attempt to implement a 'just deserts' model of sentencing, which endorsed community penalties for the vast majority of offenders.
>
> (Worrall 1997: 36)

Despite the significance placed upon the 1991 Act, its impact was short lived and the resultant difficulties of trying to implement a number of the reforms led to a complete reversal of policy under the Major administration in the early 1990s. Although there was a reported drop in the prison population (Home Office 1993) there was a rise in the number of fines and community sentences. However, it was the difficulties associated with administering the unit fine, managing the 'two offence rule' and restrictions on the consideration of previous convictions that undermined the direction of the 1991 Act. As a result of these difficulties the 1993 Criminal Justice Act abolished the unit fine, the 'two offences rule', which allowed the courts to consider only one other associated offence when determining a sentence, and abandoned restrictions on the consideration of previous offences.

Consequently, 1993 witnessed a dramatic reversal in the rhetoric and practice behind criminal justice policy. Against a backlash of public anger about the incidence of juvenile crime and the failure of government to incarcerate these youths, a re-emphasis on the legitimacy of the prison sentence as an effective method of punishment emerged. The highly publicised incidence of 'joyriding' and the appalling murder of Jamie Bulger by two children caused a moral panic about youth crime. The effect of this outrage was an increased public perception that prison was the only effective method for dealing with such anti-social individuals. Community punishments were criticised for their overly liberal and 'wishy-washy' approach to deviancy that was clearly not deterring criminality or protecting the public. In response to this public concern the Home Secretary, Michael Howard, pursued a policy that Bottoms has referred to as 'populist punitiveness':

> Generally speaking, this factor is probably of appeal to some politicians for one of three main reasons: first, because they believe that resort to increased

punitiveness will have an effect in reducing the crime rate through general deterrence and/or incapacitation; secondly, because they believe that it may help to strengthen the moral consensus in society against certain kinds of activity – especially where, as in the field of drugs, there is a degree of moral contestation as regards the activity in question; and thirdly because they believe that the adoption of a 'populist punitive' stance will satisfy a particular electoral constituency.

(Bottoms 1995: 39)

This particular approach to policy was explicitly stated by the Home Secretary at the 1993 Conservative Party conference at Blackpool with the now famous (or infamous) assertion 'prison works'. This statement was followed by twenty-seven pledges intended to 'tighten up' the criminal justice system. Of these twenty-seven pledges seventeen found their way into the 1994 Criminal Justice and Public Order Act. In general, the 1994 Act had none of the overall structure of the 1991 Act and was largely perceived as a collection of measures designed to respond to the media-led public outcry for more punitive sanctions:

The Act includes, amongst others, provisions for secure training orders for 12–14 year olds; increases the grounds for refusing bail; allows inferences to be drawn from the use of the right to silence; and introduces a new offence of aggravated trespass. Although as a piece of legislation it has little coherence and is, in many ways, merely a mish-mash of largely unconnected provisions, it clearly belongs within the Thatcherite 'law and order' crime control tradition.

(Newburn 1995: 124)

One of the more controversial aspects of the 1994 Act was the criminalisation of entirely new groups of individuals, namely demonstrators, squatters and those attending 'raves'. This factor can perhaps be seen as a not very subtle attempt to appease the media and the moral majority by outlawing certain types of youth culture deemed unsavoury. In this respect, the allegation that the 1994 Act was little more than an appeal to the 'populist punitiveness' prevalent at the time is justified. The aim of the 1991 Act to structure and organise the criminal justice system around a graduated system of punishment with the emphasis on community sanctions and 'just deserts' had been quickly and effectively subverted. The 1994 Act witnessed the return to the 'traditional' model of justice that has at its core the use of custody as the most effective method of punishment. Whilst the early 1990s emphasis on punishment still remained, the 1994 Act represented a shift towards a system of justice that was not so concerned with the reduction of crime but more interested in being seen to protect the public:

Prison works. It ensures that we are protected from murderers, muggers and rapists – and it makes many who are tempted to commit crime think twice . . . this will mean that many more people will go to prison. I do not flinch from that. We shall no longer judge the success of our system of justice by a fall in our prison population.

(Michael Howard, Home Secretary, Conservative Party Conference 1993)[3]

In 1995 the government produced the consultation document *Strengthening Punishment in the Community* (Home Office 1995). The central recommendation of this document was the replacement of existing community sanctions with a single overarching 'community sentence'. This proposal allowed the courts greater discretion in deciding what the components of a community sentence ought to be and placed the Probation Service firmly within the court's power. Furthermore, this paper proposed that community sentences no longer needed the consent of the offender, thus making the notion of 'contract' obsolete. One major criticism of this suggestion is that by removing the necessity of compliance by the offender you clearly place in jeopardy their co-operation. The overall thrust of this document has much in common with the 1988 Green Paper (Home Office 1988a) and is largely concerned with toughening up the perception of community sentences so as to increase public confidence in these measures:

> The criminal justice system can only operate effectively if it retains the confidence of society as a whole. It is the view of the Government that the role of community sentences is poorly understood and – perhaps as a result – that they have failed to command the confidence of the public despite the greater prominence and extra resources given to the probation service in recent years. Probation supervision is still widely regarded as a soft option. Although in many cases, this perception may be misconceived, it must be addressed.
>
> (Home Office 1995, para. 4.4)

Continuing in this trend, and with the general election looming, the government produced the White Paper *Protecting the Public* (Home Office 1996). This paper reiterated the government's concern to promote the severity of community sentences and the need to view such sentences as punitive rather than rehabilitative. In a further effort to reinforce the government's law and order policies the White Paper introduced several new sentencing practices that clearly reflected the 'prison works' ideal. These practices included: the abolition of the automatic early release, automatic life sentences for second-time serious violent or sexual offences, mandatory seven-year sentences for third-time drug-trafficking offences and mandatory three-year sentences for third-time burglary offences. With these changes the government firmly and undeniably reasserted the role of the prison within the criminal justice system and substantiated its punitive rhetoric.

Both the 1995 Green Paper and the 1996 White Paper clearly pursue policies and ideals that are based upon the previously disputed notion that 'prison works'. The underlying aim of this policy direction was to promote public confidence in the government's ability to deal harshly and effectively with society's anti-social elements. Whether or not these policies have actually had a positive effect upon rates of criminality is another issue. What government policy between 1988 and

1996 has done is to shift the aim of policy from controlling and preventing crime to managing the whims of public opinion. Whilst there is clearly a strong political motivation for this shift, it is less clear that a consistent and logical framework designed to safeguard the public from crime has been progressed. By pandering to public opinion rather than the needs of criminal justice the fear of crime has soared and an unfortunate precedent has been set. This precedent asserts that the purpose of criminal justice policy to reduce criminality is secondary to the management of public opinion for political advantage. It is within this context that the notion of 'anything works' is applicable. Providing that policy effectively responds and reassures the public, it does not actually matter if it affects the reality of crime. If the public wants it, then it works.

Engendering responsibility for crime control

In 1997 the Labour Party rose to power after eighteen years of Conservative government. The Labour Party in opposition had largely failed to provide an effective radical alternative to the law and order policies of the Conservative Party. Indeed the Labour Party had endorsed the consensus that increasingly punitive methods of punishment were the most appropriate response to rising crime. In this respect it too had succumbed to a political agenda over a crime control agenda. However, after such a prolonged period of Conservative rule, and given the huge Labour majority, an atmosphere of optimism and hope for change pervaded. Although the newly appointed Home Secretary, Jack Straw, was perceived to be on the right of the party and sharing many of the previous administration's law and order ideals, the rhetoric of New Labour suggested a new vision for criminal justice.

In 1998 the Crime and Disorder Act came into being. There are four main sections to this Act dealing with: youth crime, combating crime and anti-social behaviour, measures to reduce delays and more effective sentencing. In general this Act shares very little of the punitive message of the 'just deserts' model of justice progressed under the Conservative administration. However, it is far more difficult to detect if any kind of ideological vein exists within the Crime and Disorder Act. According to James and Raine (1998), much of the direction of the Act seems to stem from several Home Office-commissioned studies. However, commentators such as Nellis (2000) and Driver and Martell (1998) have argued that both the Crime and Disorder Act and the Labour administration have been heavily influenced by the communitarian movement.

Firstly, it is necessary to provide a brief commentary concerning the two main areas of the Act. The first section, on youth, introduces a number of new child regulations. The Act introduces local child curfews, youth offending teams, final warning cautions, parenting orders, child safety orders, reparation orders, action plan orders and police powers against truancy. It is noticeable that these recommendations do not concern themselves with juvenile crime but, rather, with preventative strategies for reducing the rate of juvenile delinquency. This concern is largely the product of two studies, one conducted by the Audit Commission, entitled *Misspent Youth* (Audit Commission 1996), and one conducted by

NACRO, entitled *A New Three Rs for Young Offenders: Towards a New Strategy for Children who Offend* (NACRO 1997). The Audit Commission study concerns itself with the escalating cost to the police and the courts of dealing with juveniles and endorses a strategy of crime prevention to redistribute expenditure on a criterion of efficiency. This approach avoids a return to welfare justice by focusing on the cost-effectiveness of criminal justice, yet the conclusions of the Audit Commission have much in common with the welfare ideal. The NACRO report delved into the possible advantages of using a restorative model of justice for young offenders and was largely based upon the successes of family group conferencing in New Zealand and Australia. The report has a distinct emphasis on prevention, rehabilitation and reintegration. Both of these studies endorse a largely preventative approach to criminal justice policy and therefore provide a more holistic analysis of crime. Each study places emphasis on social, economic and cultural factors that lead to criminality. In essence, they progress a strong preventative ethos coupled with the effectiveness of the multi-agency partnership approach.

The second section of the Act is concerned with combating crime and anti-social behaviour. To this end the Act discusses crime and disorder partnerships, racially aggravated offences, anti-social behaviour orders and sex offender orders. Of major interest is the discussion of crime and disorder partnerships. Within this outline the Act concerns itself with an integrated partnership approach to crime prevention that must be based in local communities:

> There are three key messages which we want to emphasise here. The first is the importance of involving the local community at every stage in the process . . . The second is the importance of avoiding the risk of becoming preoccupied with structures . . . The third point is related, and we make it because there appears to have been some confusion about it on the ground. It is simply this: the Act places the legal duty to ensure that the work of preventing crime and disorder locally gets underway, and is maintained, on the police and local authorities.
>
> (Home Office 1998, Foreword, p. 1)

Again, these issues are ones that were previously raised by the document *Manifesto for Community Safety and Crime Prevention* (Local Government Association 1997). This document endorsed the need to create safer communities by instilling a sense of responsibility and citizenship back into communities. This was to be achieved by improving the physical and social environment:

> A deterioration of the physical and social fabric of our communities creates a haven within which crime and anti-social behaviour can flourish. Public spaces that are strewn with rubbish, defaced by graffiti and debilitated by vandalism are profoundly demoralising places in which to live. Social deterioration follows if such spaces are abandoned by the law abiding public, especially after dark. These proposals aim to halt the spiral of decline by mar-

shalling the substantial planning, regulatory and enforcement powers of local government to reclaim a decent physical environment and promote responsible and caring behaviour.

(Local Government Association 1997: 6)

To summarise, the 1998 Crime and Disorder Act seems to lack the strong ideological underpinnings of previous Criminal Justice Acts. It does, however, promote a largely preventative strategy for crime that focuses upon juvenile delinquency and community involvement. To do this there is a very heavy emphasis on increased partnership between criminal justice agencies and local authorities. Further, some of the new sentencing options are geared towards involving the community and devolving responsibilities to the community (e.g. parenting orders, restorative conferencing). Many of the policy suggestions are supported by continual references to existing schemes that have successfully met this criterion of co-operation at the local level. This emphasis on community is complemented by the administration's general focus on the need to balance individual rights with responsibilities. This consideration is taken directly from the Etzioni 'manual' of communitarianism and clearly reflects the strong influence of this ideology within the Labour administration. Whilst this connection is never explicitly stated, communitarian thought nevertheless remains a pervasive influence on the government's agenda within the crime control arena:

The modern world offers freedoms and opportunities unheralded a generation ago. But with new freedoms come new fears and threats to our security. Our progressive case is that to counter these threats we need strong communities built on mutual respect and the rule of law. We prize the liberty of the individual; but that means protecting the law-abiding majority from the minority who abuse the system. We believe in being tough on crime and its causes so we will expand drugs testing and treatment, and tackle the conditions – from lack of youth provision to irresponsible drinking – that foster crime and anti-social behaviour. In a third term we will make the contract of rights and responsibilities an enduring foundation of community life.

(Labour Manifesto 2005: 43)

The Crime and Disorder Act does not say how to utilise the community, only that it must be utilised. There is in general a more holistic approach to the problem of crime that incorporates aspects of social and economic exclusion, and it seeks to empower communities by enhancing those structures that are perceived to effectively prevent crime. If any shift in the direction of policy can be ascertained this early in the process, it must be a move away from punishment-orientated 'just deserts' to:

an holistic approach to intervention; a focus on participatory approaches to citizenship and community in tackling the problem; and a strong basis in evidence of what works.

(James and Raine 1998: 102)

From state to citizen: the case of restorative justice

It is difficult to condense what restorative justice is into a simplistic statement, and controversial within the restorative movement to try and do so. However, a not too reductionist or partisan summary might be that restorative justice is a set of principles and practices that prioritise voluntary, inclusionary and communicative approaches to overcoming conflict and harm (Zehr, 1990, Marshall, 1999, Van Ness, 2003).

Restorative justice emerged in the mid-1970s amongst penal reformers seeking to improve the way in which criminal justice is delivered. Concerns about the alienating, stigmatising and adversarial nature of criminal justice have long been a worry for both criminologists and criminal justice professionals. In response to these concerns restorative justice offered an alternative model of doing justice that sought to address the harm caused by crime in an inclusionary and humanist fashion. Taking inspiration from a combination of radical Christian teachings about justice, forgiveness and repentance and various indigenous tribal systems of justice amongst Navajo, Maori and Aborigine peoples, restorative justice is premised on bringing people together to resolve and repair the harm caused by crime and wrong-doing (Johnstone, 2011). Traditionally, this has operated as a form of mediated encounter between victim, offender and other community members affected by the crime (such as family members, partners, local community members, social workers and so on).

At its heart restorative justice is designed to return responsibility and authority for deciding how a crime is dealt with from state authorities and professionals to ordinary citizens with a personal interest in the matter. The archetypal model for a restorative encounter begins with a facilitator or mediator bringing together the relevant parties in a meeting. Restorative encounters are often called 'circles', 'conferences' or 'mediation'.[4] At an encounter the offender (usually having taken responsibility for the offence) explains why they did it; the victim explains how they were affected; and the other people at the meeting explain further the context and harm caused by the offence. The aim of the meeting is for the offender to directly see the damage they have caused and for the victim to understand why they were harmed (Green, 2007). The ideal outcome from such an encounter is that victim and offender agree on how to deal with crime and move forward with their lives. Such encounters are supposed to be entirely voluntary and based on a mutually understood agreement that everyone will be given the opportunity to speak. Through this more communicative forum the aim is to restore relationships between the injured parties and the wider community. In theory this can also help to reintegrate offenders back into the community as they regain a sense of self-respect and community acceptance (Braithwaite 1989). Similarly, the victim can also be restored through the encounter, which gives them a voice and influence not traditionally available through the courts.

At its heart restorative justice is concerned with addressing the harm caused by a wrong-doing (Baker 1994). As this definition implies, restorative justice is not a process applied only to criminal cases. It has been successfully employed in schools, the workplace, neighbourhood disputes (Braithwaite 2003) and for broader political conflicts such as post-Apartheid South Africa (South African Truth and Reconciliation Commission 1998). Yet, in most contemporary criminological debates it is within the criminal justice jurisdiction that restorative justice is most commonly applied. Restorative justice aims to restore victims, restore offenders and restore the community by 'repairing the breach' caused by criminal behaviour (Burnside and Baker 1994). As such, restorative justice represents a shift in focus. No longer are crimes committed against a remote and impartial state but against individuals, specific victims in specific contexts:

> Crime then is at its core a violation of a person by another person, a person who himself or herself may be wounded. It is a violation of the just relationship that should exist between individuals. There is also a larger social dimension to crime. Indeed, the effects of crime ripple out, touching many others. Society too has a stake in the outcome and a role to play. Still these public dimensions should not be the starting point. Crime is not first an offence against society, much less against the state. Crime is first an offence against people, and it is here we should start.
>
> (Zehr 1990: 182)

Thus, crime and conflict are seen as affecting relationships between individuals, rather than between individuals and the state (Zehr and Mika 2003). This process fundamentally transforms the role of the victim from a largely ignored bystander to an involved participant.

Restorative justice therefore begins with a voluntary agreement (Van Ness 2003) by both victim and offender to meet and discuss the harm caused by the crime and the various ways in which this harm can be repaired. For this process to start it is necessary for the offender to have taken responsibility for the offence and to be willing to enter into some form of victim–offender mediation (Wright 1991). The purpose of this mediation is to allow the victim to express directly to the offender the consequences of their offending and for the offender to explain what led them to commit the offence. Thus, the process has at its core communication between involved parties (Van Ness 2002). In addition to the victim and offender, other relevant parties also often attend mediation. Usually, there is a trained mediator to facilitate the process, relevant family members for both the victim and offender and other involved individuals or agencies (e.g. local community leaders, social workers, youth workers, police officers etc.). The intended outcomes are:

- To attend fully to *victims' needs* – material, financial, emotional (including those who are personally close to the victim and may be similarly affected)
- To prevent re-offending by *reintegrating offenders* into the community
- To enable offenders to assume active responsibility for their actions
- To recreate a *working community* that supports the rehabilitation of offenders and victims and is active in preventing crime

- To provide a means of *avoiding escalation* of legal justice and the associated costs and delays.

(Marshall, 2003: 29; emphasis in original)

Within this restorative framework there are a variety of different mediation models that include direct, face-to-face contact between the victim and offender; mediation via a third party or go-between; mediation with an offender or victim group that does not include the direct victim or offender; or mediation via a correspondence course. Within the range of international restorative programmes (see Miers 2001) the exact practices and composition of mediation vary considerably but they all contain some form of communication between 'stakeholder' parties. The practical outcome of such mediation is the agreement by all parties of some form of reparation contract that is deemed an appropriate way to make amends for the harm caused by a particular offence. The content of these contracts varies widely and can include anything from a direct apology from the offender to the victim through to compensation by the offender (either financial or work based). In the United Kingdom restorative justice has been almost exclusively used within the context of juvenile justice. Although there are various local and voluntary schemes that have broadened the application of restorative schemes (e.g. Liebmann 2000, McEvoy and Mika 2002), it has mainly been used to introduce a range of new youth justice disposals. Chief amongst these is the Referral Order, which was introduced in the Youth Justice and Criminal Justice Act 1999. Only nationally rolled out in 2002, the order involves a first-time young offender, having admitted responsibility for his or her offence, being 'referred' to a youth offending panel. These panels are made up of lay members of the community who are provided with training for these panels. The young offender then attends along with family members and, where appropriate, the victim. The aim of these panels is to agree a 'contract' which will outline activities and work that the young offender has agreed to undertake (Crawford and Newburn 2003). This contract is designed to fit with the broad restorative principles outlined above and is, in essence, the sentence the young offender receives. In addition to the referral orders there are a number of other youth justice sanctions that incorporate restorative proceedings (e.g. final warnings, reparation orders, action plan orders and supervision orders).

Where, then, in this process does community fit? Victim–offender mediation requires the participation of only these two individuals, yet restorative justice supposes a third participant, the community. Why is this, and what purpose does this community have in dispute resolution? To answer this question it is perhaps necessary to begin with the notion of reintegration. As Zehr and Mika (2003) state:

> The community has responsibilities to support efforts to integrate offenders into the community, to be actively involved in definitions of offender obligations and to ensure opportunities for offenders to make amends.

(Zehr and Mika 2003: 42)

Whilst Zehr and Mika (2003) include other themes of community involvement (that will be returned to), reintegration is often seen as the underpinning theoretical device that justifies community participation in restorative processes (Johnstone 2001). This aspect of community participation evolved out of Braithwaite's (1989) compelling thesis on reintegrative shaming. This form of shaming, Braithwaite (1989) argues, avoids the stigmatising effects of a criminal label and instead seeks to denounce the crime whilst maintaining respect for the criminal:

> Reintegrative shaming communicates disapproval within a continuum of respect for the offender; the offender is treated as a good person who has done a bad deed. Stigmatisation is disrespectful shaming; the offender is treated as a bad person. Stigmatisation is unforgiving – the offender is left with the stigma permanently, whereas reintegrative shaming is forgiving.
>
> (Braithwaite 2000: 281)

For this process to operate effectively it requires a social consensus that the community must take some responsibility for the reintegration of offenders back into society (Braithwaite 1989). In other words, for the harm caused by a particular crime to be fully restored not only must the offender accept responsibility; the victim's needs be met but also the community should embrace the offender back into civil society. Only then will the harm caused to community relations be restored (Walgrave 2002). Within this context the community is therefore invested with a clear mandate in terms of achieving restoration and it is in this capacity that the inclusion of community is justified as the third component of restorative justice.

Within Braithwaite's (1989) original discussion of reintegrative shaming he very clearly cites the type of social conditions that are a prerequisite for effective community involvement in reintegrating offenders. For Braithwaite (1989), it is societies that demonstrate very high levels of social interdependence that respond most reintegratively to criminal or anti-social behaviour. Braithwaite (1989) refers to these social conditions as communitarian:

> Crime is best controlled when members of the community are the primary controllers through active participation in shaming offenders, and, having shamed them, through concerted participation in ways of reintegrating the offender back into the community of law-abiding citizens. Low crime societies are societies where people do not mind their own business, where tolerance of deviance has definite limits, where communities prefer to handle their own crime problems rather than hand them over to professionals.
>
> (Braithwaite 1989: 8)

This conception of communitarianism, whilst sharing some common themes with others, should not be confused with Etzioni's (1995) communitarianism. Braithwaite cites Japan as an ideal example of a communitarian society where:

The conclusions of the leading scholars who have studied the social context of Japan's low and declining crime rate can be read as support for the notion of high interdependency in Japanese society (with employers and neighbours as well as families), highly developed communitarianism, and these two characteristics fostering a shaming of offenders which is reintegrative.

(Braithwaite 1989: 62)

Hence it is these informal networks of interdependent relationships that foster the culture in which reintegration can occur. For the proponents of restorative justice the participation of the community is therefore a necessary component in the delivery of a fully restorative outcome. Yet, what is apparent from Braithwaite's (1989) description of these social conditions is that they are not always evident in every society in which restorative justice has taken root (Braithwaite 1993, Crawford 1996). This has led some restorative justice advocates to explore the capacity of the process to help reinvest stronger community relations in society (Strang 1995, Van Ness and Strong 1997, Braithwaite 1998, Clear and Karp 1999). Therefore, in addition to the community as an agent of reintegration there is also a growing literature on other virtues that community participation can offer the restorative process.

Johnstone (2001) distinguishes between two powerful rationales for community participation. The first is the capacity of the offender's community to influence the offender and thus help repair the harm done. This most closely reflects the broad reintegrative thesis outlined above. The second is that by involving communities in criminal conflicts you empower them and, as such, strengthen them. This notion of community empowerment is explained by Crawford and Clear (2003), who suggest that the motivation for this 'reinvigoration of community through restorative justice' (p. 220) is the creation of strengthened social bonds that will inhibit anti-social and criminal behaviour. Thus, cohesive community is conceived not only as tool of restorative justice but also as a goal (Crawford and Clear 2001).

Therefore, the literature on community participation within the restorative paradigm is varied and often overlapping. It is seen as having a variety of different values and applications. Walgrave (2002) suggests that there are at least four distinct ways in which community plays a part in restorative justice. The first of these is as an extension of the victim and offender, where it is represented by relevant family members. The second is the community as a tool, where it is required for reintegrative shaming to work. The third is as a stakeholder in the wrong-doing, where the community is secondary victim and may have suffered its own harm. The fourth is as goal of restorative justice, where communities are regenerated via the healing aspects of the restorative process.

These various approaches to community participation have been recently summarised by Dzur and Olson (2004), who categorise them into three groups: efficacy, empowerment and education. Efficacy refers to the belief that laypeople rather than professionals are better at certain key restorative tasks such as reprobation, reintegration and communicating sympathy for victims. Empowerment means that the more the community or public participate, the more they are able to retake from the state authority for social control. Finally, education concentrates on the capacity of community participation to teach people more about offenders, victims and criminal justice. Although there are, according to Dzur and Olson (2004), interpretive differences about what these three categories are intended to achieve, there is little doubt that, in the literature at least, community participation plays an important part in restorative justice. However, there continues to be an on-going debate about how fully this participation has been realised in practice:

> Without a clear account of community participation, reform-minded criminal justice professionals may believe that superficial or merely symbolic community participation can suffice for their programs to be considered restorative. Without a clear account, restorative justice can easily be seen as requiring only that a few community members be added to an otherwise overwhelmingly professionalized procedure.
>
> (Dzur and Olson 2004: 104)

Further, other commentators (McCold 1996, Crawford 2002) have criticised the restorative movement for failing to consider some of the negative or restrictive elements of over-bearing communities. Yet, whilst these debates continue it is clear that restorative justice provides yet another sphere in which justice has been effectively devolved from the state:

> One of the aims of the restorative justice movement is to replace forms of state justice for a wide range of offences and offenders. This means changing the focus of the term 'criminal justice' itself, away from the assumption that it is a matter concerning only the state and the defendant/offender, and towards a conception that includes as stakeholders the victim and community too.
>
> (Ashworth 2002: 578)

The purpose of this section has been to describe the ways in which restorative justice incorporates the community in its approach to addressing crime and criminality. This demonstrates another forum in which responsibility for crime control has shifted away from the state and towards the community. Together with community safety, restorative justice provides two of the best examples of how the communitarian ethic is translating into crime control strategies. What is clear is that neither can be understood purely in terms of communitarian thinking but both contain elements that strongly resonate with the idea of community building and mobilisation as strategies for both controlling crime and reinvigorating civil society. As such, both place an emphasis, or a responsibility, on the community to engage in criminal justice arenas that previously were the sole remit of the state.

Conclusion: governance, responsibility *and* morality

The overall impression of this chapter is that criminal justice policy has changed in response to two distinct factors. The first is the pragmatic necessity of dealing with changes in the crime landscape. This type of shift is represented by the pro-liferation of alternatives to custody that developed in response to the rising prison population in the 1960s. The second is the equally pragmatic political motive that seeks to appease public opinion for electoral gain. This is arguably the type of approach that led to the development of an increasingly retributive criminal jus-tice policy during the early 1990s. Whilst it is very difficult to ever fully separate the one from the other it is clear that the uneven development of criminal justice policy is a result of these competing tensions.

The inclusion of the community within the criminal justice system was evident in the eighteenth and nineteenth centuries and is represented by the expansion of alternatives to custody in the twentieth century. However, the use of community sentences did not seek to incorporate the wider society and largely remained at a remote distance from the general public. It is only more recently that the use of community has been perceived as an effective method for preventing crime. This shift in emphasis represents the inclusion of the general public within the criminal justice system and squarely places the responsibility for crime prevention at the feet of all citizens.

This particular approach is one that is endorsed within the 1998 Crime and Disorder Act and its associated restorative practices. The ideas of communitarians such as Amitai Etzioni (1995, 1997) have clearly influenced the incorporation of both a moral and a social element within the aims of New Labour. Notions of responsibility, civic virtue and citizenship have permeated into criminal justice policy. In such a climate restorative justice has gathered momentum. Whilst the origins and goals of restorative justice do not derive from communitarian think-ing, its recent success can arguably be explained in terms of its obvious similari-ties with the New Labour and communitarian projects (Green 2002, 2007).

This shift towards responsibilising citizens for crime control represents only one half of the New Labour approach to crime. The other half is made up of an increasingly punitive, 'tough on crime' mentality that shares the previous Con-servative government's commitment to 'just deserts'. Consequently, the New Labour approach to crime and punishment seems split along two quite separate lines. The first is harsher punishment, with its underlying neo-liberal ethic of free-dom and choice governing our actions, and the second is community governance and its underlying communitarian and socially conservative ethic of civic respon-sibility and shared values. These two ideological positions of neo-liberalism and neo-conservatism arguably constitute the ideological character of all British gov-ernments since 1979. This is discussed in further detail in Chapter 4, but for the purposes of concluding this chapter it begins to demonstrate the focus of this book and how it differs from others.

This focus is very definitely upon the latter ideological position, that of neo-conservatism and its explanation of the causes of crime being located in moral collapse. Whilst neo-liberal politics have certainly played an important role in shaping explanations of both crime and punishment (Taylor 1999, Wacquant 2009, Currie 2013), the impact of neo-conservative values upon understanding about why people commit crime and how we should respond to it has received much less attention. To be clear, insightful discussion of strategies of community governance by Cohen (1985), Crawford (1997), Hughes (2007) and Simon (2007) does discuss in persuasive detail how successive governments on both sides of the Atlantic have increasingly sought to harness the community for the purposes of both social and criminal control.

These studies are about technologies of control. They are about government and governance. They are about power and penality. Despite dealing with the same subject matter as these analyses, this book is not concerned with these topics but with a different dynamic altogether. This book is interested in exploring the values that underpin community governance and what they tell us about the causes of crime and the logic of how it is dealt with. What role does morality and responsibility have in shaping beliefs about the causes of crime? If we understand criminality as a consequence of moral decline, what are the implications of this for how we respond to it? What evidence is there to suggest that morality is in decline? How does this explanation fit with social and cultural conditions? How sound is the logic behind strategies designed to reduce crime by rebuilding shared morality? These are the questions of this book. The dynamic is crime–community–morality, whereas the ground-breaking work of Cohen (1985) and more recently Simon (2007) is crime–community–control. Inspired by their penetrating analysis, I want to look at how the public debate has shifted as the locus of responsibility for crime control has shifted and explore in detail the veracity and implications of this largely uncharted terrain.

Notes

1 Gattrell (1994) and McGowen (2000) are returned to in Chapter 7 in the discussion of maladapted justice.
2 Originally the suspended sentence was made mandatory for all prison sentences of up to six months, though after fierce opposition from the Magistrates' Association this particular insistence was rescinded in 1972.
3 I could not find a full transcript of this speech but the now (in)famous quotation can be found at: www.independent.co.uk/news/uk/howard-seeks-to-placate-angry-majority-home-secretary-tells-party-that-balance-in-criminal-justice-system-will-be-tilted-towards-public-colin-brown-reports-1509088.html.
4 See www.restorativejustice.org.uk/resource/rj_models/ for a short summary of the different models of restorative justice or read Bazemore and Umbreit's (2001) discussion of four types of restorative conference.

References

Advisory Council on the Penal System (1970) *Non-custodial and Semi-custodial Penalties*, London: HMSO.
Ashworth, A. (1997) Sentencing, in M. Maguire, R. Morgan and R. Reiner *The Oxford Handbook of Criminology* (2nd edn), Oxford: Clarendon Press.
Ashworth, A. (2002) Responsibilities, Rights and Restorative Justice, *British Journal of Criminology*, 42 (3): 578–95.
Audit Commission (1996) *Misspent Youth: Young People and Crime*, London: Audit Commission.

Baker, N. (1994) Mediation, Reparation and Justice, in J. Burnside and R. Baker (eds) *Relational Justice: Repairing the Breach*, Winchester: Waterside Press.

Bazemore, G. and Umbreit, M.S. (2001) *A Comparison of Four Restorative Conferencing Models*, Washington, DC: United States Department of Justice, Office of Justice Programs, Office of Juvenile Justice and Delinquency Prevention.

Bottoms, A. (1977) Reflections on the Renaissance of Dangerousness, *Howard Journal of Penology and Crime Prevention*, 16: 70–96.

Bottoms, A. (1981) The Suspended Sentence in England: 1967–1978, *British Journal of Criminology*, 21: 1–26.

Bottoms, A. (1995) The Philosophy and Politics of Sentencing, in C.M.V. Clarkson and R. Morgan (eds) *The Politics of Sentencing Reform*, Oxford: Clarendon Press.

Boyson, R. (1971) *Down with the Poor*, London: Churchill Press.

Braithwaite, J. (1989) *Crime, Shame and Reintegration*, Cambridge: Cambridge University Press.

Braithwaite, J. (1993) Shame and Modernity, *British Journal of Criminology*, 33 (1): 1–18.

Braithwaite, J. (1998) Restorative Justice, in M. Tonry (ed.) *Handbook of Crime and Punishment*, New York: Oxford University Press.

Braithwaite, J. (2000) Shame and Criminal Justice, *Canadian Journal of Criminology*, 42 (3): 281–98.

Braithwaite, J. (2003) Restorative Justice and a Better Future, in E. McLauglin, R. Fergusson, G. Hughes and L. Westmarland (eds) *Restorative Justice: Critical Issue* s, London: Sage.

Brownlee, I. (1998) *Community Punishment: An Introduction*, London: Longman.

Burnside, J. and Baker, N. (1994) (eds) *Relational Justice: Repairing the Breach*, Winchester: Waterside Press.

Cavadino, M. and Dignan, J. (1997) *The Penal System: An Introduction*, London: Sage.

Clear, T.R. and Karp, D.R. (1999) *The Community Justice Ideal: Preventing Crime and Achieving Justice*, Boulder, CO: Westview.

Cohen, S. (1979) The Punitive City: Notes on the Dispersal of Social Control, *Contemporary Crises*, 3: 339–63.

Cohen, S. (1983) Social Control Talk: Telling Stories about Correctional Change, in Garland, D. and Young, P. (eds) *The Power to Punish: Contemporary Penality and Social Analysis*, London: Heinemann.

Cohen, S. (1985) *Visions of Social Control*, Cambridge: Polity Press.

Crawford, A. (1996) The Spirit of Community: Rights, Responsibilities and the Communitarian Agenda, *Journal of Law and Society*, 2 (23): 247–62.

Crawford, A. (1997*) The Local Governance of Crime, Appeals to Community and Partnership*, Oxford: Clarendon Press.

Crawford, A. (2002) The State, Community and Restorative Justice: Heresy, Nostalgia and Butterfly Collecting, in L. Walgrave (ed.) *Restorative Justice and the Law*, Collumpton: Willan.

Crawford, A. and Clear, T.R. (2001) Community Justice: Transforming Communities through Restorative Justice? in G. Bazemore and M. Schiff (eds) *Restorative Community Justice: Repairing Harm and Transforming Communities*, Cincinnati, OH: Anderson Publishing.

Crawford, A. and Clear, T.R. (2003) Community Justice: Transforming Communities through Restorative Justice, in E. McLauglin, R. Fergusson, G. Hughes and L. Westmarland (eds) *Restorative Justice: Critical Issues*, London: Sage.

Crawford, A. and Newburn, T. (2003) *Youth Offending and Restorative Justice: Implementing Reform in Youth Justice*, Collumpton: Willan.

Currie, E. (2013) *Crime and Punishment in America* (rev. edn), New York: Picador.

Driver, S. and Martell, L. (1998) *New Labour: Politics after Thatcherism*, Cambridge: Polity Press.

Durkheim, E. (1893 [1964]) *The Division of Labour in Society*, New York: The Free Press of Glencoe.

Dzur, A.W. and Olson, S.M. (2004) The Value of Community Participation in Restorative Justice, *Journal of Social Philosophy*, 35 (1): 91–107.

Etzioni, A. (1995) *The Spirit of the Community: Rights, Responsibilities and the Communitarian Age*, London: Fontana.

Etzioni, A. (1997) *The New Golden Rule: Community and Morality in a Democratic Society*, London: Profile Books.

Foucault, M. (1977) *Discipline and Punish: The Birth of the Prison*, London: Allen Lane.

Garland, D. (1996) The Limits of the Sovereign State, *British Journal of Criminology*, 36 (4): 445–71.

Gatrell, V.A.C. (1994) *The Hanging Tree: Execution and the English people 1770–1868*, Oxford: Oxford University Press.

Green, S. (2002) Ideology and Community: The Communitarian Hi-jacking of Community Justice, *British Journal of Community Justice*, 1 (2): 49–62.

Green, S. (2007) Restorative Justice and the 'Victims' Movement, in G. Johnstone and D. Van Ness (eds) *A Handbook of Restorative Justice*, Collumpton: Willan.

Home Office (1962) *Report of the Departmental Committee on the Probation Service* (The Morison Committee), Cmnd 1650, London: Home Office.

Home Office (1984) *Probation Service in England and Wales: Statement of National Priorities*, London: Home Office.

Home Office (1988a) *Punishment, Custody and the Community*, Cmnd 424, London: HMSO.

Home Office (1988b) *Tackling Offenders: An Action Plan*, London: Home Office.

Home Office (1989) National Standards for Community Service Orders, Circular 18/1989, London: Home Office.

Home Office (1990a) *Crime, Justice and Protecting the Public*, Cmnd 965, London: Home Office.

Home Office (1990b) *Supervision and Punishment in the Community: A Framework for Action*, Cmnd 966, London: Home Office.

Home Office (1993) *Monitoring of the Criminal Justice Act 1991*, Statistical Bulletin 25/93, London: HMSO.

Home Office (1995) *Strengthening Punishment in the Community*, London: HMSO.

Home Office (1996) *Protecting the Public: The Governments Strategy on Crime in England and Wales*, Cmnd 3190, London: HMSO.

Home Office (1998) *The Crime and Disorder Act. Guidance on Statutory Crime and Disorcer Partnerships*, Home Office Communication Directorate, archived at www.nationalarchives.gov.uk/ERORecords/HO/421/2/P2/CDACT/CDAGUID.HTM.

Hudson, B.A. (1993) *Penal Policy and Social Justice*, Basingstoke: Macmillan.

Hughes, G. (2007) *The Politics of Crime and Community*, Basingstoke: Palgrave Macmillan.

Ignatieff, M. (1978) *A Just Measure of Pain*, London: Macmillan Press.

James, A. and Raine, J. (1998) *The New Politics of Criminal Justice*, New York: Longman.

Johnstone, G. (2001) *Restorative Justice: Ideas, Values, Debates* (2nd edn) Collumpton: Willan.

Labour Manifesto (2005) *Ambitions for Britain.*

Liebmann, M. (2000) History and Overview of Mediation in the UK, in M. Liebmann (ed.) *Mediation in Context*, London: Jessica Kingsley Publishers.

Local Government Association (1997) *Manifesto for Community Safety and Crime Prevention*, London: LGA.

Mair, G. (1997) Community Penalties and the Probation Service, in M. Maguire, R. Morgan and R. Reiner *The Oxford Handbook of Criminology*, 2nd edn, Oxford: Clarendon Press.

Marshall, T.F. (1999) *Restorative Justice: An Overview*, London: Home Office.

Marshall, T.F. (2003) Restorative Justice: An Overview, in G. Johnstone (ed.) *A Restorative Reader: Texts, Sources, Context*, Collumpton: Willan.

Martinson, R. (1974) What Works? Questions and Answers about Prison Reform, *The Public Interest*, 35: 22–54.

McCold, P, (1996) Restoring Justice and the Role of the Community, in B. Galaway and J. Hudson (eds) *Restorative Justice: International Perspectives*, Monsey: Criminal Justice Press

McEvoy, K. and Mika, H. (2002) Restorative Justice and the Critique of Informalism in Northern Ireland, *British Journal of Criminology*, 42 (3): 534–62.

McGowen, R. (2000) Revisiting the Hanging Tree, *British Journal of Criminology*, 40 (1): 1–13.

Miers, D. (2001) *An International Review of Restorative Justice*, Crime Reduction Research Series Paper 10, London: Home Office.

NACRO (1997) *A New Three Rs for Young Offenders: Towards a New Strategy for Children who Offend*, London: National Association for the Care and Resettlement of Offenders.

Nellis, M. (2000) Creating Community Justice, in S. Ballintyne, K. Pease and S. McLaren (eds) *Key Issues in Crime Reduction and Community Safety*, London: IPPR.

Newburn, T. (1995) *Crime and Criminal Justice Policy*, London: Longman.

Oatham, E. and Simon, F. (1972) Are Suspended Sentences Working? *New Society*, 21: 233.

Pitts, J. (1988) *The Politics of Juvenile Crime*, London: Sage.

Report on the Departmental Committee on Prisons (1895) (the Gladstone Report), *Parliamentary Papers*, LVII.

Sanders, A. and Senior, P. (eds) (1994) *Jarvis' Probation Service Manual* (5th edn), Sheffield: PAVIC Publications.

Scull, A. (1984) *Decarceration: Community Treatment and the Deviant – a Radical View*, 2nd edn, Cambridge: Polity Press.

Simon, J. (2007) *Governing through Crime: How the War on Crime Transformed American Democracy and Created a Culture of Fear*, Oxford: Oxford University Press.

South African Truth and Reconciliation Commission (1998) *The Report of the Truth and Reconciliation Commission*, available from: www.doj.gov.za/trc/trc_frameset.htm (accessed 24/10/2004).

Strang, H. (1995) Replacing Courts with Conferences, *Policing*, 11 (3): 212–20.

Taylor, I. (1999) *Crime in Context*, Cambridge: Polity Press.

Tonnies, F. (1887 [1963]) *Community and Society*, trans. and ed. C.P. Loomis, New York: Harper and Row (First published as *Gemeinschaft und Gesellschaft*, 1887).

Van Ness, D. (2002) The Shape of Things to Come: A Framework for Thinking about a Restorative Justice System, in G.M. Weitekamp and H.J. Kerner (eds) *Restorative Justice: Theoretical Foundations*, Collumpton: Willan.

Van Ness, D. (2003) Proposed Basic Principles on the Use of Restorative Justice: Recognising the Aims and Limits of Restorative Justice, in A. Hirsch, J. Roberts, A.E. Bottoms, K. Roach and M. Schiff (eds) *Restorative Justice and Criminal Justice: Competing or Reconcilable Paradigms*, Oxford: Hart Publishing.

Van Ness, D. and Strong, K.H. (1997) *Restoring Justice*, Cincinnati, OH: Anderson Publishing.

Vass, A. (1990) *Alternatives to Prison: Punishment, Custody and the Community*, London: Sage.

Wacquant, L. (2009) *Punishing the Poor*, London: Duke University Press.

Walgrave, L. (2002) From Community to Dominion: In Search of Social Values for Restorative Justice, in G.M. Weitekamp and H.J. Kerner (eds) *Restorative Justice: Theoretical Foundations*, Collumpton: Willan.

Worrall, A. (1997) *Punishment in the Community: The Future of Criminal Justice*, New York: Longman.

Wright, M. (1991) *Justice for Victims and Offenders*, Milton Keynes: Open University Press.

Young, J. (1997) Left Realist Criminology: Radical in Its Analysis, Realist in Its Policy, in M. Maguire, R. Morgan and R. Reiner *The Oxford Handbook of Criminology* (2nd edn), Oxford: Clarendon Press.

Zehr, H. (1990) *Changing Lenses: A New Focus for Crime and Justice*, Waterloo, ON: Herald Press.

Zehr, H. and Mika, H. (2003) Fundamental Concepts of Restorative Justice, in E. McLaughlin, R. Fergusson, G. Hughes and L. Westmarland (eds) *Restorative Justice: Critical Issues*, London: Sage.

3 Community, ideology and utopia

Chapter 1 outlined the various different ways in which explanations of crime and crime control strategies have interacted with community. Chapter 2 focused on the progression of policy and ideology towards the dispersion of crime control responsibility from the state to its citizenry. This chapter explores the underlying influences and ideology that have informed this development by considering the ways in which community has been incorporated into the crime control and governmental agendas. In particular, the influence of North American communitarianism (Etzioni 1995) will be looked at closely in terms of what its central tenets are and how these shape understanding of the community in the crime control process.

At the centre of recent New Labour and Coalition policies has been a drive towards the devolution of responsibility for justice from the state to communities. Encapsulated in political motifs like Respect, the Big Society and localism there has been a concerted effort to inculcate the community in the fight against crime. Whilst the values and politics of this process are discussed in detail in Chapter 4, the aim of this chapter is to explore the ideological and governmental impetus that drives this devolution of responsibility.

I am in no way implying that this is a total shift, but a gradual process of change that goes hand in hand with new public management, public-private partnership, community governance, crime prevention and restorative justice. By the same token, it would be naive and reductionist to suggest that one model of justice had been replaced by another. As Garland (2001) discusses, old trends continue alongside the introduction of new ones. The old penology and the new penology co-exist, for example as does governmental and community responsibility for crime control. But what I am arguing is that the two are merging and, as a consequence of this merger, new political and ideological ambitions arise that contain within them new explanations for crime and how we respond to it. To make this argument, I am therefore beginning with the most explicit ideological driver of this trans-Atlantic trend, namely Etzioni's (1995, 1997) communitarianism, as well as exploring a broadly Foucauldian analysis of strategies of governmentality that increasingly exercise power through, rather than on, individuals and communities.

A sizeable body of literature (e.g. Crawford 1997, Garland 1997, Johnston and Shearing 2003, Hughes 2007) has begun to document this shift in responsibility for justice and the ways in which it manifests itself in the crime control apparatus. Most of this literature concentrates on the local or community governance of crime. This is where the chapter will begin, with a review of what these terms mean and discussion of the various competing explanations given for the growth of these new forms of governance. This will then be followed by a short review of Garland's (1996) concept of responsibilisation and the evolving nature of community safety in relation to these shifts in governance.

Alongside the growing literature on governance an arguably overlapping literature on community justice has also been developing in the UK and USA. Community justice is perhaps best described as an umbrella term for those strategies emanating from the attempted shift in the governance of crime:

> In America during the 1990s, a so-called 'community justice' movement gained popularity. In theory, this movement offers a means to 1) bring less formal justice processes to neighborhoods, and 2) increase citizen involvement in crime control efforts.
>
> (Altschuler 2001: 28)

Although the phrase can mean different things in different contexts and contains a range of features (Williams 2002), many of these overlap with community governance of crime and strategies of responsibilisation. Both preventative and restorative strategies fit within the broad framework of community justice, as both draw heavily on the notion of community participation.

Communitarianism and the ideas of Amitai Etzioni

Communtarianism has been used in a variety of different ways that carry with them different values and applications. For example, Braithwaite (1989) talks about Japan as a communitarian society, by which he means that it has strong sense of tradition and social interdependence that provides high levels of informal social control. Hughes (1996) and Driver and Martell (1997) have pointed to the range of different ways that the term communitarianism has been deployed in crime control policies and political ideology. To complicate matters still further, communitarianism is often used to describe a group of political philosophers (MacIntyre 1981, Sandel 1984, Taylor 1985) engaged in a long-standing critique of liberalism as set out in the work of John Rawls (1971), Robert Nozick (1974) and Ronald Dworkin (1977). Developed in response to a neo-liberal individualistic conception of justice, this conception of communitarian philosophy helped to rekindle a debate between the two opposing paradigms of individualism and collectivism. On the one side, the liberals keenly support the supremacy of the market and the rights of the individual as the only fair and equitable method of distribution. They see the autonomy and freedom of the individual as a fundamental prerequisite of the good society. They believe the only way to guarantee this is to reduce state interference to a bare minimum and allow the market free reign in the allocation of goods and resources. The political representation of this ideology is referred to as the New

Right, although there is also a strong neo-conservative element contained within this paradigm (Levitas 1986). The New Right is characterised by a belief in laissez-faire capitalism, market freedom and individual liberty. During the 1980s the Thatcher and Reagan administrations strongly pursued a New Right agenda that sought to advance the rights of the individual and diminish the role of the community. In this period the political rhetoric encouraged individuals to think in terms of self-help, personal interests and individual rights. With these factors fast becoming the dominant values, communitarianism responded to this ideology of self. In many respects communitarianism took on the mantle of a counter-culture, warning against the dangers of excessive liberty and individual anonymity.

More recently, however, communitarianism seems to be moving from the margins of political thought to occupy a more prominent position. In the USA the work of Amitai Etzioni (1995, 1997) and his colleagues at the Centre for Communitarian Policy Studies at George Washington University progresses a mainstream conception of communitarianism based on a carefully balanced equilibrium between individual rights and community-based social and moral values. This particular approach appears to have influenced the direction and language of the New Labour administration (e.g. the stakeholder society or parenting schools), clearly giving communitarianism a more central expression in the United Kingdom.

It is in response to the neo-liberal politics of the New Right that communitarianism has developed (Kymlicka 1989). The liberal belief in the importance of the individual and the liberal assertion that the human race is essentially selfish and self-seeking is strongly contested by communitarians. Unlike liberals, communitarians:

> make descriptive claims about the nature and essence of persons, arguing that individuals are social creatures whose identity is shaped by their community ... Secondly, communitarians make normative claims and defend the value of the community, public participation and civic values ... Thirdly, communitarians make a meta-ethical claim about the status of political principles and they eschew liberalism's universalism, arguing that correct values for a given community are those that accord with the shared values of that community.
>
> (Caney 1992: 273–4)

Essentially, communitarianism refutes the liberal conception of the self and the market as the most important components in society. As a political philosophy, communitarianism asserts that the real self is not autonomous but constituted through interactions with the community. Further, it argues that universal laws are not pertinent to societies in which each community's view of rights will be relative to their circumstances (Kymlicka 1989). Communitarianism stresses the importance of the community in shaping individual ideas and practices and upholds the values of social obligation and civic behaviour.

Within the communitarian movement there are a number of competing paradigms. Hughes (1996) distinguishes between the 'moral authoritarian' version espoused by Amitai Etzioni (1995, 1997) and the more radical ways in which communitarianism has developed. Hughes (1996) identifies three alternative communitarian agendas: new local governance, radical egalitarianism and restorative justice. Each of these approaches veers away from Etzioni's (1995, 1997) 'moral authoritarianism' whilst maintaining a belief that communities are the medium in which the good society can be realised. These other forms of communitarianism will be returned to in Chapter 6 when considering alternatives to the current popularity of Etzioni's (1995) philosophy.

The ideas of Amitai Etzioni are most clearly expressed in his text *The Spirit of Community* (1995), in which he articulates the core themes of his manifesto. Central to this version of communitarianism is the belief that America and other parts of the Western world are suffering from excessive individualism and a severe overemphasis on personal rights, which in turn leads to the collapse of the civil society. Manifestations of this include: 'increases in the rate of violent crime, illegitimacy, drug-abuse, children who kill and show no remorse, and yes, political corruption' (Etzioni 1995: x). In other words, the communitarians believe that most social ills are a product of the imbalance between personal rights and responsibilities. Etzioni (1995) believes that American society has developed an unhealthy preoccupation with individual rights and liberties at the expense of responsibilities. This leads Etzioni (1995) to advocate a regeneration of community life concerned with balancing individual freedoms with moral responsibilities:

> If there is no civil order we risk a police state. We must aim for a moral dialogue and agreement on what is right. We cannot leave everything to the state. We must take responsibility in our families and communities.
>
> (Interview with Amitai Etzioni in New Statesman 1995: 21)

The belief is that we have become preoccupied with our individual entitlements, the cost of which is the loss of a shared moral voice that provides both social control and a sense of community. Hence, the communitarian agenda contains three interlocking strategies for addressing the decline in community that are designed to 'attain a recommitment to moral values – without puritanical excesses' (Etzioni 1995: 1). These strategies are:

*   the shoring up of morality in civil institutions such as the family, the school and voluntary associations
*   the addressal and reversal of the problem of 'too many rights, too few responsibilities
*   the assertion of the importance of the public interest against special interests in political life.

> (Adapted from Hughes 1996: 21)

At the heart of the communitarian thesis is a belief that during the 1960s the American values of the 1950s, where 'we had a clear set of values that spoke to most Americans, most of the time, in a firm voice' (Etzioni 1995: 1) were challenged and discarded. To be clear, Etzioni (1995) is not suggesting that this challenge was not important or necessary, but that no new moral values emerged to replace the loss of older ones. As a result the permissive society arose, a product of both the undermining of traditional American value begun in the 1960s and the growth of neo-liberal, New Right thinking, where 'The eighties tried to turn vice into virtue by elevating the unbridled pursuit of self-interest and greed to the level of social virtue' (Etzioni 1995: 24). For Etzioni (1995) this period ushered in the era of market dominance, where the economy may well have thrived, but at the cost of society:

> The eighties was a decade in which 'I' was writ large, in which the celebration of the self became a virtue. (The period was not unique, however, since such tendencies run far and deep in our national tradition.) Now is the time to push back the pendulum. The times call for an age of reconstruction, in which we put a new emphasis on 'we,' on values we share, on the spirit of community.
>
> (Etzioni 1995: 25)

What is apparent from this brief overview of communitarianism is that community is regarded as the locus for morality. The breakdown of community and the decline of morality go hand in hand, though it is not necessarily clear which one causes the other (a theme that will be returned to later). To recreate community, Etzioni (1995) believes that morality must first be re-established. Communities provide for the 'good society' by acting as the site of shared moral values that create social obligations which in turn will help to overcome the 'me-istic' culture of contemporary modern life. For Etzioni (1995) the key to achieving this turnaround is found primarily in parenting, and secondarily in schooling. Hence, the communitarian ethic is rooted in the belief that rearing children needs revaluing above wealth and success if delinquency and moral ambiguity are to be avoided.

Devolving justice: from government to governance

Within the context of both Etzioni's (1995) communitarianism and the associated shift in responsibility from the state to its citizenry the term 'governance' refers to the arena from which crime is managed. Situated within a much wider debate on the process and changing nature of governing society (Foucault 1982, Rose and Miller 1992, Garland 1997), the issue of governance has come to have a particular salience within recent crime control debates. In terms of organising this debate there are arguably two interconnected branches of the governance of crime. On the one hand, what has come to be known as the local or community governance of crime (Crawford 1997, Edwards and Benyon 2000) discusses the particular politics and characteristics of changes in the management of, and responsibility for, crime. On the other hand, a Foucauldian discussion of 'governmentality' (O'Malley 1992, Stenson 1993, Rose 2000) tries to analyse the wider socio-political conditions that result in the reconfiguration of the crime control landscape.

Whilst these two branches share a common interest with the process of enlisting and creating active communities to help govern (Rose 1996, Edwards and

Hughes 2002), they can be divorced from each other. The community governance of crime is more directed towards understanding the contours of new crime control strategies. It is therefore primarily concerned with describing and analysing these strategies, whereas governmentality is not specific to crime and is focused on explaining how social agency is enlisted in the service of governmental aims and objectives (Foucault 1982, Garland 1997). Therefore, both the community governance of crime and the governmentality discourse provide useful frameworks for understanding what devolved justice looks like and how it can be understood.

In broad terms, community justice refers to informal neighbourhood justice and increased citizen participation in crime-related matters (Altschuler 2001). This entails the involvement of a large range of individuals and community groups working in partnership with the statutory agencies to help deliver a more inclusionary form of justice. It is often held up as a viable alternative to an increasingly retributive, exclusionary and managerial conventional justice (Williams 2002). As such, it advocates reintegrative processes (Braithwaite 1989) that address the harm caused by offending without stigmatising the individual. Restorative justice would therefore be a good example of community justice. In essence community justice, believes that justice should be administered from within the community, involving the participation and co-operation of community members. If this process is to be successful it demands that the community must take some responsibility for crime control. This is what is meant by the devolution of justice: the devolution from state to community for crime control responsibilities.

The devolution of justice involves what has been referred to as 'strategies of responsibilisation'. Garland (1996) suggests that these strategies reflect one of the ways in which the state has adapted to its inability to control high crime rates in modern or late-modern society. Essentially, Garland (1996) argues that the normality of high crime in contemporary societies undermines the myth that the state is able to ensure 'security, law and order, and crime control within its territorial borders' (Garland 1996: 448). On the one hand, the state pursues what Garland refers to as 'adaptations', whilst on the other it behaves as if in denial of the problem. Garland identifies five adaptations. The first is what he refers to as 'the new criminologies of everyday life', which presumes the normality of offending in modern societies rather than a more orthodox explanation that assumes criminality is a type of deviation. The second is the 'responsibilisation strategy', which seeks to devolve criminal justice responsibilities from the state:

> Its key phrases are terms such as 'partnership', 'inter-agency co-operation', 'the multi-agency approach', 'activating communities', creating 'active citizens', 'help for self-help'. Its primary concern is to devolve responsibility for crime prevention on to agencies, organisations and individuals which are quite outside the state and to persuade them to act appropriately.
>
> (Garland 1996: 452)

The third is 'adapting to failure', which describes how the statutory agencies have had to modify themselves to cope with the increased demand on their services.

The fourth is 'defining deviance down', which effectively decriminalises some petty offences and reduces the sanctions associated with others. This then relieves the burden on the system. The fifth is 'redefining success and failure'. This involves altering the criteria by which success and failure are measured.

Garland (2001) reiterates and elaborates on this perspective, arguing that in a complex, late-modern society the sovereign state can no longer provide security or social control for its citizens without devolving power and responsibility to the community. Garland (1996, 2001) therefore provides a structural explanation for the state's need to redefine both the nature of the crime problem and where responsibility for its prevention lies. This leads Garland (1997) to consider the existence of the 'criminogenic situation', which is the site of intervention for governmental practice about crime control. The criminogenic situation is the place in which crime occurs; it is not individual offenders but a particular location or domain with its own features and characteristics. It is populated by active subjects and usually provides some form of economic or social function outside of its criminogenic features. According to Garland (1997), examples include: unsupervised car parks, football games, bus stops and subway stations. This, Garland (1997) argues, presents a problem for government, as the site generally has some form of social or commercial value and must, therefore, be allowed to function normally despite any crime-reduction projects. The criminogenic site must therefore be governed but not coercively controlled. In response to this conundrum he argues that the government pursues strategies of responsibilisation where:

> state authorities (typically the police or Home Office) seek to enlist other agencies or individuals to form a chain of coordinated action that reaches into criminogenic situations, prompting crime control conduct on the part of 'responsibilized' actors.
>
> (Garland 1997: 188)

In a similar fashion, Hughes (2007) has drawn on both Garland (2001) and Johnston and Shearing (2003) to explore what he refers to as the 'preventative turn' in criminology. Like Garland (2001), Johnston and Shearing (2003) argue that responsibility for policing has been part devolved from central government across a range of local and community organisations to create 'community networked governance' (Johnston and Shearing 2003: 11) instead of the traditional model of a state-led police service.[1] Hughes (2007), Garland (2001) and Johnston and Shearing (2003) epitomise this shift from state government to local governance. Hughes describes this shift as the preventative turn that has at its core:

> The enrolment of new actors, from a wide range of organisations, statutory, voluntary, commercial, into local multi-agency partnerships has been interpreted in contemporary criminological theory as representing a shift from state-centred government to governance.
>
> (Hughes 2007: 27)

Hughes (2007) argues that it is with the fields of community safety and crime and disorder reduction partnerships that this shift is most commonly associated. Hughes (2007) believes that this preventative turn has been overstated. However, of key importance to this discussion is his assertion that these preventative strategies are understood in terms not only of proven techniques but of the political, ideological and normative influences that both shape and direct crime control and prevention activities.

This articulation of the process of responsibilisation draws its theoretical potency from Foucault's (1982) and others' (Miller and Rose 1990) conception of governmentality. Fundamentally, this issue of governmentality represents a technology of control whereby the state seeks to govern from a distance, exercising its power by shaping the active choices made by its citizens. Nowhere is this more true than in the Labour administration's proselytising about the need to build strong and responsible communities.

When Labour was elected in 1997 there was persistent speculation regarding its ideology and motivations. The aim here has been to explore the New Labour rhetoric of 'rights and responsibilities' and its focus on building 'strong and safe communities' (Labour's manifesto 2001). The intention is to demonstrate that New Labour's effort to engender individual responsibilities in the crime control arena derived from a communitarian ideology developed in the United States by Amitai Etzioni (1995, 1997).

Within the criminological sphere Crawford (1996), Gilling (2007) and Hughes (2007) have all argued that this approach broadly reflects a communitarian ideology, and this relationship has been widely confirmed by Giddens (2000) and Driver and Martell (1998, 2002). Public statements from Prime Minister Blair also suggested a continuing commitment to rights and responsibilities. His suggestion that child benefit should be removed from parents who fail to ensure their children attend school (Observer, 5 May 2002) is but another example in a long list of policy suggestions that attempted to impose individual responsibilities through the threat of sanctions. If New Labour drew some of its ideas from communitarianism, then, given the particular salience of communitarianism to community justice, a closer inspection of the communitarian values and their influence on politics is required to help understand how and why community is being deployed within public debate (Green 2002).

Governing through communities: advanced liberalism and governmentality[2]

Advanced liberalism and governmentality provides a valuable insight into how governments exercise power in contemporary society (Stenson 1993, 2000, 2001, Rose and Miller 1992, Rose 1996, Simon 2007). Their relevance to this chapter is that they provide a compelling theoretical explanation for the growing significance of community in the crime control arena. In essence, they describe why the above-mentioned strategies of responsibilisation have emerged and how they are linked to new forms of governance.

Advanced liberalism has been defined by Rose (2000) as:

> a widespread recasting of the role of the state, and the argument that national governments should no longer aspire to be the guarantor and ultimate provider of security: instead the state should be a partner, animator, and facilitator for a variety of independent agents and powers, and should exercise only limited powers on its own, steering and regulating rather than rowing and providing.
>
> (Rose 2000: 323–4)

Stenson (2001) summarises advanced liberalism as a move away from the notion that the state should provide top-down bureaucratic government to one where increasingly informal and interconnected networks of control exist. Rather than the state providing for its citizenry, people are expected to provide for themselves. Yet, this self-government is not conducted in a vacuum but in a regulated environment where policy still determines the boundaries for activities.

Advanced liberalism is therefore a strategy of governing. It is not a political philosophy in the sense that it outlines a notion of what constitutes the 'good' society (Rose 1993), nor is it a simple reiteration of the neo-liberal assertion that the role of the state should remain as minimal as possible (Rose 1993). Instead, it denotes government at a distance (Miller and Rose 1990, Garland 1997, Dean 1999), where:

> Advanced liberal government entails the adoption of a range of devices that seek to recreate the distance between the decisions of formal political institutions and other social actors, and to act upon these actors in new ways, through shaping and utilizing their freedom.
>
> (Rose 1993: 295)

This conception resonates strongly with Foucault's (1982, 1991) notion of governmentality, which provides Rose (1993, 1996, 2000) with an analytical tool to consider advanced liberalism.

Foucault's (1982) discussion of governmentality is presented as a revised concept of power. He attempts to side-step the long-standing criticism that he neglects the role of the state and of his tendency to over-emphasise citizens as 'docile bodies' rather than active subjects (Garland 1997). Governmentality is thus construed by Foucault (1982) as the process by which active choices by individuals are the mechanism by which power is exercised. Therefore, government creates individuals who will exercise their choices in line with governmental priorities. In other words, to govern is to 'shape' the way in which individuals exercise their choices:

> To govern, in this sense, is to structure the possible field of action of others.
>
> (Foucault 1982: 221)

Within this analysis Foucault (1982) locates a range of governmental authorities who have responsibility for regulating people's conduct. These include the family, medicine, psychiatry, education and employers. As Garland (1997) states, this means that traditional boundaries between state and civil society or between public and private become blurred. The business of governing is thus diverted through those 'social bodies' that have responsibilities for providing modern forms of 'pastoral' care (Foucault 1982). To this list of governmental authorities community has been added by Rose (1996).

Rose (1996) argues that in recent years most advanced industrial societies have witnessed a transformation of their welfare systems:

> One sees the privatization of public utilities and welfare functions, the marketization of health services, social insurance and pension schemes, educational reforms to introduce competition between schools and colleges, the introduction of new forms of management into the civil service modelled upon an image of methods in the private sector, new contractual relations between agencies and service providers and between professionals and clients, a new emphasis on the personal responsibilities of individuals, their families and their communities for their own future well-being and upon their own obligations to take active steps to secure this.
>
> (Rose 1996: 327–8)

For Rose (1996), this represents the end of social government in the sense that its aim should be the national provision of collective welfare. The welfare agenda was criticised for its cost, injustices and burdens. Too much power was centralised in the hands of the welfare system and its agents. Instead, a libertarian consensus emerged which focused on the rights and empowerment of 'active citizens', which led to a fundamental shift in the locus of responsibility (Green 2008). No longer was civic responsibility to be understood in terms of an obligation between citizen and society, rather:

> it was to be a relation of allegiance and responsibility to those one cared about the most and to whom one's destiny was linked. Each subject was now located in a variety of heterogeneous and overlapping networks of personal concern and investment – for oneself, one's family, one's neighbourhood, one's community, one's workplace.
>
> (Rose 1996: 331)

Thus Rose (1996) is led to the inevitable conclusion that collective relations have been reconfigured away from the social and in favour of the community. Increasingly, governmental strategies operate 'at a distance' through our community structures. It is the community that has been 'governmentalised'. For this process to be fully realised it requires a renewed emphasis on the importance of community as a locus of activity. Community becomes the forum in which mutual relations are constructed and fostered. Therefore, according to the doctrine of governmentality, we are to be governed through community, and it is in this way that the new technologies of advanced liberalism will operate. The 'death of the social'

(Rose 1996) has therefore led to the birth of community, and it is through this community that governing takes place.

Within the criminological discourse this analysis has been adopted by other commentators. Amongst these are O'Malley (1992, 1996), and Stenson (1993) and Simon (2007), who have both taken the concept of governmentality and applied it to crime. For Stenson (1993), policing is the subject of interest. He argues that contemporary notions of community policing represent a governmental technology in which the government attempts to harness a range of social bodies that 'create their own regulatory strategies' (Stenson 1993: 384). Within this framework it is the community in which policing operates and responds, and it is the community in which these moral authorities are situated. Therefore, by aligning itself with the particular needs and concerns of a community the governmental strategy is to create active citizens who will self-govern by directing the activities of the police service. Stenson's (1993) argument echoes the earlier work of Miller and Rose (1990), in which the characteristic of advanced liberal governmentality is government at a distance, and demonstrates a further example of how the boundaries between public and private space have become increasingly blurred.

Similarly, O'Malley (1992) comments on the ways in which crime prevention can be understood in terms of the governmentality thesis. According to O'Malley (2001), this dynamic explains how the decline of the welfare state had led to the growth of individualised risk management or 'prudentialism'. This shift represents a move away from social strategies of welfare (or social insurance) to individualised forms. For O'Malley (1992, 2001), this is connected to a neo-liberal agenda where individual responsibilities and active citizens:

> foster devolution of crime prevention to the citizenry and promote risk-based models of governing crime in the community.
>
> (O'Malley 2001: 89)

Without wishing to over-egg the issue, this fits well with the model of community safety outlined in Chapter 1. Whilst O'Malley (1992) is primarily concerned with the growth of individualised risk-based actuarialism, it appears that along with Rose (1996) and Stenson (1993) he also acknowledges that a core part of this governmental strategy is the creation of active, responsible citizens. This encompasses a crucial shift from the state to the community as the locus of government.

Simon (2007) makes a powerful contribution to this debate in his careful analysis of how the United States government has stage-managed public fears about victimisation to create a 'war on crime' that justifies state intrusion into the family, community, workplace and education system. Simon (2007) argues that, building on the threat of victimisation, the state increasingly governs through crime. He cites numerous examples that have created crime and punishment categories that intrude into families in the form of domestic violence and child custody; into schools in the form of school violence and zero-tolerance policies; and into the workplace in the form of drug testing, sexual harassment and fraud-screening practices. Simon's (2007) work draws on Foucault's (1977) conception of technologies of control to demonstrate how the war on crime and the fear of victimisation have been used to legitimate governmental power over, and intrusion into, a range of social institutions outside of the penal system. Consequently, crime and the fear of crime have reshaped the governance of American society and provided a legitimising rationality for the state's intrusion into non-penal spheres of the social world.

Of course, this governmentality literature has not been without its critics. Garland (1997) has pointed to conceptual problems in the use of terminology (for example, how the term liberalism is understood and deployed), as well as criticising the notion that the 'governmentalised state' has not always existed. Crawford (1997) criticises Rose and Miller's (1992) rejection of sociological realism, arguing that by so doing their governmentality debate has a tendency to ignore the:

> lived experiences of material realities, the interactions, interpersonal behaviour and the meanings accorded to them by actors.
>
> (Crawford 1997: 210)

Crawford (1997) also suggests that the approach of Miller and Rose (1995) has a tendency to marginalise the sites for resistance and doesn't address the issue of legitimacy in the exercise of power. Further, Crawford (1997) points to three other limitations of the governmentality literature. First, he argues that the political rationalities of liberalism, welfarism and neo-liberalism are conceived as too all-encompassing, neglecting possibilities for contradiction and unintended outcomes. Second, power is over-rationalised, implying intention which is not always evident in the exercise of power, and neglects non-rational forces and values. Third, an over-emphasis on 'language' at the expense of 'realist' accounts of social behaviour and action fails to acknowledge the significant differences between what people say and do, the distance between 'rhetoric' and 'reality' (Crawford 1997).

What these criticisms highlight is that the governmentality thesis fails to properly acknowledge that there may be other forces outside of governmental technologies of control that may affect the exercise of power. In this sense they are too deterministic in their explanation. Yet, in terms of the dynamics of power in community justice and community safety they provide an important theoretical explanation for the shift in responsibility (Hughes 2002, Stenson 2001, 2002, Stenson and Edwards 2001). The community therefore is not just an ideological good to be pursued for the betterment of society but a tool to be used in the exercise of power and social control (Cohen 1985). It fills the gap left by the decline of social welfare policies and introduces a new form of social relations that are both mutual (internally) and competitive (externally). This shift in orientation raises questions about the assumptions, limits and potential dangers of utilising the community in the crime control arena.

Assumptions and tensions in communitarian thinking about community[3]

Amitai Etzioni's (1995, 1997) version of communitarianism extols the virtues of community and its capacity to 'shore up moral values' (Etzioni 1995: 31). These ideas appear to have influenced New Labour's ideology and provide a platform upon which the Coalition government has launched its Big Society logo. However, because this is a normative vision of what communities ought to look like there is very little acknowledgement, within either communitarianism or public life, of the possible problems that accompany appeals to community.

A range of sociological, anthropological and political observations call into question the exclusively positive imagery engendered by the invocation of community. These observations concern the exclusionary potential of communities and their restrictions on individual freedoms. Whilst Etzioni (1995) does disavow authoritarian and puritanical communities, these are dealt with as contrary to the communitarian vision and easily put to one side. Etzioni (1995) does distinguish between coercive and persuasive communities, the first being the unacceptable pressure of community, the second, legitimate pressure to conform to shared moral values. However, Etzioni (1995, 1997) is less clear about how coercive communities are to be protected against, or at what point shared moral values oppress those who do not, or cannot, conform.

Kymlicka (1989) expresses concern about the communitarian assertion that there are shared ends that can be utilised to realise the common good for all groups in society. His concerns are twofold. The first is that communitarians have never provided examples of such shared ends, arguably because there probably are none. The second is with the communitarian belief that these shared ends can be found in historical practices and roles. Kymlicka (1989) argues that these practices and roles are founded on the interests of propertied white men. Even when women, ethnic minority groups and the working class are allowed to participate, these practices remain gender, race and class coded:

> The problem of historically marginalized groups is endemic to the communitarian project. As Hirsch notes, 'any "renewal" or strengthening of community sentiment will accomplish nothing for these groups'. On the contrary, our historical sentiments and traditions are 'part of the problem, not part of the solution'.
>
> (Kymlicka 1989: 87)

In a similar vein, Crawford (1996) points out that Etzioni (1995) fails to appreciate the ways in which 'community membership and the process of inclusion and exclusion' (Crawford 1996: 253) are bound to the power structures embedded in society. He goes on to say that the process of inclusion is accomplished by reference to outside 'others'. In this sense Crawford reiterates Anthony Cohen's (1985) interpretation of community, which includes the ways in which members of one group define their identity by distinguishing themselves from members of other

'putative groups' (Cohen 1985: 12). For Crawford (1996), the failure to acknowledge that discourses of community are intrinsically linked to assessments of 'us
and them', inclusion and exclusion, ignores the difference between the social and
the communal and invites bigotry and racism. This point is reiterated by Hughes
(1996), who argues:

> 'community' used in this context sounds like a prescription for bigotry and
> parochialism, given its attempt to resolve the complexity and antagonisms
> of an increasingly diverse population through the ideological device of a
> 'regressively imagined people' which excludes 'aliens', 'lone mothers' and
> the 'underclass' from its naturalised ranks.

> (Hughes 1996: 25)

The general point is that communitarians do not adequately engage with the
ways in which individuals construct their sense of identity or the implicit power
structures that exist within communities. To clarify, it is not that Etzioni (1995)
is unaware of the potential dangers of community but that he sees these dangers
deriving from extreme forms of coercion and repression rather than as being integral to the nature of community. Exclusion, competition and power differentials
exist both within communities and between communities (Crawford 1997).

This may seem a little harsh on Etzioni (1995), yet there are persistent and on-
going concerns that whilst he rejects bigotry and discrimination, his commitment
to moral cohesion and two-parent families fails to either explain or engage with
how such conditions can be achieved without some degree of coercion. Levitas
(1998) picks up on the issue of coercion in relation to two broad themes that
are central to Etzioni's ideas (1995). Firstly, Levitas (1998) argues that although
Etzioni (1995) promotes the two-parent family as best able to raise children, he
fails to explain how this could be achieved equitably, given on-going inequalities
between the sexes. He justifies this commitment to such a family structure on the
basis that bringing up children is both labour intensive and works best when there
is an emotional division of labour where one parent will be the primary carer and
the other work focused. For Etzioni (1995), how these roles are divided is a private
matter for parents to negotiate. Yet Levitas (1998) criticises this position, arguing
that quite apart from stigmatising single-parent families further, it ignores the fact
that women still do most of the unpaid work in society. Again, the criticism is that
Etzioni (1995) ignores existing power structures within society, in this case those
that disadvantage women. Levitas (1998) states:

> This situation is underpinned both ideologically, through beliefs that women
> are naturally nurturing, and economically, through gender segregation in the
> labour market and the financial dependence of women on men.

> (Levitas 1998: 95)

Secondly, Levitas (1998) questions how effective any community can be at
maintaining social order if there is not some degree of coercion that ensures

conformity to the group's values. Etzioni (1995) argues that individuals can move between communities if they find themselves in disagreement with the dominant values of the community and suggests that the process by which common values are achieved is through what he calls 'megalogues', where members of the public come together to determine shared common ground. Yet, as Levitas (1998) argues, this fails to address the fundamental question of who has the power to impose these standards and how they are to be implemented in an equitable and just fashion. Further, she suggests that Etzioni's (1995) belief that communitarian society will not be coercive is misplaced, at best, and disingenuous at worst. How is the social order to be maintained if there is not some form of coercive pressure that can exact conformity? Levitas (1998) argues that for communitarianism to ensure moral cohesion and conformity to group values coercion is implicit, otherwise there will be no basis for controlling dissenting attitudes or behaviour.

The distribution of power is therefore conspicuously absent from Etzioni's (1995) vision of community. How established power inequalities are managed and overcome is not explained. In Etzioni's (1995) world community life, with its moral fabric, social control and civic obligation, appears to have no negative connotations or potential downsides. It is presented as an ideal state of social relations, the cure to the social ills that he sees as endemic in contemporary society. In this sense, community itself becomes both an ideology and a utopian image. An ideology because it presents a notion of what community ought to be, as distinctly different from what it may actually be, and a utopia because he appears to present communitarianism as the ideal society to which we should aspire. This level of normative commitment seems to gloss over the negative elements of community life, the intra- and inter-community conflict; the unequal distribution of power and resources within communities; the potential subjugation of self-expression and creative thinking; and the potential for communities to foster anti-social or deviant values as well as law-abiding, conformist ones. Hence, community seems an odd vehicle for advancing the 'good' society, riddled with as many questions as answers and, in this context, having virtually nothing to say about material conditions or structural inequalities (Levitas 1998, Young 1999).

In addition to this Bauman (2001) has commented on the relationship between community and freedom. Bauman (2001) essentially argues that community represents 'a warm place, a cosy and comfortable place' (p. 1). It offers security and safety. Within it there is no danger, no strangeness and no ill will. Community stands for:

> the kind of world which is not, regrettably, available to us – but which we would dearly wish to inhabit and which we hope to repossess.
>
> (Bauman 2001: 3)

Community therefore signifies a type of utopia; a medium in which conflict and risk are swept away. Unfortunately, Bauman (2001) argues that to obtain the security available from community there is a cost. This cost is the loss of freedom and autonomy. For Bauman (2001) this cost is inoffensive up to the point at which community is realised. He sees both freedom and security as equally valuable but cannot imagine a society that manages to provide both:

> we will never stop dreaming of a community, but neither will we ever find in any self-proclaimed community the pleasures we savoured in our dreams.
>
> (Bauman 2001: 5)

Bauman (2001) sees no resolution to this dilemma but asserts instead that we must not deny its existence, lest we face the consequences. The significance of this discussion to Etzioni's (1995, 1997) communitarianism is that it demonstrates a further obstacle to his notion of the good society. Firstly, the idea that community represents an unobtainable yearning suggests that the communitarian vision is striving for an impossible goal, and secondly, that, should it ever be realised, then it would not fulfil our needs, as individual autonomy would be compromised.

Bauman (2001) also issues a warning that there is a difference between the 'community of our dreams' and the 'really existing community' (p. 4). The 'really existing community' is a collective that masquerades as the real thing and demands the submission of personal freedoms in return for security. Non-compliance with these demands is considered tantamount to treason and therefore social pressure is applied to relinquish autonomy for the common good. Yet this does not provide community but, rather:

> a besieged fortress being continuously bombarded by (often invisible) ene-mies outside while time and again being torn apart by discord within; ram-parts and turrets will be the places where the seekers of communal warmth, homeliness and tranquillity will have to spend most of their time.
>
> (Bauman 2001: 15)

This vision appears to have a particular salience to the New Labour claims that we can create stronger, safer communities by engendering individual responsibili-ties. Whilst the intention is that we develop communities that will foster shared moral values that apply subtle forms of social control, instead we will sacrifice freedom and autonomy by shutting ourselves away within 'gated communities' (Garland 2001). The implication of this, and other concerns, is that by pursuing an ideologically infused notion of community, both Etzioni (1995, 1997) and New Labour pursued social conditions that instead of providing security and belonging, create the conditions for division and exclusion.

The conflation of moral philosophy with moral authoritarianism

The critique offered of communitarianism in this work has been a critique of what is often referred to as moral authoritarian communitarianism. This is closely associated with a neo-conservative political philosophy aligned with the work of Amitai Etzioni (1995, 1997) and the Institute for Communitarian Policy Studies at George Washington University. The focus has been upon this particular 'brand' of communitarianism because of its influence on modernising left-of-centre politicians on both sides of the Atlantic over since the early to mid-1990s. Of particular concern to this analysis is the link between this type of communitarianism and its framing of public debates about crime, anti-social behaviour and the breakdown of morality and civil society.

The moral commonwealth refers to a substantial piece of work by Philip Selznick (1994). In this comprehensive text Selznick (1994) plots out the social and ethical basis of a moral communitarianism. By far the most well thought-through attempt to intellectually ground a communitarian agenda, Selznick's (1994) work strongly resonates with Etzioni's (1995) subsequent moral authoritarianism and they share a concern with developing a moral framework against which the inequities of modernity, or perhaps, more accurately, late or postmodernity, can be resisted. For Selznick (1994) the moral commonwealth is therefore a loose-knit or possibly federal system of communities that shares a common and on-going sense of commitment and endeavour to the preservation of human well-being and public life. He is at pains to avoid the accusation of either authoritarianism or moral dogma, instead seeing the moral community as the basis for resisting the insidious relativism and individualism that he sees as infecting social life.

Selznick's (1994) work provides a clear agenda for a communitarian vision. Whilst he might not provide all the answers or all the conditions under which communitarianism might be realised, he proffers the notion of a moral commonwealth as the basis from which the relativism, fragmentation and individualism of modernity can be overturned. Yet, despite his far more thoughtful elucidation of the grounds on which his moral commonwealth might rest, he is guilty of the same criticisms levelled against Etzioni (1995). These are a failure to really grapple with the limitations of community and a failure to address the social conditions that herald the arrival of late-modernity. Whilst much of the late-modern theory considered in Chapter 5 was only just 'hitting' the open market at the time when Selznick (1994) was writing, his two-page critique of postmodernity and postmodernism is telling. For Selznick (1994), postmodernism seems to equate to little more than an overstated expression of the forces of modernity that provide only a depressing and cynical outlook on human conditions. None of its emancipatory discourse or theoretical insight is given more than the most cursory attention and Selznick (1994) seems quite content to dismiss such perspectives before moving on to develop his stratagem for reinvesting the social world with a moral commonwealth. Yet, what is most interesting about this dismissal, and about Selznick's (1994) analysis more generally, is that it provides an insight into the root of the communitarian conviction that community is crucial to morality and therefore to society.

Selznick (1994) very sensibly says that he takes an 'ecumenical' view of sociology (p. 14) which draws on philosophy, political science, psychology and so forth. In the preface to his book Selznick (1994) claims inspiration from the work of moral philosophers like Alisdair MacIntyre (1981), Michael Sandel (1984) and Charles Taylor (1985), who, he argues, begin to redeem the relationship between morality and community as part of their critique of liberal political philosophies. Also referred to as communitarians, these moral philosophers are concerned to critique and ultimately reject the neo-liberal philosophies of John Rawls (1971), Robert Nozick (1974) and Ronald Dworkin (1977). Very briefly, this critique is based upon a refutation of the primacy of the individual's and the market's autonomy and freedom from unnecessary constraint and regulation (usually by the state). Instead these moral philosophers seek to explore the origins and nature of morality and conclude that it is within the context of community, or perhaps more accurately the environment, that morality is birthed, shared and understood. As such they argue against the universal claims of individual freedom and autonomy that are lauded by liberalism. For these moral philosophers, morality is a shared endeavour that is realised through the shared enterprise of individuals brought together in pursuit of common goals. From this they assert the claim that political principles should be based on these 'shared understandings' (Caney 1992: 273).

This work predates both Selznick's (1994) and Etzioni's (1995) communitarianism and is of an entirely different ilk from the moral authoritarianism espoused by either. Yet both Selznick (1994) and Etzioni (1997) claim some connection with these moral philosophies. It is in this claim that the intellectual or philosophical credentials of moral authoritarianism mistakenly locate themselves. This mistake is based on a misappropriation of moral philosophy because of its apparent resonance with the themes of morality and community so strongly adhered to by the moral authoritarians. Yet moral philosophy is geared towards a different type of debate that follows a different type of logic to that of the moral authoritarians. The subtleties of political thought and the implications of it for how conceptions of the good society are realised are at the roots of moral philosophy. At heart these questions are metaphysical – first-order questions that deal directly with the nature of being and how life itself is understood. Moral authoritarianism is premised upon the development of a political agenda, namely that of conservatism. It has its roots in a critique of social conditions and the associated political ideology that, they believe, has led to these social conditions.

The similarities and differences between these two perspectives are instructive when considering the problems of moral authoritarian communitarianism. On the face of it they seem to share some significant common ground. Both moral philosophy and moral authoritarianism share a normative commitment to a notion of the community and its intrinsic worth in shaping morality. Similarly they both operate in the political sphere, sharing a dislike of rights-based liberalism. And finally they both draw on a sociological notion of community from which to make their political appeals (Cochran 1989, Caney 1992).

Yet closer examination of these points of similarity tells a different story. For example, whilst both may indeed share a normative commitment to community, this is expressed very differently. Moral philosophy is concerned with exploring where morality is generated and how this presents a different logic for political philosophy. It is therefore not concerned with a particular morality or a particular set of social conditions but with community as the forum in which morality is generated and developed. Its normative commitment is therefore to a notion of the political community, or solidarity, in which people come together to develop shared common goals. Moral authoritarianism, on the other hand, is making an empirical claim about the nature of social conditions and the decline of morality. It seeks to advance a conservative morality through rebuilding strong communities which will impart the sorts of values that moral authoritarians see as missing in a culture where individual rights have come to dominate over shared responsibilities. This conflation between moral philosophy and moral authoritarianism has compelled MacIntyre (2007) to state in the Prologue to the third edition of his classic *After Virtue*:

> I see no value in community as such – many types of community are nastily oppressive – and the values of community, as understood by the American spokespersons of contemporary communitarianism, such as Amitai Etzioni, are compatible with and supportive of the values of the liberalism that I reject . . . And, where liberalism by permissive legal enactments has tried to use the power of the modern state to transform social relationships, conservatism by prohibitive legal enactments now tries to use that same power for its own coercive purposes. Such conservatism is as alien to the projects of After Virtue as liberalism is.
>
> (MacIntyre 2007: xii–xiii)

In other words, a shared normative commitment to community disguises the very real differences in what is meant by this. In fact, it is not a shared normative commitment at all but two entirely separate normative commitments to two entirely different notions of community based on two entirely separate sets of questions. There are certainly parallels but they are unconnected, except insofar as they use the same concepts (whilst meaning different things) and have attracted the same label of communitarianism.

Another apparent similarity is that both perspectives operate in the political sphere. Yet again this masks an important difference. Moral philosophy is an attempt to reject the premise on which neo-liberalism rests. The aim of this is to undermine a pervasive political individualism and replace it with a perspective that highlights the essence of mutual experience and endeavour as at the heart of social and political life. Moral authoritarianism is about the replacement of one political will that is seen as permissive and immoral with another political will that is seen as progressive and moral. Hence moral philosophy has nothing to say about the rights or wrongs of particular forms of social life that might be considered moral or immoral, nor does it have anything to say about the strength or otherwise of community life. It is therefore entirely specious to use moral philosophy in support of moral authoritarianism. The one does not inform the other and they do not share a common agenda.

This is an important point, as it removes a perception of philosophical credibility from moral authoritarianism and demonstrates a dangerous conflation of perspectives that seem mutually supportive but in fact are anything but. Moral authoritarian communitarians mistakenly conflate philosophical questions about the nature of morality with conservative moralising about the virtue of community. This leads to a dangerous belief that more community equals more morality and less morality less community. This is not the argument being made by the moral philosophers, though the reason for this conflation is perhaps partially explained by the following shared flaw in both schools of thought.

A final point of convergence between moral philosophy and moral authoritarianism is that they both rely on a sociological notion of community (Cochran 1989). Unlike the previous two points of similarity, where there is in fact no real convergence, this is an important similarity between both perspectives. However, this similarity is undermined because neither the moral philosophers nor authoritarians have managed to provide a fully worked-through theory or conception of community. This is perhaps where the root problem that leads to the conflation between the two begins. Without some clear articulation of how they deal with the binary dynamics of inclusion and exclusion, both approaches fail to provide a convincing articulation of their perspectives. Thus they fail to distinguish themselves from each other, as both provide such limp articulations of community that they are virtually indistinguishable, as neither really attempts to deal with the problems inherent in the concept of community. This criticism of moral authoritarianism has been covered extensively and is perhaps best described in relation to moral philosophy in the following way:

> Authority is one of the constituent features of community, so community cannot be understood without unpacking the meaning of authority. Yet certain concepts travel with authority, concepts such as loyalty, commitment, obedience, law and coercion, all ideas that seem to demand sacrifice of individuality, to diminish agency. There are other concepts as well that make community 'thick': ritual, tradition, common good and common action. Communities cannot exist without these; therefore, properly speaking, the theory of community is the description of these concepts and of their relationships between and the distinctions amongst them. None of the communitarians has provided this description.
>
> (Cochran 1989: 434)

At one level it might be legitimately suggested that the concept of community is heavily contested and it is therefore unhelpful to overly dwell on its constituent parts and characteristics. Yet this would seem an entirely disingenuous position for philosophers to take, as it could just as easily apply to any philosophical question. Even if one of the characteristics of community is that it is fundamentally contested, this does not preclude an attempt to at least address those aspects of community that either support or challenge the argument of either moral philosophy or authoritarianism. Yet neither manages to convincingly do so.

Despite the differences between moral philosophy and moral authoritarianism, they share a common flaw in a sociologically limited understanding and expression of community. As Bauman (2001) argues, community evokes a sense of warm sanctuary in which people live together in harmony. Yet this is an imagined place, rhetorically powerful but sociologically weak. Cochran (1989) articulates this point further in relation to moral philosophy, arguing:

> The history of community includes sorrow and tragedy, as well as progressive development in terms of its purposes and shared beliefs. Nothing in the theory of community should suggest that the positive qualities indicated are guaranteed.
>
> (Cochran 1989: 434)

Both perspectives are therefore guilty of this uncritical and, arguably, romanticised conception of community, and it is this shared guilt which in part explains the conflation of their very separate arguments and goals. The moral commonwealth is thus built on a rather flimsy bedrock. Not only is its philosophical inspiration at odds with its purported goals, but it utilises a vague and ill-conceived notion of community that largely fails to address the dangers inherent in the concept and which is at odds with the conditions of late-modernity. Yet the problems for moral authoritarianism do not stop here. Not only is it fundamentally flawed in its conception of community, it is also fundamentally flawed in its belief that high crime and its associated problems can be understood in terms of a breakdown of morality. As will be argued, the combination of these two flaws actually leads communitarianism to exacerbate the very thing it seeks to remedy.

Conclusion: community as utopian, or dystopian?

This chapter has sought to provide a detailed examination of the concept of community and the communitarian ideas of Amitai Etzioni (1995, 1997). What has emerged is that the concept of community being used is both normative and ideological and, as a result, contains some contradictions and value assumptions. This conception of community contains a grand, even utopian vision of the good society brought about by reinvesting a stronger sense of shared values and commitment to the common good. Yet precisely because of this vision and the values that drive it the sort of community on offer contains many unanswered questions about both the potential costs of creating them and the sometimes exclusionary, intolerant and constraining aspects often associated with strong communities. On the one hand, strong communities might instil greater levels of control on irresponsible and criminal behaviour but, on the other hand, the type of informal social control offered by strong communities can be both stifling and inhibitory to people who either aren't able or don't wish to conform.

How can you create a strong sense of community without teetering towards something illiberal? What values should they hold? Where does individualism and self-identity fit within such communities? How do you avoid strong deviant, or socially undesirable communities emerging? These questions seem to be almost entirely ignored by the communitarians. The vision of strong, safe and cohesive communities may be instinctively attractive and politically appealing, but what is the evidence that such communities are compatible with contemporary social and cultural conditions or that trying to create them won't lead to a form of social engineering that either backfires badly and creates outcasts or comes at too high a cost and begins to resemble something out of *The Stepford Wives*?

These are some the questions this chapter begins to tease out. The aim has been to look at some of the ways in which community has been inculcated in strategies of governance and to consider the extent to which communitarian thinking progresses a distinctive notion of community that contains within it a set of assumptions and normative commitments. What emerges is a particular imagining of community that is treated as an ideological construct that can create the good society. This communitarian ideology can be critically analysed at three levels:

1   *Implementation.* There appears to be little within the communitarian image of community that addresses how moral consensus is to be achieved, or how discrimination and bias is to be avoided. In this sense implementation refers to the fundamental failure of communitarianism to articulate how it will equitably bring about its new moral order.

2   *Structural.* How compatible is communitarianism with social conditions? Communitarianism strives to build strong and morally cohesive communities that will provide both social order and shared support. What is not clear is whether social relations in late-modern society can sustain such communities or whether contemporary social structures will support them.

3   *Ideological.* The value commitment to community pays scant attention to its negative features. The notion of community that is progressed by Etzioni (1995) is therefore ideologically infused and utopian in scale. This casts a question mark over, firstly, whether this ideology is empirically and theoretically sound and, secondly, whether it is achievable in any meaningful way.

These concerns are important. If community is to continue playing such a prominent part in political rhetoric and crime control policy it must be critically investigated. This chapter has begun that process by outlining some of the problems and assumptions of both community and communitarianism. Three key questions emerge out of this chapter that will be tested over the second half of this book. First, how close is the communitarian conception of community to sociological accounts about the nature and character of community? Second, whether the conditions of late-modernity are incompatible with the conception of community offered by both Etzioni (1995) and New Labour; and third, to what extent is immorality linked with both community decline and high crime? These critical themes will be charted across Chapters 5, 6 and 7, but before this, Chapter 4 will continue by demonstrating the relationship between contemporary political values and public policy and the commitment to an ideologically driven conception of community.

Notes

1   For example see the Casey Report (2008) *Engaging Communities in Fighting Crime* or the 2008 Home Office Green Paper *From the Neighbourhood to the National: Policing Our Communities Together.*

2 A part of this section was first published in Green, S. (2008) Discrimination and the Poor: Using Incentives and Privileges as a Framework for Anti-discriminatory Practice, in S. Green, S. Feasey and E. Lancaster (eds) *Addressing Offending Behaviour* (pp. 426–44) Collumpton: Willan. A similar passage can also be found more recently in Green, S. (2011) Vengeance and Furies: Existential Dilemmas in Penal Decision-making, in J. Hardie-Bick and R. Lippens (eds) *Crime, Governance and Existential Predicaments* (pp. 61–84), Basingstoke: Palgrave Macmillan.

3 An earlier version of this discussion was originally published as part of Green, S. (2002) Ideology and Community: The Communitarian Hi-jacking of Community Justice, *British Journal of Community Justice*, 2 (1): 49–62.

References

Altschuler, D.M. (2001) Community Justice Initiatives: Issues and Challenges in the US Context, *Federal Probation*, 65 (1): 28.

Bauman, Z. (2001) *Community, Seeking Safety in an Insecure World*, Cambridge: Polity Press.

Braithwaite, J. (1989) *Crime, Shame and Reintegration*, Cambridge: Cambridge University Press.

Caney, S. (1992) Liberalism and Communitarianism: A Misconceived Debate, *Political Studies*, 40: 273–89.

Casey, L. (2008) *Engaging Communities in Fighting Crime*, Independent Report for Crime and Communities Review, London: Cabinet Office.

Cochran, C.E. (1989) The Thin Theory of Community: The Communitarians and Their Critics, *Political Studies*, 32: 422–35.

Cohen, A.P. (1985) *The Symbolic Construction of Community*, London: Tavistock.

Crawford, A. (1996) The Spirit of Community: Rights, Responsibilities and the Communitarian Agenda, *Journal of Law and Society*, 2 (23): 247–62.

Crawford, A. (1997) *The Local Governance of Crime: Appeals to Community and Partnership*, Oxford: Clarendon Press.

Dean, M. (1999) *Governmentality: Power and Rule in Modern Society*, London: Sage.

Driver, S. and Martell, L. (1997) New Labour's Communitarianisms, *Critical Social Policy*, 17 (3): 27–46.

Driver, S. and Martell, L. (1998) *New Labour: Politics after Thatcherism*, Cambridge: Polity Press.

Driver, S. and Martell, L. (2002) *Blair's Britain*, Cambridge: Polity Press.

Dworkin, R. (1977) *Taking Rights Seriously*, Duckworth: London.

Edwards, A. and Benyon, J. (2000) Community Governance, Crime Control and Local Diversity, *Crime Prevention and Community Safety: An International Journal*, 2 (3): 35–55.

Edwards, A. and Hughes, G. (2002) Introduction: The Community Governance of Crime Control, in G. Hughes and A. Edwards (eds) *Crime Control and Community: The New Politics of Public Safety*, Collumpton: Willan.

Etzioni, A. (1995) *The Spirit of Community*, Hammersmith: Fontana Press.

Etzioni, A. (1997) *The New Golden Rule, Community and Morality in a Democratic Society*, London: Profile Books.

Foucault, M. (1977) *Discipline and Punish: the Birth of the Prison*, London: Allen Lane.

Foucault, M. (1982) The Subject and Power, in H.L. Dreyfus and P. Rabinow (eds) *Michel Foucault Second Edition*, Chicago: Chicago University Press.

Foucault, M. (1991) Governmentality, in G. Burchell, C. Gordon and P. Miller (eds) *The Foucault Effect: Studies in Governmentality*, London: Harvester.

Garland, D. (1996) The Limits of the Sovereign State: Strategies of Crime Control in Contemporary Society, *British Journal of Criminology*, 36 (4): 445–71.

Garland, D. (1997) Governmentality and the Problem of Crime: Foucault, Criminology, Sociology, *Theoretical Criminology*, 1 (2): 173–214.

Garland, D. (2001) *The Culture of Control*, Oxford: Oxford University Press.

Giddens, A. (2000) *The Third Way and its Critics*, Cambridge: Polity Press.

Gilling, D. (2007) *Crime Reduction and Community Safety: Labour and the Politics of Local Crime Control*, Cullompton: Willan.

Green, S. (2002) Ideology and Community: The Communitarian Hi-jacking of Community Justice, British Journal of Community Justice, 1 (2): 49–62.

Green, S. (2008) Discrimination and the Poor: Using Incentives and Privileges as a Framework for Anti-discriminatory Practice, in S. Green, S. Feasey and E. Lancaster (eds) *Addressing Offending Behaviour*, Cullompton: Willan.

Home Office (2008) *From the Neighbourhood to the National: Policing Our Communities Together*, London: Home Office.

Hughes, G. (1996) Communitarianism and Law and Order, *Critical Social Policy*, 16: 17–41.

Hughes, G. (2002) Plotting the Rise of Community Safety: Critical Reflections on Crime Prevention and Community Safety, in G. Hughes and A. Edwards (eds) *Crime Control and Community: The New Politics of Public Safety*, Cullompton: Willan.

Hughes, G. (2007) *The Politics of Crime and Community*, Basingstoke: Palgrave Macmillan.

Johnston, L. and Shearing, C. (2003) *The Governance of Security: Explorations in Policing and Justice*, London: Routledge.

Kymlicka, W. (1989) *Liberalism, Community and Culture*, Oxford: Clarendon Press.

Labour Manifesto (2001) *Ambitions for Britain*.

Levitas, R. (1986) *The Ideology of the New Right*, Cambridge: Polity Press.

Levitas, R. (1998) *The Inclusive Society? Social Exclusion and New Labour*, Basingstoke: Macmillan.

MacIntyre, A. (1981) *After Virtue*, London: Duckworth.

MacIntyre, A. (2007) *After Virtue* (3rd edn), London: Duckworth.

Miller, P. and Rose, N. (1990) Governing Economic Life, *Economy and Society*, 19 (1): 1–31.

Miller, P. and Rose, N. (1995) Political Thought and the Limits of Orthodoxy: A Response to Curtis, *British Journal of Sociology*, 46 (4): 590–7.

New Statesman (1995) *Tough on Crime*, 3 March.

Nozick, R. (1974) *Anarchy, State and Utopia*, Oxford: Blackwell.

Observer (2002) We Should Link Benefits to Duties: Mr. Blair's Way Can Be Made to Work, 5 May.

O'Malley, P. (1992) Risk, Power and Crime Prevention, *Economy and Society*, 21 (3): 253–75.

O'Malley, P. (1996) Risk and Responsibility, in A. Barry, T. Osborne and N. Rose (eds) *Foucault and Political Reason: Liberalism, neo-Liberalism and Rationalities of Government*, London: UCL Press.

O'Malley, P. (2001) Policing Crime Risks in the Neo-liberal Era, in K. Stenson and R.R. Sullivan (eds) *Crime, Risk and Justice: The Politics of Crime Control in Liberal Democracies*, Collumpton: Willan.

Rawls, J. (1971) *A Theory of Justice*, London: Oxford University Press.

Rose, N. (1993) Government, Authority and Expertise in Advanced Liberalism, *Economy and Society*, 22 (3): 283–99.

Rose, N. (1996) The Death of the Social? Re-configuring the Territory of Government, *Economy and Society*, 25 (3): 327–56.

Rose, N. (2000) Government and Control, *British Journal of Criminology*, 40 (2): 321–39.

Rose, N. and Miller, P. (1992) Political Power beyond the State: Problematics of Government, *British Journal of Sociology*, 43 (2): 172–205.

Sandel, M. (1984) *Liberalism and Its Critics*, Oxford: Basil Blackwell.

Selznick, P. (1994) *The Moral Commonwealth: Social Theory and the Promise of Community*, London: University of California Press.

Simon, J. (2007) *Governing through Crime: How the War on Crime Transformed American Democracy and Created a Culture of Fear*, Oxford: Oxford University Press.

Stenson, K. (1993) Community Policing as a Governmental Technology, *Economy and Society*, 22 (3): 373–89.

Stenson, K. (2000) Crime Control, Social Policy and Liberalism, in G. Lewis, S. Gewirtz and J. Clarke (eds) *Rethinking Social Policy*, London: Sage.

Stenson, K. (2001) The New Politics of Crime Control, in K. Stenson and R.R. Sullivan (eds) *Crime, Risk and Justice: The Politics of Crime Control in Liberal Democracies*, Collumpton: Willan.

Stenson, K. (2002) Community Safety in Middle England – the Local Politics of Crime Control, in G. Hughes and A. Edwards (eds) *Crime Control and Community: The New Politics of Public Safety*, Collumpton: Willan.

Stenson, K. and Edwards, A. (2001) Crime Control and Liberal Government: The 'Third Way' and the Return to the Local, in G. Hughes and A. Edwards (eds) *Crime Control and Community: The New Politics of Public Safety*, Collumpton: Willan.

Taylor, C. (1985) *Philosophy and the Human Sciences: Philosophical Papers 2*, Cambridge: Cambridge University Press.

Williams, B. (2002) Community Justice: Where Do the Victims of Crime Fit in? *British Journal of Community Justice*, 1 (2): 1–10.

Young, J. (1999) *The Exclusive Society*, London: Sage.

4 The politics of moral degeneration

The last chapter charted the rise of communitarianism in the 1990s and debated where it sat in relation to sociological, political and philosophical thought about community and morality. What this demonstrated is that communitarianism sits uncomfortably next to this wider canon of research. The communitarian commitment to rebuilding communities and their concomitant commitment to rebuilding shared values and responsibilities resonates with governmental strategies of control that treat community as a mechanism by which order and the good society are created. Consequently, community becomes the locus and generator of both morality and control. The two are then implicated with each other and this begins to explain the significance of community to crime control debates, providing an important clue about how morality has become a central theme in political and public explanations for criminality.

This theme of declining morality (or values) as a key explanation for criminality needs carefully unpacking, and this chapter is intended to begin this by looking at the influence of these ideas on the policy and rhetoric of successive governments and party leaders over the 1980s. Before starting this analysis, a few qualifying statements need to be made. First, my goal in this chapter is to demonstrate an emerging political consensus that understands criminality as a consequence of moral decline. As discussed at the end of Chapter 1, the focus on community decline can mask this emphasis and easily be misread as the economic or material decline of a community. My purpose in demonstrating the relationship between crime, community and morality is to show that this replaces an older, post-war welfare consensus about both the causes of crime and how to create the good society. To be clear, I am in no way suggesting that the link between morality and crime is new: it is not. A sizeably body of criminological research is testament to this link (e.g. Cohen 1973, Hall et al 1978, Pearson 1983, Emsley 2005, Jewkes 2011). But what is new is the link between crime, community and morality and the corresponding attempt to control crime by building and involving the community in crime control and penal decision making. This is therefore not about media or political representations of particular crime problems but a culturally ingrained construction of criminality as a consequence of individual choice and depravity that is borne of broken communities and a permissive society. I am not suggesting that this explanation is typically given by criminologists but that, *despite* how criminologists might investigate, explain or articulate the crime problem, this is the explanation that currently holds weight in the public imagination.

My second caveat is that whilst this book is a critical discussion of this conception of criminality it is not an ideological attack upon it. I am not interested in asserting an alternative or preferable political or normative explanation for crime but instead seek to demonstrate, examine and consider the implications of this explanation. Criminological thought often seems to engage in an ideological tug-of-war that seeks to argue against neo-liberal explanations of criminality and the associated oppressive, state-sanctioned responses to it, replacing them with socially situated explanations that are rooted in inequality, exclusion and deprivation. Regardless of the merits of either position, this seems to me to offer little in terms of driving the debate forward and is unlikely to convince anybody who holds strong views about the causes of crime and criminality. Furthermore, I find that both positions tend to essentialise human behaviour as either voluntary or determined and, as a result, neither provides a compelling starting point for understanding why people behave in particular ways. If I were addressing this question, the work of Pierre Bourdieu (1977, 1984, 1990) or perhaps Norbert Elias (2000) would seem like a solid starting point, but that is not what I am striving for in this chapter or book. Not because this is not an important question; it most certainly is; but because it deals with a different dynamic than the one I am addressing here.

My concern is to locate the political explanation for criminality in both community and moral decline as the basis for understanding why the community has been inculcated in crime control strategies. This is therefore not about the rights or wrongs of a particular political or ideological perspective but about establishing a clear link in both the rhetoric and policy of political parties between criminality and immorality.

From Butskellism to broken Britain: a new political consensus?

In the 1950s a political consensus emerged that has been referred to as 'Butskellism'. Butskellism was driven in large part by the need for Britain to rebuild itself in the aftermath of the Second World War and is the blending of two politicians' names, Rab Butler and Hugh Gaitskell, who both held high office as Chancellor of the Exchequer in the first half of the 1950s. Butler was Conservative and Gaitskell Labour, and between them they forged a consensus that blended private ownership and individual initiative concerns with social security and trade unionism and led to the formation of a mixed economy and the creation of the welfare state. This consensus dominated until the 1970s, when it slowly began to unravel during economic depression and the rise of the New Right under the leadership of Margaret Thatcher in the UK and Ronald Reagan in the USA.

Of importance to this discussion is that during this period of political consensus law and order played a comparatively minor part in political and public life (Downes and Morgan 2012). Crime and punishment were therefore wrapped up within this wider political consensus and its focus upon welfare, full employment and economic growth. Yet, from the 1960s onwards crime increasingly returned to the political agenda and the consensus gradually began to erode as the crime rate rose and politicians felt pressed to show they were aware of, and tackling, the problem. By the mid to late 1970s law and order had become an important political bone of contention between the Conservatives and Labour, with Margaret Thatcher using the turmoil of the winter of discontent (1978–79) as political ammunition, pointing to the lawlessness and disorder created by the industrial action under the Labour government (Brake and Hale 1992).

The victory of the Conservative Party in 1979 and the rise to power of Margaret Thatcher spelt the end of the last remnants of Butskellism and the beginning of a trans-Atlantic New Right, neo-liberal agenda concerned with rolling back the size of the state and its welfare system. Asserting the primacy of the marketplace and individual choice, Thatcherism mounted an effective and sustained attack on the welfare state, trade unions and Keynesian economics. Taking inspiration from the monetary theory of Milton Freedman in the USA, the government adopted a position of light-touch, laissez-faire market economics combined with a social and moral neo-conservatism committed to 'traditional values'. This coalesced into a political rhetoric and value system that gave primacy to the individual and the free market as the space in which the individual could succeed through dint of their own merit and hard work (Kavanagh 1990).

The corollary of this credo is that criminality, anti-social behaviour and all forms of unwanted behaviour are also the consequence of individual choice. Put simply, society is not to blame, the individual is:

> I think we've been through a period where too many people have been given to understand that if they have a problem, it's the government's job to cope with it. 'I have a problem, I'll get a grant.' 'I'm homeless, the government must house me.' They're casting their problem on society. And, you know, there is no such thing as society. There are individual men and women, and there are families. And no government can do anything except through people, and people must look to themselves first. It's our duty to look after ourselves and then, also, to look after our neighbour. People have got the entitlements too much in mind, without the obligations. There's no such thing as entitlement, unless someone has first met an obligation.
>
> (Margaret Thatcher in an interview with *Woman's Own* magazine,
> 31 October 1987, courtesy of the Margaret Thatcher Foundation)

This famous (or infamous, depending on your perspective) statement provides a clear indication of Thatcherism and British New Right politics. The idea that social problems required social policy solutions was overtly discredited by the Conservative government, and with this went the argument that crime and criminality had their roots in social problems rather than in individual depravity. As Norman Tebbit neatly puts it, the problem of inner-city life can be solved by:

> Bringing back personal responsibility (through ownership), security (through law and order) and stability (through strengthening a sense of personal obligation, most notably through families).
>
> (Tebbit 1985, taken from Brake and Hale 1992: 14)

This is well-trodden ground that needs little further elaboration to make the point. Thatcherism broke the economic and welfare consensus of the post-war period and asserted individual, rather than collective, responsibility for social problems, and the free market as the only viable solution to them.

During this period the Labour Party was left in the political wilderness on law and order and struggled to find a palatable alternative that was electorally viable. Whilst Farrall and Hay (2010) have persuasively argued that the law and order policies of the Thatcher years rarely lived up to the political rhetoric of her administration, it is precisely this rhetoric and its underlying ideological drivers that is of interest to this discussion. Despite the relative absence of a compelling body of criminal justice legislative reform to back up the rhetoric, the Conservative government of the 1980s shifted the centre of the political spectrum, which in turn had a very clear legacy on the formation and policies of New Labour. Following successive election defeats, the Labour Party engaged in a prolonged and sometimes bitter internal battle to 'modernise' itself, during which it moved from the left towards the centre ground in British politics and effectively purged the most militant left-wing trade unionists and socialists from its party structure.

As Farrall and Hay (2010) rightly state, the impact of the 1980s on criminal justice policy was not through legislative reform but on the ideological values that rose to prominence. The ideological and political vogue shifted away from explanations of human behaviour rooted in social conditions to individual choice and human depravity. From determinism to voluntarism. This vogue drove the reformation of the Labour Party's own ideological stance as it sought to negotiate the ideological and electoral space between Thatcherism and its own political roots. Drawing on a combination of social democratic values and neo-liberal assertions about individual responsibility, New Labour developed its 'third way' under the veneer of Anthony Giddens' (1998) the sociological wisdom. This third way sought to temper individual responsibility with a commitment to tolerance, opportunity and community (Blair 1998). Hence the values of New Labour recast individual responsibility in the context of social responsibility, or a responsibility that each of us has not only to ourselves, our families and our material wealth but also to each other and civil society:

> In recent decades, responsibility and duty were the preserve of the Right. They are no longer; and it was a mistake for them ever to become so, for they were powerful forces in the growth of the labour movement in Britain and beyond. For too long, the demand for rights from the state was separated from the duties of citizenship and the imperative from mutual responsibility on the part of individuals and institutions.
>
> (Blair 1998: 3–4)

Consequently, New Labour did not seek to reject the emphasis on responsibility introduced during the Thatcher administrations but to cast personal responsibility alongside civic responsibility: 'Human nature is co-operative as well as competitive, selfless as well as self-interested; and society could not function if it was otherwise' (Blair 1998: 4). New Labour and what later became known as 'Blairism' has various strands which evolved over the course of Tony Blair's leadership and some of these are considered later in this chapter when trying to consider the policy implications of these values and how they then begin to shape criminal justice policy. But the primary purpose of this discussion is to demonstrate the emergence of an evolving political narrative about the causes of crime that persists to this day. Key to understanding this narrative is the emphasis that New Labour attached to tackling anti-social behaviour. For New Labour, anti-social behaviour is that kind of socially inconsiderate and damaging behaviour that can blight peoples' lives that often goes unchallenged. Graffiti, noisiness, littering, verbal harassment, nuisance behaviour such as petty acts of criminal damage, parking (without grounds) in disabled bays or letting your dog foul the pavement would all be good examples of anti-social behaviour. This type of behaviour indicates a casual disregard for the community and civil society more generally and can have a profound effect on the quality of people's lives:

> In conjunction with tackling the underlying causes of crime, the community has the right to expect more responsible and less anti-social behaviour from its citizens. That means less intimidation, bullying and loutish behaviour on the streets and in our towns and city centres.
>
> (Jack Straw, Shadow Home Secretary, 1995)

The language of responsibility and community remains a constant theme through New Labour's subsequent governments and, whilst the policy buzzwords may have changed, the rhetoric that crime and anti-social behaviour are types of irresponsible behaviour born of a sense of too much entitlement and not enough duty persists: 'But ultimately, the change has to come from within the community, from individuals exercising a sense of responsibility. Rights have to be paired with responsibilities' (Blair, 2006). There are numerous examples dotted throughout New Labour ministerial speeches, election manifestos and radio and magazine interviews that pair together not only rights and responsibilities but also communities and crime. Without wishing to over-egg the pudding, here are a couple of representative statements made at the beginning of both Blair's and Brown's leadership about the relationship between community and crime:

> I have no doubt that the breakdown of law and order is intimately linked with the break up of a strong sense of community. And the break up of community in turn is, to a crucial degree, consequent on the breakdown of family life. If we want anything more than a superficial discussion of crime and its causes, we cannot ignore the importance of the family.
>
> (Blair 1993)

> We are determined to take immediate action to fight crime and disorder, to make our communities safe. But we also know that the communities with the lowest crime are most likely to be the ones with the most active citizens. Citizens who are inspired by a sense of belonging, shared values, and duty to others; by a sense of justice.
>
> (Straw, Justice Secretary, speech at Labour Party conference 2007)

These two quotes make the key point that high crime is seen as a consequence of community decline, and vice versa. This in turn is symptomatic of a decline in personal responsibility and civic duty which implicates a decline in shared values.

Whilst Tony Blair was succeeded by Gordon Brown as Prime Minster, I shall not dwell over-long on his term in office, as, firstly, it wasn't very long and, secondly, whilst there were some differences between Blair and Brown, they aren't particularly relevant to this discussion. Thirdly, both were key architects in the New Labour project, and there is nothing to say that the Brown administration changed either the rhetoric or policy direction in relation to crime control; and Louise Casey's (2008) *Engaging Communities in Fighting Crime* review and the Home Office's (2008) Green Paper *From the Neighbourhood to the National: Policing Our Communities Together* signalled a renewed appetite for community engagement in crime control and provided the forerunner for the Coalition government's introduction of Police and Crime Commissioners (PCCs).

This brings the discussion up to the present. In 2010 the Coalition government took office, constituting a majority Conservative and a minority Liberal Democrat government that contains an unusual blend (at least in terms of post-war British politics) of two political doctrines. Whilst there are some sizeable differences between the two parties over matters such as electoral reform and membership of the European Union, they have generally managed to co-operate in government, and this is certainly true of law and order policies. Yet, whilst there may be a legislative meeting of minds, it is the Conservative Prime Minister, David Cameron, who has picked up the baton from Tony Blair and Gordon Brown and perpetuated the crime–morality connection. In particular, whilst in opposition and in the run-up to the general election he made reference to 'broken Britain' or 'broken society' as a sound bite designed to invoke moral bankruptcy. Consequently, broken Britain is perhaps best understood as a political device designed to invoke a sense of social decay and moral collapse and as primarily existing at the rhetorical level. Yet this should not be misunderstood as insignificant, as it perpetuates the legacy of 'politicking' about crime and disorder that goes back to the late 1970s and strengthens the connection between criminality, anti-social behaviour, community decline, responsibility and morality.

In the context of the Conservative Party, 'broken Britain' emerges alongside Cameron's vision of the 'Big Society' and his sense of a both an economic and social imperative to engender a different ethic in public life. In particular, a reformatory approach to state spending and welfarism underpins a strategy for social justice that has much in common with Blair's ambitions whilst in office.

Iain Duncan Smith's Centre for Social Justice think-tank produced a series of strategic and policy documents from 2006 onwards which begin to spell out some of these issues in more detail. For example, the Social Justice Policy Group (2006) produced *Breakdown Britain*, which outlines the relationship between welfare decline, family breakdown, educational failure, economic dependence, indebtedness and addiction. This report is an unashamedly political analysis designed to begin building a platform for electoral success. Putting aside its critical stance towards the Labour government, it is nevertheless an interesting insight into Conservative thinking about the relationship between inequality, welfare, work and family values. In particular, the link between welfare dependency, worklessness and other social problems is explicit, as is the response which seems to be premised on a combination of removing welfare disincentives to work and traditional family values. The report concludes:

> For too long governments have stripped responsibility from citizens and been indifferent to the important local structures that surround them and give them their quality of life. This is what Dr Dick Atkinson refers to in his excellent book, 'Mending the Hole in the Social Ozone Layer.' In this book he describes how when the bonds that tie people together, such as marriage, loosen, not only families suffer but whole communities decay as well.
>
> (Social Justice Policy Group 2006: 106)

Broken or breakdown Britain is therefore a place where the welfare state has robbed its citizens of personal responsibility and the incentive to work. It is a place where social decline has its roots in family breakdown, drug abuse and educational disparities. But it also has obvious and explicit links to crime. These links are made explicit in the aforementioned *Breakdown Britain* and were never more evident than in the aftermath of the London riots of 2011. The reaction of both the Coalition government and the Labour opposition clearly signalled a broad consensus about what and who was to be blamed for this public disorder. Whilst the inevitable tit-for-tat between the parties ensued, the reactions of the three main parties provide an interesting narrative on the riots which can be broken down into two parts.

The first is the inevitable condemnation of the rioters' criminal conduct. From across the political spectrum a condemnatory rhetoric emerged that clearly demonstrated the party leaders' law and order credentials and established that there would be no excuses or leniency for those involved in the riots:

> these riots were not about poverty: that insults the millions of people who, whatever the hardship, would never dream of making others suffer like this.
>
> No, this was about behaviour . . . people showing indifference to right and wrong . . . people with a twisted moral code . . . people with a complete absence of self-restraint.
>
> (Cameron, 2011a)

Let me be clear. There is no excuse for this behaviour. None. As a liberal, I see violence and disorder of this kind as an attack on liberty, on the freedom for individuals to live and trade in peace in their own communities.

(Clegg 2011)

There can be no excuses for the violence, the intimidation of people. That can never be excused, that can never be justified. That is why the immediate priority is to restore public order and public safety.

(Miliband 2011a, cited on BBC News website)

This type of statement may well be a political necessity in the aftermath of riots. It symbolises affinity and sympathy with the victims (see, for example, Garland 2000) and the law and order credentials of the party leaders. Behind these headline-grabbing sound bites is a message that reinforces the wrongness of the criminal, their personal responsibility for what they've done and the sense that there can be no excuses made for such behaviour. In other words, it was voluntary and personal choice to become involved in the riots. When thought about in these terms, any wider explanation for why someone might behave in such a way is effectively circumvented. If criminality is a choice and if criminality is by definition an immoral act, then the only logical explanation can be that people choose to behave criminally because they are immoral. Tautological though this may be, it neatly constrains explanations of criminality to the individual.

Yet it is perhaps only Cameron who continues this initial statement into his more full-blooded motif of moral collapse. For Cameron, such criminality appears to be indicative of a wider moral decline across society. In the popular press Cameron and Blair locked horns in the aftermath of the riots. Tony Blair criticised Cameron for implying with his broken Britain mantra that Britain was in the 'grip of some general moral decline' (Observer 2011) and that this wrongly represented the nature of the problem and the character of the British people. Cameron retorted on BBC Radio 4's flagship news programme, the *Today* programme, that Blair was wrong, and defended his position to talk about moral collapse, arguing instead that it wasn't the hardcore of rioters but those people who just got dragged into the rioting, taking advantage of an opportunity to loot, damage and hurt that indicated moral decline. For Cameron (Guardian 2011), this moral decline is not limited to a deprived and depraved underclass, but connected to a much broader cultural shift that has led to a loss of personal responsibility and consequence for our actions. This debate between former and current Prime Ministers demonstrates both the similarity and difference between their political doctrines.

Blair explicitly uses the word 'responsibility' whereas Cameron opts for 'morality'. But it is difficult to really see what the difference is, as the two are similar types of values about ethical standards of behaviour. The only difference is the extent to which these values have permeated into British society, not the fundamental cause of the problem itself. The blurring of language and terminology around the themes of responsibility, values, morality and community is often used for political advantage rather than substantive difference, and suggests at least a degree of commonality about the causes of crime that are locked, however expressed, in the breakdown of our moral fabric:

> Do we have the determination to confront the slow-motion moral collapse that has taken place in parts of our country these past few generations? Irresponsibility. Selfishness. Behaving as if your choices have no consequences. Children without fathers. Schools without discipline. Reward without effort. Crime without punishment. Rights without responsibilities. Communities without control.
>
> (Cameron 2011a)

This quote from Cameron's speech hits pretty much every single theme and buzzword about values that has been expressed over since the 1980s. Ultimately, they all mean the same thing: criminality is a consequence of individual immorality.

The second theme that emerges from analysis of political speeches in the aftermath of the riots is how this moral deterioration has come about. Our political leaders know that they cannot leave this question unanswered, as it provides the basis for policy responses that go beyond harsher punishment to try to deter the morally deficient. Consequently, the three largest parties all have what appear to be quite different views on this question:

> For me, what was most striking about the disorder was that so many of those involved clearly felt like they had nothing to lose.
>
> (Clegg 2011)

> This is not about poverty, this is about culture.
>
> (Cameron 2011b)

> I am clear: both culture and opportunity matter.
>
> (Miliband 2011b)

These three short statements would seem fairly indicative of the modern political range. The Conservatives focus on values, Labour on a balance between values and opportunities and the Liberal Democrats on opportunities. And there are clear differences in emphasis across these three speeches about how to explain the rioters' behaviour. But they are only matters of emphasis and underneath there is a shared sense of what the problems are and how they should be addressed.

Families, schools, welfare, employment and communities are commonly given by all three parties as the roots for crime and anti-social behaviour. However, these are generally reduce to broad statements about the need to engender responsibility and help people to take advantage of opportunities by providing greater stability, structure, self-discipline and personal motivation. They are not, as is perhaps easy to mistake them for, concerns about social inequality or deprivation and, despite talking in a language that evokes these concerns, the emphasis appears to be very much on making sure that improvements are made to how these social institutions instil a responsible, hard-working set of values into young people:

Schools and family life are just two areas where I believe we can strengthen our society's ability to encourage and reward the right values which the vast majority of us share.

But it shouldn't stop there. We should be taking every opportunity to demonstrate to our young people that if you work hard and do the right thing the opportunities will be there for you.

(Miliband 2011c)

I think the best defence against this kind of nihilistic behaviour is to ensure that everyone has a stake in society, and everyone feels a sense of responsibility towards their own community. That, in turn, means giving people the opportunities to get ahead so they feel they have a stake in their own future.

That is why this Government has decided to focus our social policies on social mobility, because having opportunity – real opportunity – gives people the drive, discipline and responsibility to do the right thing.

(Clegg 2011)

The next part of the social fight-back is what happens in schools.

We need an education system which reinforces the message that if you do the wrong thing you'll be disciplined.

. . . but if you work hard and play by the rules you will succeed.

(Cameron 2011a)

What these quotes indicate is that across the three main political parties there is, underneath the differences in rhetoric, a much closer consensus than is obvious as first glance. Whilst there is still a clearly evident difference between the political parties' emphasis on inequality and opportunity, this masks a deeper qualitative consensus of meaning that often locates questions of social and cultural inequalities within debates about values.

This is perhaps unsurprising, given the trajectory of British politics since the 1980s, but it nevertheless demonstrates an important point in the central argument of this book, which is that explanations of criminality are now increasingly couched in terms of individual morality. This also drives the response to criminality, which on the one hand is an increasingly punitive ethic born out of a belief that our behaviour is a choice and, on the other hand, is a strategy driven by a neo-conservative value-set that seeks to instil responsibility and hard work by strengthening families, schooling, communities and any other types of social institutions that can be used to induce informal social control. In recent years this has manifested itself in early intervention schemes with 'troubled families' (Department for Communities and Local Government 2012), localism, devolution of authority and active citizenship (Localism Act 2011) or revolutionising rehabilitation (Ministry of Justice 2011) and public sector reform (Her Majesty's Government 2011), but the trend was established during the late 1970s and 1980s and clearly denotes a political explanation for criminality that is rooted in the decline of responsibility and shared values.

This decline is often associated with the decline of the traditional family and community through which we are socialised and our moral compass is developed. This in turn leads to a logical crime control response which seeks to strengthen both families and communities by involving them in crime prevention and penal decision making. As we saw in the previous chapter, this then becomes part of a governmental strategy that harnesses informal social control mechanisms to address and reduce criminality. It is this new axis of crime, community and morality that I have sought to demonstrate in the above analysis of political speeches and statements, as I believe it represents a new dimension in crime control politics and policy that sees the purpose of community regeneration as a strategy of moral regeneration. The rest of this chapter seeks to ground some of this political rhetoric in the policies and underpinning ideas of the New Labour and Coalition governments.

New Labour: rights, responsibilities and social inclusion[1]

In 1997 the Labour Party rose to power after eighteen years in opposition. Since then there has been persistent speculation regarding New Labour's ideological points of reference. This discussion aims to tackle this question by exploring the New Labour rhetoric of 'rights and responsibilities' and its focus on building 'strong and safe communities' (Labour Manifesto 2001). The intention is to demonstrate that New Labour's efforts to engender individual responsibilities derive from the communitarian ideology developed in the United States by Amitai Etzioni (1995, 1997).

Over the last 200 years there has been significant discussion of ideology. The most prominent and enduring discussion probably dates back to Marx and Engels (1845), who argued that ideology was a shared set of ideas or beliefs that reflected the interests of the ruling class. Such ideologies therefore provided a distorted image of the world that was used to justify the subordination of one group by another. There has been significant elaboration on the early works of Marx and Engels (Mannheim 1960 [1929], Althusser 1969, Gramsci 1971), but in essence they remain within the Marxist tradition. Whilst the tensions between political economy, power and conflict may well remain a central concern to critical discussions of ideology, the aim here is to explore to what extent Etzioni's (1995) communitarianism has influenced the trajectory of New Labour and subsequent governments. Consequently, the more critical questions about power relations are deliberately left unaddressed, as the goal is to explore ideological influences rather than ideological oppression. However, critical analysis of the assumptions and dangers about an ideologically driven conception of community are begun in Chapter 3 and continued in Chapters 6 and 7.

Across the 1990s Tony Blair and New Labour repeatedly talked of the need to balance individual rights with responsibilities. This emphasis is apparent within both their general policy framework and their criminal justice rhetoric. For example, the 2001 Labour Manifesto states:

> We all know the sort of Britain we want to live in – a Britain where we can walk the streets safely and know our children are safe. We have a ten-year vision: a new social contract where everyone has a stake based on equal rights, where they pay their dues by exercising responsibility in return, and where local communities shape their own futures.
>
> (Labour Manifesto 2001: 31)

The implication of this is that a lack of responsibility is somehow to blame for society's ills. In his pamphlet *The Third Way, New Politics for the New Century*, Blair (1998) reiterates this theme, calling for the need to create a strong civil society based on a balance of rights and responsibilities.

In addition to the rhetoric of New Labour, Anthony Giddens (1998, 2000) has significantly contributed to the development and formation of 'The Third Way'. His two influential texts concern themselves with the political, economic and social challenges of contemporary society. Within them Giddens (1998, 2000) details the 'death of socialism' in the light of the neo-liberal domination of the Thatcher–Reagan administrations. As a result of the impact of these New Right ideologies the traditional left had to modernise in an effort to respond to both electoral pressures and a shift in the political landscape. Giddens (1998) views 'The Third Way' as the basis from which social democracy can be renewed. Within this context, Giddens refers to the need to reinvest in the civil society, a society where there are '*no rights without responsibilities*' (Giddens 1998: 65). Underpinning this assertion is the belief that 'The Third Way' requires:

> a new social contract, appropriate to an age where globalisation and individualism go hand in hand. The new contract stresses both the rights and responsibilities of citizens. People should not only take from the wider community, but give back to it too.
>
> (Giddens 2000: 165)

Whilst by no means the total extent of Giddens' (1998, 2000) commentary, his two texts are peppered with references to rights and responsibilities and the importance of community in providing a locus in which these rights and responsibilities are practised.

What this suggests is that there is, at least, a set of ideas underpinning New Labour's policies. Tony Blair's notion of the 'stakeholder' society strongly resonates with the '*no rights without responsibilities*' mantra. Giddens (2002) responds to the criticism that New Labour exists in an ideological vacuum by arguing that it may well have done itself harm by asserting 'what counts is what works' (p. 36), a position that suggests New Labour has no ideological basis for the advancement of policy. This 'what works' principle is heavily infused within current criminal justice reform (Crow 2001, Underdown 2002) and is based on the idea that improvements to the criminal justice system should be led by examples of best or most effective practice (Chapman and Hough 1998).

The ideological ambiguity of such an approach can be used to refute the notion that New Labour is ideologically driven. Yet this is at odds with the normative commitment to community and civil society promoted in the rhetoric and vision of New Labour. However, there is enough evidence to suggest that there is a New Labour ideology underpinning the development of community, namely, strategies of responsibilisation and community participation in crime control. The growth of restorative practices, particularly in the field of youth justice and parenting orders, are examples of such strategies. These are complemented by an approach to community safety that vigorously endorses a zero-tolerance stance on anti-social and disorderly behaviour (McLaughlin 2002).

Whilst in power New Labour repeatedly called for communities to take responsibility for crime. Jack Straw, the former Home Secretary, called for the end of the 'walk on by' society where we ignore our responsibilities to confront low-level disorder and anti-social behaviour (Guardian 1999). Underpinning these calls is a persistent rhetoric regarding the importance of family and its ability to defend itself against anti-social behaviour (Levitas 1998). These features have manifested themselves in a package of legislative reform that attempt to engender responsibility in parents. The 1998 Crime and Disorder Act introduced a range of such measures including local child curfews, final warning cautions, parenting orders and reparation orders.

This plethora of reforms share a common theme in that they are designed to engender parental responsibility for juvenile delinquency. This is coupled with public statements from the government regarding the value of traditional two parent families (Guardian 1998). New Labour's early years are a catalogue of similar moralising statements, strongly reflecting the communitarian commitment to the family as a basic institution for civic renewal. This reflects an ideological agenda concerned with developing strong communities via the social institution of the family. For example:

> History will call it the Decent Society, a new social order for the Age of Achievement for Britain. We will respect family life, develop it in any way we can, because strong families are the foundations of strong communities.
>
> (Blair 1996, Labour Party Conference)

> The family is the bedrock of a decent, civilised society. But it is under enormous strain. Divorce, and separation have increased, lone parenthood has risen and child poverty has worsened. The reasons for this may be varied, but the impact is clear: more instability, more crime, greater pressure on housing and social benefits.
>
> (Frank Field, Secretary of State for Social Security and Minister for Welfare Reform 1998: 13)

A host of academic commentators, including: Crawford (1996, 1997), Driver and Martell (1997), Levitas (1998), Nellis (2000), Bevir (2005) and Jordan (2010) have argued that this approach broadly reflects a communitarian ideology. This relationship has been confirmed by Giddens (2000). Public statements from then

Prime Minister Tony Blair also suggest a continuing commitment to rights and responsibilities. His suggestion that child benefit should be removed from parents who fail to ensure their children attend school (Observer 2002) is but another example in a long list of policy suggestions that attempt to impose individual responsibilities through the threat of sanctions. Arguably, it is therefore Etzioni's (1995) version of communitarianism that most strongly reflects New Labour values. As Driver and Martell state:

> Labour increasingly advocates conditional, morally prescriptive, conservative and individual communitarianisms at the expense of less conditional and redistributional, socioeconomic, progressive and corporate communitarianisms.
>
> (Driver and Martell 1997: 43)

This issue is also raised by Levitas (1998) and Young and Matthews (2003). Levitas (1998) highlights an important shift in New Labour's thinking regarding social exclusion. Levitas (1998) points to three different discourses on social exclusion: a redistributionist discourse (RED); a moral underclass discourse (MUD); and a social integrationist discourse (SID). Essentially, Levitas (1998) argues that New Labour has shifted from the redistributionist discourse to a confused meshing of the moral underclass and social integrationist discourse. According to Levitas (1998), all three of these discourses prioritise paid work as the major component of social integration, but differ in terms of what the excluded are deemed to be lacking. In RED, they have no money; in MUD, they have no morals; and in SID, they have no work. She goes on to argue that both SID and MUD are more narrowly defined than RED with regard to what constitutes social exclusion. In SID it is largely economic exclusion, whilst in MUD it is cultural.

The relevance of this analysis to this discussion is that Levitas' (1998) assertion that New Labour has shifted towards a blend of both SID and MUD is that MUD, in particular, closely resonates with the moral discourse proposed by Etzioni (1995). Etzioni's (1995) manifesto prioritises similar issues and solutions to that of MUD, whereby a strong family unit, moral cohesion and community organisation are the routes out of social disorder. In this sense, Etzioni (1995) endorses a version of social inclusion that places significance on moral inclusion, over economic or social inclusion. Hence, Levitas' (1998) work maps out a further relationship between New Labour and communitarianism, one where New Labour's approach to social inclusion shares many of the same moral overtones and commitment to a notion of community that Etzioni (1995) endorses:

> What distinguishes MUD is that it defines the boundary between included and excluded in terms of moral deficiency, and thus implies the imposition of moral order on the excluded. Communitarianism claims to seek a consensual moral order, but tends to rely on formal and informal imposition when the consensus fails or the conditions are absent. The parallels with MUD are thus both partial and covert. Etzioni is the most conservative and the closest to MUD.
>
> (Levitas 1998: 111)

Levitas (1998) is not suggesting that Etzioni's (1995) communitarianism is the only influence on New Labour thinking, but is clearly delineating an important relationship that at the very least accords with Etzioni's (1995) principles for achieving social reform. In addition, as with New Labour's approach to social exclusion and Etzioni's (1995) communitarianism, very little regard is given to economic inequalities as a cause of social exclusion. The emphasis is on integration and moral cohesion, rather than economic conditions. Of course, Levitas (1998) also points to aspects of SID that inform New Labour strategies for inclusion, and whilst these do indeed focus on 'participation in paid work' (Levitas 1998: 26) this tends to divert attention from the poverty suffered by the unemployed (that in RED is addressed through benefits) and significant inequalities between different forms of paid employment (as well as deprioritising unpaid work).

This blurring of both MUD and SID is further demonstrated by Young and Matthews (2003), who suggest that New Labour's approach to tackling social exclusion is based on three interrelated strategies: 'the *prevention* of social exclusion, the *reintegration* of the excluded, and the delivery of *basic minimum standards*' (Young and Matthews 2003: 10; emphasis in original). Young and Matthews (2003) consider these various themes in relation to New Labour policies for achieving social inclusion policies. Two of their policy themes, (1) children, families and schools and homes, and (2) neighbourhoods and communities, echo the themes that Etzioni (1995) prioritises, namely the family and the community. A third theme, skills, jobs and income, sits more comfortably with Levitas' (1998) argument that New Labour pursues SIDs that prioritise paid work, whilst the fourth theme, on crime, can arguably be seen as both a cause of social exclusion (as a result of known about offending) and a consequence (exclusion leading to criminality). What these four themes demonstrate is that there is at least an attempt to address social exclusion by seeking to prevent the conditions that cause it and to reintegrate those suffering from it. Yet Young and Matthews (2003) go on to agree with Levitas (1998) that these strategies represent a fundamental shift in New Labour's approach to social exclusion, from redistributionist to integrationist policies. This, they argue, divorces structural debates about inequality and material conditions from the causes of social exclusion, choosing instead to focus on the need to tackle the 'excluded people's handicapping characteristics' (Young and Matthews 2003: 18) rather than focus on the ways in which individuals and groups are excluded.

In common with Etzioni (1995), this approach largely side-lines economic inequalities and their structural causes when seeking to explain social problems, and reinforces the notion of the excluded area: 'group of people outcast, spatially cut off from the rest of society, with perhaps different values and motivations' (Young and Matthews 2003: 17). This suggests that the MUD also plays a part in the creation of New Labour's approach towards social exclusion. As Young and Matthews (2003) argue, such an approach focuses attention on a socially, economically and culturally excluded group who are cut off from mainstream society. In accord with Levitas (1998), this begins to concentrate attention on the characteristics of the poor, rather than the structural conditions in society. Inequalities across the rest of the society are ignored and the socially excluded become increasingly presented as a definite group, distinctively different from the rest of society. The links between this approach to social exclusion and the ideas of Etzioni (1995) are strong, if not all-encompassing. The parallel themes of moral cohesion, community regeneration and social integration permeate through Etzioni's (1995) work into New Labour, at both the ideological and policy levels.

Whilst it would be over-stating the case to suggest that Etzioni's (1995) communitarianism is the sole influence on New Labour's thinking it certainly does seem to have exerted an influence. In terms of both its rhetoric of responsibility and its moralising on family and civic behaviour, New Labour shares much in common with the concerns of moral authoritarian communitarianism of Etzioni's (1995) school of thought.

As Crawford (1996) has commented, it is Etzioni's (1995) political 'vision' that New Labour has latched onto. For Etzioni (1995) it is the decline of community that is responsible for the decline of public morality. As such, he sees the revaluation of families and schools as the fundamental community institutions that can lead to the regeneration of public morality and the civil society. For New Labour, these also appear be fundamental concerns; whether in terms of a wider discourse on public morality or more specifically in relation to the advancement of policies designed to address social exclusion or crime and anti-social behaviour, the parallels are compelling.

Making sense of the New Labour project: moral conservatism and the third way

The New Labour project is comprised of various different themes that attempt to weave a 'third way' politics somewhere between first and second way politics of the Old Left and New Right (Driver and Martell 2002). Trying to define exactly what constitutes the New Labour project, or third way politics is no straightforward task, as it has changed over time and there are differences of opinion both within New Labour and without as to what the defining core of values might be.

Yet Driver and Martell (1998, 2002) suggest that New Labour can be initially understood in terms of its attempt to avoid the politics of free market liberalism and state-directed regulation and redistribution. Blair (1998) in the early days of his premiership defined the third way in terms of a new reconciling politics that aims to respond to the challenges of the contemporary social world whilst avoiding the ideological dogma on both the left and right of the political spectrum. Across Blair's term in office several key themes seemed to crystallise. These remained largely unaltered during Brown's incumbency and include but are not necessarily limited to:

- a recognition of changing social conditions, in particular globalisation, information and individualism
- a commitment to fiscal prudence, competitiveness and new public management
- a moral conservatism that strongly endorses traditional community and family life

- a shift from redistributive welfare to employment-based social integration
- evidence-based practice, public-private co-operation and joined-up government
- a recalibration of welfare that ties entitlements to responsibilities (to search for work for example)
- devolution of democracy and the administration of social welfare provision to the local or community level.

(Adapted from Driver and Martell 1998, 2002)

This list begins to give some insight into the political ground that New Labour treads. The third way articulates its political ethos in terms of new challenges posed by wider global forces. This position is sustained and reinforced through the work of Anthony Giddens (1998), who provides a useful map of contemporary social conditions from which New Labour legitimates its new policy agenda.[2]

Emerging from this platform are the broad themes of welfare reform, moral conservatism and devolution of democracy and public administration. At one level these themes appear to complement each other nicely. Welfare reform is achieved by empowering communities to manage and direct their local schools and hospitals, which in turn reinforces the New Labour commitment to both devolution and community life. This commitment is clear in much of New Labour's thinking between the mid-1990s and the mid-2000s. Hazel Blears (2003) articulates this most clearly in what can only be described as an aspirational account of community mobilisation and empowerment:

> What seems clear is that if we do nothing to pass power to local communities, the result will not be apathy; it will be alienation and anger. Our choice is between giving people control over their lives, or failing to deliver the transformation we want. The great lesson from the successes and failures of social democracy in Britain and around the world is that social change cannot come simply by pulling the levers and pressing the buttons in central government departments, or by relying on an enlightened and altruistic political class. Social change must be a common endeavour of all citizens, if change is to be progressive and lasting. We need to breathe new life into our neglected neighbourhoods, we need to spread a message of hope that politics matters, and we need to put communities in control.
>
> (Blears 2003: 46–7)

Whilst this all seems very exciting and entirely in keeping with an older, more left-wing Labour tradition, this aspiration has run up against another strong theme within New Labour, namely new public management, public-private co-operation and evidence-based practice. These themes emphasise strong central government which directs public expenditure. Whilst this expenditure may well be administered at the local and community level it remains governed from the centre (Pitts 2001). Public-private co-operation and reform of the competition laws has also both introduced tight controls over how services are provided and brought the private sector with its profit-driven logic into service provision. Hence big business and big government, with their shared focus on managing costs and hitting targets, seem entirely at odds with the community empowerment and ownership sentiments expressed so powerfully by Hazel Blears (2003).

This tension calls into question New Labour's ability to deliver the sorts of community governance that would meaningfully achieve political pluralism and local democracy. This tension has led Driver and Martell (2002) to query Blair and New Labour's commitment to devolution, arguing that it is only skin deep, masking both an elective dictatorship mode of governance and a control-freakery over the fiscal levers of power that is 'quite out of touch with modern pluralistic social democratic thinking' (Driver and Martell 2002: 158).

Yet, within this context, and largely in spite of these tensions, moral conservatism remains a consistent theme of New Labour. Inspired by the communitarian thinking of Amitai Etzioni (1995) and its influence on the Clinton administration, this moral conservatism has appeal at a number of levels. Its focus on civic responsibility means that it sits well alongside the theme of community ownership and empowerment and its moral overtures regarding individual responsibilities resonate with much of New Labour's social welfare reforms. Further, communitarianism appeals to those on the radical left who opposed the Thatcherite doctrine of rampant self-interest and individualism whilst simultaneously appealing to the conservative centre-right with calls for the remoralisation of society.

Thus the moral conservatism of New Labour occupies a convenient political space between laissez-faire liberalism and redistributive socialism. The broad appeal of moral conservatism is that it invokes a language that strikes a chord with both the Left and Right. This is the language of community, a language which appears to resonate across the political spectrum and has been used in reference to different political agendas whilst drawing on the same words and concepts. Yet there are different meanings within communitarian discourses and despite, the apparent universal appeal of community, New Labour derives its political direction from a very particular moral authoritarian perspective (Hughes 1996, Little 2002). Driver and Martell (2002) provide a useful framework in which the relationship between New Labour and Etzioni's (1995) moral authoritarian communitarianism is clearly demonstrated.

This combination of community and morality also finds a clear home in the New Labour approach to crime and anti-social behaviour. The intuitive relationship between morality and criminality and between the breakdown of community and moral decay means that the moral conservative voice of New Labour is at its strongest when talking about crime and anti-social behaviour. Although the other themes and tensions briefly outlined in the above discussion also play an important part in the crime control policies, the moralising sentiments of New Labour about community decline, broken families, anti-social behaviour, self-centredness and high crime continue to play an important part in the development of criminal justice policy (see, for example, Crawford 1997, Hughes 1998, Labour Manifesto 2001 and 2005, McLaughlin 2002, Respect Task Force 2006, Gilling 2007). Hence, whilst the principle of devolution has spread into the criminal

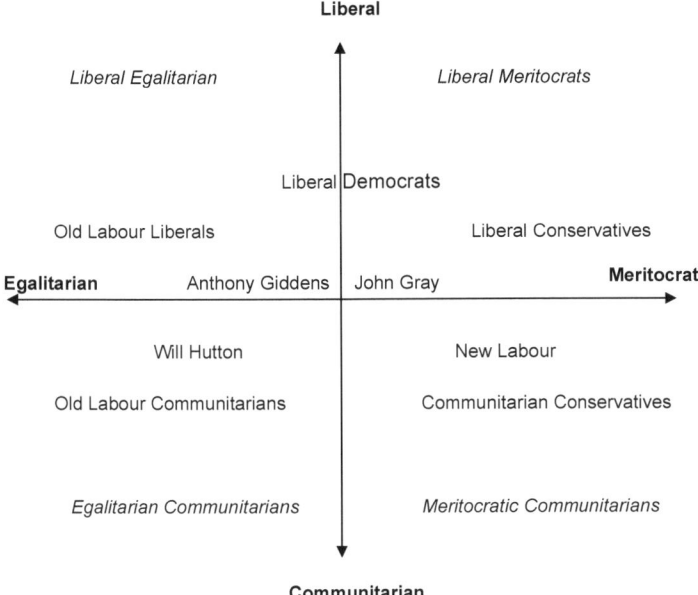

Liberal

Liberal Egalitarian   *Liberal Meritocrats*

Liberal Democrats

Old Labour Liberals   Liberal Conservatives

Egalitarian   Anthony Giddens   John Gray   **Meritocrat**

Will Hutton   New Labour

Old Labour Communitarians   Communitarian Conservatives

Egalitarian Communitarians   *Meritocratic Communitarians*

Communitarian

Figure 4.1 Liberty, equality and community in contemporary British political debates (Adapted from Driver and Martell 2002: 93)

justice arena, this devolution is both partial and imperfect. A range of crime and punishment-related activities have shifted responsibility for crime control from the state downwards. These need exploration, in terms of both the devolutionary trend and the sociological perspectives that begin to shed some light on how this might be explained beyond simple electoral politics.

The values of the Big Society

In 2010 a new Coalition government was formed between the Conservative and Liberal Democrat parties. In the run-up to the election the Conservative Party introduced themes of broken Britain and the Big Society. As discussed earlier in the chapter, broken Britain alludes to the deterioration of economic and social conditions alongside the decline of the welfare state and personal responsibility. As a political motif, broken Britain was mainly used in the run-up to the general election as a form of political accusation levelled against the Labour government (Conservative Party Election Manifesto 2010) but received comparatively little attention subsequently, apart from in the aftermath of the 2011 riots. The Big Society, on the other hand, seems to have remained a more constant, albeit sometimes rather vague, theme in the Coalition government, and with Conservative ministers in particular.

The Big Society is a rather amorphous concept that contains various threads within a broad narrative about the character of the Conservative Party under David Cameron's leadership. According to Morgan (2012), its keywords are: 'devolution, localism, restored discretion, partnership working, and responsibility' (p. 467). Glasman (2010) has gone further, arguing that the Big Society could have profound implications for both democracy and devolution and seeks to establish a new relationship between the state and its citizenry. He adds mutualisation and social entrepreneurialism to responsibility and localism as the key ingredients of the Big Society.

In the context of the wider economic conditions of economic downturn and fiscal deficit much of the current debate around what the Big Society is revolves around whether it is 'code' or a 'mask' for government cuts and free market Thatcherite public sector cuts (Morgan 2012) designed to introduce private investment and big business into the criminal justice sector. Whilst it is clear that this is happening, it would be a mistake to reduce the Big Society to a cynical ploy to progress a New Right ideology, and Jordan (2010) makes this point strongly, arguing that the Big Society is also a moral vision about local decision making, voluntarism, active engagement and mutuality. For Jordan (2010), the Big Society is therefore not just about economics but also about values, and it is this that resonates with the earlier values espoused by both New Right and New Labour governments. Maguire (2012) makes a similar point, commenting that the focus upon active citizenship, civic renewal and 'the greater participation of local individuals and communities in matters affecting their lives' (p. 485) were also salient themes under New Labour. In fact, Maguire (2012) goes a step further, drawing out the similarities between the New Labour and Big Society emphasis on community engagement, voluntary sector involvement and the introduction of new service-sector markets through the advancement of new public management and public-private partnership. Under the auspices of community engagement and generating a sense of community, Maguire (2012) concludes that both Labour and Coalition administrations share a concern with transforming the public sector through the introduction of market forces and third sector organisations.

In the context of criminal justice reform the aspects of the Big Society that are most in evidence are the introduction of Police and Crime Commissioners (PCCs), the extension of Payment by Results (PBR) and Social Impact Bonds (SIBs) into youth justice and third sector rehabilitation projects. PBR is being piloted in Peterborough and Doncaster prisons and the looming privatisation of most of the Probation Service will probably follow suit, though at the time of writing this plan leaves as many questions unanswered as it does answered.

However, under the rubric of the Big Society, the introduction of PCCs can easily be understood in terms of localism, accountability and the opening up of criminal justice to new forms of public engagement through the political process. Introduced in the tellingly entitled Police Reform and Social Responsibility Act (2011), the first election of PCCs was a rather underwhelming event with very low turn-out at the polling stations (15 per cent average) and a rather mixed range of candidates standing for election (Guardian, 2012). Yet the precedent has been set and the overt local politicisation of criminal justice introduces a new form of electoral and public debate into criminal justice matters. Time will tell exactly what kind of fruit this will bear but the PCC election campaigning suggests a combination of populist and tabloid-style headlines about cutting crime and protecting communities, underscored by a more measured engagement (for the most part) with criminal justice agencies.[3]

The introduction of PBR, large security companies and third sector organisations is arguably much more about public sector cuts and reducing the fiscal deficit. But to suggest that this is wholly separate from the Big Society would be disingenuous, as they contain Big Society themes as well. For example, a modest amount of support has been made available to help probation staff to set up mutual businesses that can then begin to bid for the rehabilitation contracts in 2014/15 (Cabinet Office 2013). Similarly, PBR and SIB provide a space for new forms of private investment into the third sector and a basis on which to roll out further innovation and partnership between communities, charities and private enterprise (Third Sector 2013). In drawing attention to these aspects, my aim is to draw attention to the wider value base of the Big Society that underscores not only the social but also the economic policy of the Coalition government.

Doubtless, debate will continue about what is meant by the Big Society and exactly what policies can be attributed to it. But what is clear is that, regardless of whether or not there is a more cynical ideological underpinning to the rhetoric of the Big Society, it does provide a very particular political purpose, which is to distinguish between the Conservative and New Labour values. In this way the Big Society becomes an important organising theme around which the Coalition government organises its political message. The Big Society stands in contrast to the big government of New Labour (Bochel 2011). When set alongside the broken Britain election mantra, the Big Society becomes the solution to the overweening and over-controlling nanny state that robs people of their independence and responsibility. Whilst the language of broken Britain may have taken a back seat since the Coalition government came into office, it remains there in the background, rearing its head in tabloid outrage and sound-bite politics in the aftermath of particular heinous or irresponsible behaviour, whether it be phone-tapping, rioting or benefit fraud. And the Big Society is a constant reminder that New Labour under Blair and Brown was responsible not just for the economic mess but also for the social mess that has led to the moral decline we sometimes witness.

These values are perhaps best expressed by the Prime Minister himself, who in 2011 gave a speech on the Big Society in which he said:

> There are too many parts of our society that are broken, whether it is broken families or whether it is some communities breaking down; whether it is the level of crime, the level of gang membership; whether it's problems of people stuck on welfare, unable to work; whether it's the sense that some of our public services don't work for us – we do need a social recovery to mend the broken society. To me that's what the Big Society is all about.

To me, there's one word at the heart of all this; and that is responsibility. We need people to take more responsibility. We need people to act more responsibly, because if you take any problem in our country and you just think: 'Well, what can the government do to sort it out?', that is only ever going to be half of the answer.

(Cameron 2011c)

This is perhaps one of the clearest messages of what Cameron's Conservative Party is focused on. Its 2010 Election Manifesto is called *Invitation to Join the Government of Britain* and is explicitly intended to invoke a sense of each person's responsibility to contribute to their society. It echoes President John F. Kennedy's inaugural address in 1961, when he uttered the now immortal lines: 'Ask not what your country can do for you but what you can do for your country'. Consequently, whatever else it might be, the Big Society is a moral vision about reducing the size, role and cost of government and encouraging each of us to help fill the gap left behind. Regardless of what each of us may think about this; regardless of whether or not it matches with our own individual political values; regardless of whether it is used to progress ideologically driven public sector cuts, it is about individual responsibility; about strengthening families and communities; and about living hard-working, law-abiding lives that contribute to civic society.

Conclusion: crime, immorality and a time machine

The aim of this chapter has been to chart the development of contemporary political values, with the intention of demonstrating how they have increasingly come to rely on a combination of morally conservative communitarian thought and neo-liberal conceptions of personal responsibility. This blend of personal responsibility and community values is not specific to the Coalition government and a large part of this chapter has been designed to demonstrate the consistency of these values across the three major political doctrines that have developed since the 1980s. Starting with the New Right politics of the Thatcher years, then the New Labour reforms of the 1990s and culminating with the Big Society rhetoric, what we have witnessed is a commitment to individual responsibility and shared values. This has shaped the political, media and public sense of what causes crime and how it should be responded to. Crime and anti-social behaviour is caused by increasing irresponsibility and immorality. It is therefore controlled by finding ways to rebuild both through the medium of community governance.

In particular, I have explored the thought and values of New Labour as marking a watershed moment during when responsibility and morality became coterminous with community cohesion, social inclusion and employment. By rebuilding community and civic responsibility New Labour made explicit the link between declining shared values and social problems. It appears that Cameron's Big Society continues this theme, albeit within a different set of policies in a different economic context. The purpose of demonstrating these links has been to show that political and public explanations for crime have been recalibrated. It's not about inequality, deprivation and opportunity. It's about family, community, responsibility and morality. This of course comes as no surprise whatsoever, and of itself it is not a particularly original or remarkable observation. Yet my purpose in demonstrating this link is to show how profound this change is and how it then begins to affect the construction of the crime problem. As discussed in Chapter 2, a dual strategy of neo-liberal-inspired harsh punishment and neo-conservative community responsibilisation emerges in relation to the emphasis on responsibility and values.

In terms of the argument that I wish to progress over the next three chapters it is the second of these two themes, community responsibilisation, that I shall take issue with. Not because it is represents a set of ideological values that I find unpalatable or because I dislike the extension of both formal and informal social control through strategies of community governance. These would essentially be normative claims about the political values I hold and subject to comprehensive counterclaims based on the political values others hold. No, I wish to argue that this strategy of community governance rests on a fundamental misunderstanding about the nature of society that is both theoretically and empirically unfounded. This misunderstanding is that criminality is caused by immorality and irresponsibility.

In the next chapter I shall begin this analysis by seeking to expose the contradictions and differences between what sociologists and criminologists know about the nature and character of community and the assumptions contained in this ideological commitment to community. The purpose of this analysis is to challenge the perspective that crime and anti-social behaviour can be explained in terms of a net loss in either morality or responsibility. Rather, it can be explained in terms of new cultural conditions that are embedded in technological, social, emotional and economic developments. Whilst these may change the form and character of our families, communities and identities they cannot simply be reversed by rebuilding some sense of lost community. Or at least, not without a time machine.

Notes

1 An earlier version of this discussion was originally published as part of Green, S. (2002) Ideology and Community: The Communitarian Hi-jacking of Community Justice, *British Journal of Community Justice*, 2 (1): 49–62.
2 Giddens (1998) means something quite different to New Labour when he refers to these conditions. For example, Driver and Martell (2002) argue that Giddens is referring to the processes of detraditionalisation and disembedding when referring to individualism. He links this to the uncertainty of late-modernity rather than the moral decay more closely aligned with the New Labour interpretation of individualism. See Chapter 6 for a full discussion.
3 Though to my horror and my 8-year-old daughter's delight, she was given an 'I'm a John Prescott Deputy' badge during the PCC campaign! He lost the election, however.

References

Althusser, L. (1969) *For Marx*, Harmondsworth: Penguin Books.
Bochel, H. (2011) Conservative Approaches to Social Policy since 1997, in H. Bochel (ed.) *The Conservative Party and Social Policy*, Bristol: Policy Press.

Bevir, M. (2005) *New Labour: A Critique*, London: Routledge.

Blair, T. (1993) Extract from speech in P. Mandelson, and R. Liddle, (1996) *The Blair Revolution: Can New Labour Deliver?* London: Faber and Faber, p. 48.

Blair, T. (1996) *Speech to the Labour Party Conference*, 1 October.

Blair, T. (1998) *The Third Way, New Politics for the New Century*, pamphlet 588, London: Fabian Society.

Blair, T. (2006) *Respect Agenda Speech*, London, available at: www.britishpoliticalspeech. org/speech-archive.htm?speech=290 (accessed 28/02/2013).

Blears, H. (2003) *Communities in Control: Public Services and Local Socialism*, pamphlet 607, London: Fabian Society.

Bourdieu, P. (1977) *Outline of a Theory of Practice*, Cambridge: Cambridge University Press.

Bourdieu, P. (1984) *Distinction. A Social Critique of the Judgement of Taste*, London: Routledge and Kegan Paul.

Bourdieu, P. (1990) *The Logic of Practice*, Cambridge: Polity Press.

Brake, M. and Hale, C. (1992) *Public Order and Private Lives: The Politics of Law and Order*, London: Routledge.

Cabinet Office (2013) *Government Awards £500,000 to Support Probation Mutuals*, 3 July, available at: www.gov.uk/government/news/government-awards-500000-to-support-probation-mutuals (accessed 27/07/2013).

Cameron, D. (2011a) *We Are All in This Together Speech*, 15 August, available at: www. conservatives.com/News/Speeches/2011/08/David_Cameron_We_are_all_in_this_ together.aspx (accessed 12/01/2013).

Cameron, D. (2011b) Full Transcript, David Cameron Statement on Public Disorder, House of Commons, *New Statesman*, 11 August, available at: www.newstatesman. com/2011/08/police-streets-violence (accessed 12/01/2013).

Cameron, D. (2011c) *PM's Speech on the Big Society*, 14 February, available at: www.gov. uk/government/speeches/pms-speech-on-big-society (accessed 28/01/2013).

Casey, L. (2008) *Engaging Communities in Fighting Crime*, Independent Report for Crime and Communities Review, London: Cabinet Office.

Chapman, T. and Hough, M. (1998) *Evidence Based Practice*, London: Her Majesty's Inspectorate of Probation.

Clegg, N. (2011) *Speech to Party Members about the Riots*, 13 August, available at: www. libdems.org.uk/latest_news_detail.aspx?title=Nick_Clegg%3A_Speech_to_party_ members_on_the_riots&pPK=c69dd25e-6ade-4e74-b011-248db8f37401(accessed25/07/ 2013).

Cohen, S. (1973) *Folk Devils and Moral Panics*, London: Paladin (rev. edn 1980).

Conservative Party Election Manifesto (2010) *Invitation to Join the Government of Britain*, London: The Conservative Party.

Crawford, A. (1996) The Spirit of Community: Rights, Responsibilities and the Communitarian Agenda, *Journal of Law and Society*, 2 (23): 247–62.

Crawford, A. (1997) *The Local Governance of Crime: Appeals to Community and Partnership*, Oxford: Clarendon Press.

Crow, I. (2001) *The Treatment and Rehabilitation of Offenders*, London: Sage Publications.

Department for Communities and Local Government (2012) *Working with Troubled Families: A Guide to the Evidence and Good Practice*, London: Department for Communities and Local Government, December, available at: www.gov.uk/government/uploads/system/uploads/attachment_data/file/66113/121214_Working_with_troubled_families_ FINAL_v2.pdf.

Downes, D. and Morgan, R. (2012) Overtaking on the Left? The Politics of Law and Order in the Big Society, in M. Maguire, R. Morgan and R. Reiner (eds) *The Oxford Handbook of Criminology* (5th edn), Oxford: Oxford University Press.

Driver, S. and Martell, L. (1997) New Labour's Communitarianism, *Critical Social Policy*, 17 (3): 27–46.

Driver, S. and Martell, L. (1998) *New Labour: Politics after Thatcherism*, Cambridge: Polity Press.

Driver, S. and Martell, L. (2002) *Blair's Britain*, Cambridge: Polity Press.

Elias, N. (2000) *The Civilising Process* (rev. edn), Oxford: Blackwell.

Emsley, C. (2005) *Crime and Society in England 1750–1900* (3rd edn), Harlow: Pearson.

Etzioni, A. (1995) *The Spirit of Community*, Hammersmith: Fontana Press.

Etzioni, A. (1997) *The New Golden Rule, Community and Morality in a Democratic Society*, London: Profile Books.

Farrall, S. and Hay, C. (2010) Not So Tough on Crime? Why Weren't the Thatcher Governments more Radical in Reforming the Criminal Justice System? *British Journal of Criminology*, 50 (3): 550–69.

Field, F. (1998) *New Ambitions for our Country: A New Contract for Welfare*, Cm 3805, London: Stationery Office.

Garland, D. (2000) The Culture of High Crime Societies: Some Preconditions Of Recent 'Law and Order' Policies, *British Journal of Criminology*, 40 (3): 347–75.

Giddens, A. (1998) *The Third Way, the Renewal of Social Democracy*, Cambridge: Polity Press.

Giddens, A. (2000) *The Third Way and Its Critics*, Cambridge: Polity Press.

Giddens, A. (2002) *Where now for New Labour?* Cambridge: Polity Press.

Gilling, D. (2007) *Crime Reduction and Community Safety: Labour and the Politics of Local Crime Control*, Cullompton: Willan.

Glasman, M. (2010) Society not State: The Challenge of the Big Society, *Public Policy Research*, 17 (2): 58–63.

Gramsci, A. (1971) *Selections from the 'Prison Notebooks'*, London: Lawrence and Wishart.

Green, S. (2002) Ideology and Community: The Communitarian Hi-jacking of Community Justice, *British Journal of Community Justice*, 2 (1): 49–62.

Guardian (1998) *Blair and Straw Find New 'Marriage Is Best' Crusade no Bed of Roses*, 5 November.

Guardian (1999) *Take on the Criminals, Straw Urges*, 19 February, available at: www.guardian.co.uk/uk/1999/feb/19/2 (accessed 27/07/2013).

Guardian (2011) *David Cameron: Tony Blair Was Wrong about the Riots*, 2 September, available at: www.guardian.co.uk/politics/2011/sep/02/cameron-blair-wrong-about-riots (accessed 28/09/2011).

Guardian (2012) *A Phalanx of 'Stale, Male and Pale' PCC Candidates Is almost Inevitable*, 14 August, available at: www.guardian.co.uk/public-leaders-network/2012/aug/14/male-pale-police-commissioner-candidates (accessed 21/01/2013).

Hall, S., Critcher, C., Jefferson, T., Clarke, J. and Roberts, B. (1978) *Policing the Crisis: Mugging, the State and Law and Order*, London: Macmillan.

Her Majesty's Government (2011) *Open Public Services White Paper*, HM Government, available at: http://files.openpublicservices.cabinetoffice.gov.uk/OpenPublicServices-WhitePaper.pdf.

Home Office (2008) *From the Neighbourhood to the National: Policing Our Communities Together*, Green Paper, Cm. 7448, London: Home Office.

Hughes, G. (1996) Communitarianism and Law and Order, *Critical Social Policy*, 16: 17–41.

Hughes, G. (1998) *Understanding Crime Prevention*, Buckingham: Open University Press.

Jewkes, Y. (2011) *Media and Crime* (2nd edn), London: Sage.

Jordan, B. (2010) *Why the Third Way Failed: Economics, Morality and the Origins of the 'Big Society'*, Bristol: Policy Press.

Kavanagh, D. (1990) *Thatcherism and British Politics* (2nd edn), Oxford: Oxford University Press.

Labour Manifesto (2001) *Ambitions for Britain*.

Labour Manifesto (2005) *Britain Forward Not Backwards*.

Levitas, R. (1998) *The Inclusive Society? Social Exclusion and New Labour*, Basingstoke: Macmillan.

Little, A. (2002) Community and Radical Democracy, *Journal of Political Ideologies*, 7 (3): 369–82.

Maguire, M. (2012) Response 1: Big Society, the Voluntary Sector and the Marketization of Criminal Justice, *Criminology & Criminal Justice*, 12 (5): 483–505.

Mannheim, K. (1960 [1929]) *Ideology and Utopia, an Introduction to the Sociology of Knowledge*, London: Routledge and Kegan Paul.

Marx, K. and Engels, F. (1845 [1965]) *The German Ideology*, London: Lawrence and Wishart.

McLaughlin, E. (2002) The Crisis of the Social and the Political Materialisation of Community Safety, in G. Hughes, E. McLaughlin and J. Muncie (eds) *Crime Prevention and Community Safety, New Directions*, London: Sage.

Miliband, E. (2011a) *Ed Miliband: New Excuses for Rioting*, BBC News website, 9 August, available at: www.bbc.co.uk/news/uk-politics-14463246 (accessed 07/04/2013).

Miliband, E. (2011b) Full Transcript Ed Miliband Speech on the Riots, Haverstock School, *New Statesman*, 15 August, available at: www.newstatesman.com/politics/2011/08/society-young-heard-riots (accessed 20/01/2013).

Miliband, E. (2011c) *Speech at the Reading the Riots Conference, London School of Economics*, 14 December, available at: http://www.labour.org.uk/reading-the-riots-conference,2011-12-14 (accessed 20/01/2013).

Ministry of Justice (2011) *Breaking the Cycle: Effective Punishment, Rehabilitation and Sentencing of Offenders* (Green Paper) Cm. 7972, HM Government, available at: http://webarchive.nationalarchives.gov.uk/20120119200607/http:/www.justice.gov.uk/consultations/docs/breaking-the-cycle.pdf.

Morgan, R. (2012) Crime and Justice in the 'Big Society', *Criminology & Criminal Justice*, 12 (5): 463–81.

Nellis, M. (2000) Creating Community Justice, in S. Ballintyne, K. Pease and V. Maclaren (eds) *Key Issues in Crime Prevention, Crime Reduction and Community Safety*. London: IPPR.

Observer (2002) *We Should Link Benefits to Duties: Mr Blair's Way Can Be Made to Work*, 5 May, available at: http://www.theguardian.com/news/2002/may/05/leaders.politics1 (accessed 19/11/ 2013).

Observer (2011) *Blaming a Moral Decline for the Riots Makes Good Headlines but Bad Policy*, 20 August, available at: www.guardian.co.uk/commentisfree/2011/aug/20/tony-blair-riots-crime-family (accessed 28/09/2013).

Pearson, G. (1983) *Hooligan: A History of Respectable Fears*, Basingstoke: Palgrave Macmillan.

Pitts, J. (2001) *The New Politics of Youth Crime*, London: Palgrave.

Respect Task Force (2006) *Respect Action Plan*, London: Home Office.

Social Justice Policy Group (2006) *Breakdown Britain: Interim Report on the State of the Nation*, December, London: Social Justice Policy Group.

Straw, J. (1995) Straw and Order, *New Statesman and Society*, 15 September.

Straw, J. (2007) *Justice Secretary's Speech*, Labour Party Conference, Bournemouth available at: www.britishpoliticalspeech.org/speech-archive.htm?speech=302 (accessed 27/02/2013).

Thatcher, M. (1987) *Interview with Women's Own Magazine 'No Such Thing as Society'*, 23 September, available at: www.margaretthatcher.org/speeches/displaydocument. asp?docid=106689 (accessed 10/04/2013).

Third Sector (2013) *HM Prison Peterborough Social Impact Bond Has Led to a Fall in Reconvictions, Official Statistics Show*, 14 June, available at: www.thirdsector.co.uk/ news/1186265/ (accessed 27/07/2013).

Underdown, A. (2002) Making 'What Works' Work: Challenges in the Delivery of Community Penalties, in A. Bottoms, L. Gelsthorpe, and S. Rex (eds) *Community Penalties, Changes and Challenges*, Cullompton: Willan Publishing.

Young, J. and Matthews, R. (2003) New Labour, Crime Control and Social Exclusion, in R. Matthews and J. Young (eds) *The New Politics of Crime and Punishment*, Collumpton: Willan.

5   Getting a sense of community

The previous two chapters sought to consider the ideas of Amitai Etzioni and his communitarian colleagues and the influence of these types of ideas upon political values, and how this then begins to shape understanding of the crime problem. This chapter will seek to discuss the dilemmas and assumptions contained within contemporary discourses on community, and the problems of evoking a particular conception of community in relation to crime control. From this discussion several questions will emerge about the nature and character of the type of community currently progressed by academics, politicians and policy makers. These questions will form the basis of the next chapter, which will explore the social relations evident in late-modern society and whether there is any dissonance between these conditions and the assumptions contained within communitarian thought.

There are two problems with the type of community being utilised within crime control policy and practice. Firstly, there is the problem of definition and contestation regarding what community is and how it should be conceptualised. Secondly, there is the more specific problem of the communitarian commitment to a particular type of community and the implications of the normative assumptions contained within this construction of community for crime control strategies. The first of these problems is well debated within sociological, anthropological, social policy and political spheres, where community is consistently defined and redefined in reference to competing perspectives on the topic (take for example Wirth 1964, Crawford 1997 or Hoggett 1997). The second of these problems relates to the interaction between a form of communitarian thought that developed in North America (e.g. Etzioni 1995, 1997) and its application to crime control policy. This communitarian ideology contains a value-based set of assumptions regarding both the desirability and constitution of communities themselves. The contention of this chapter, and indeed the book, is that these assumptions are uncritically assimilated into political doctrine and criminal justice policy. This assimilation carries with it an explanation for criminality that drives the regeneration of community as a form of crime control. The aim, therefore, is to investigate the efficacy of these assumptions and consider other ways in which community can be, and has been, construed that challenge the logic of this type of community engagement in crime control policy. The previous two chapters explored communitarian and political values, whereas this chapter explores the concept of community in greater detail.

The objectives of this chapter are twofold. One, to provide a detailed and wide ranging discussion of the ways in which community has been understood and used, and two, to consider this understanding as it relates to criminological research about communities and crime. This begins with a brief overview of the definitional problems associated with the concept of community, before going on to look at the ways in which different authors and disciplines have theorised about community and its relationship to wider social conditions. What this demonstrates is that the concept of community varies considerably, depending on whom you read or in what context it is being applied. The chapter will conclude with a review of how community has been researched and theorised within the field of criminology and crime control. This will provide the broad empirical and theoretical background to debates about community that will form the basis for critiquing the assumptions contained within the political values currently in vogue in British politics.

Defining community

> The term 'community', like other concepts taken over from common sense usage, has been used with an abandon reminiscent of poetic licence.
>
> (Wirth 1964: 297)

Before any attempt to examine the role of community within criminal justice can be formulated some discussion of what community actually means needs to be undertaken. The above statement shows that there was recognition of the difficulties in defining and using the term 'community' some fifty years ago. The term community has been hotly contested for decades (Lee and Newby 1983, Crow and Allan 1994, Crawford 1997) and has a myriad of different meanings and definitions, depending on what purpose the term has been employed for and from which disciplinary school definitions have been derived. As far back as 1955, Hillery composed ninety-four definitions of the term, and found that the only common theme was 'all of the definitions deal with people' (Hillery 1955: 17). However, the majority of definitions did tend to point to three components of community: area, common ties and social interaction. In a similar fashion Bell and Newby (1971) reiterate this distinction by pointing to three levels of community, including 'a territorial area, a complex of institutions within an area, and a sense of belonging' (Bell and Newby 1971: 15–16).

This distinction appears to be replicated in other places. Lee and Newby (1983) distinguish between three types of community. The first is community as a geographical expression, or locality. Second, community as a local social system, consisting of social relationships broadly situated within a particular locality; and third, community as a type of relationship, or sense of identity, between individuals, that does not rely on any geographical relationship. This they refer to as 'communion'. As Lee and Newby (1983) suggest, all too often these three have been bunched together by sociologists, leaving a largely unexplored assumption that locality leads to particular forms of social relations.

Another attempt to distinguish between these different forms of community has been proffered by Peter Willmott (1986, 1987), who provides a very succinct analysis of the different types of community:

> A useful distinction can be made between the *territorial community*, defined by geography and meaning the people who live in a particular area; the *interest community*, a set of people with something in common other than just territory (the black community, the Jewish community, the gay community); and the *attachment community*, where there is the kind of attachment to people or place which gives rise to a 'sense of community'.
>
> (Willmott 1987: 2; emphasis in original)

Willmott (1987) suggests that these three types of community often overlap and that attachment communities often facilitate the 'binding together' of territorial and interest communities. Further, Willmott (1987) notes that the unravelling of these different types of communities helps us to appreciate that there are many people living in a specific locality who do not share any sense of attachment or interest with their neighbours. This in turn warns us against the 'warm, almost mystical' (Willmott 1987: 2) feelings that can be engendered by the term 'community'. Willmott (1987) concludes that the lack of clarity surrounding the term can often lead to:

> skilful jumps from one meaning to another. It can conceal more than it reveals, and is often intended to. Those advocating a new initiative, and similarly those attacking or defending a particular point of view, often invoke the community in support of their case, without making it clear which community they mean or in what sense it is likely to be affected.
>
> (Ibid.)

It is these last comments that cause the greatest concern. This concern is that the failure to define the meaning of community results in confusion about the very nature of contemporary communities. This could clearly have an impact on the effectiveness and appropriateness of criminal justice policies. However, what the combined weight of these types of definition means is that community cannot be understood purely in terms of geographical locality. Further, as Stacey (1969) states: 'Physical proximity does not always lead to the establishment of social relations' (Stacey 1969: 144). In other words people may inhabit the same space but not share any common sense of belonging (Cohen, A.P. 1982). This lesson is essential if an analysis of current conceptions of community is to be undertaken. Yet, definitional issues continue to remain a source of confusion. As Wittgenstein (1953) has stated 'For a *large* class of cases – though not for all – in which we employ the word "meaning" it can be defined as thus: the meaning of a word is in its use in the language' (p. 20, para. 43; emphasis in original). The usage of the word thus becomes critical in understanding its meaning. Hence, to properly ascertain the meaning and character of communities, study must be made of how community has been understood at both a theoretical and an empirical level.

Theorising community: tradition and modernity

There are a range of different disciplinary perspectives on community that provide sometimes complementary and sometimes competing understandings of what communities are and how they are organised. Perhaps the most established school of thought is the sociological, which has a long tradition of exploring the nature and changing character of community (Nisbet 1967, Delanty 2003).

The roots of the sociological enquiry into community can be traced back to the process of industrialisation and the development of a capitalist economy. One of the most significant early characterisations of community stems from the work of Ferdinand Tonnies (1887), who made the distinction between *Gemeinschaft* and *Gesellschaft* (community and society, respectively). Tonnies defines the difference between these two concepts as:

> All intimate, private and exclusive living together is understood as life in Gemeinschaft (community). Gesellschaft (society) is public life – it is the world itself. In Gemeinschaft (community) with one's family, one lives from birth on bound to it in weal and woe. One goes into Gesellschaft (society) as one goes into a strange country. A young man is warned against bad Gesellschaft (society), but the expression bad Gemeinschaft (community) violates the meaning of the word.
>
> (Tonnies 1887: 37)

Tonnies goes on to conclude:

> Gemeinschaft (community) should be understood as a living organism, Gesellschaft (society) as a mechanical aggregate and artifact.
>
> (ibid.: 39)

In this particular analysis Tonnies relates Gemeinschaft to pre-industrial life and Gesellschaft to industrial life. Tonnies does, however, acknowledge that Gemeinschaft can continue in industrial society, particularly in rural areas. Following on from Tonnies, Georg Simmel (1950 [1905]) applied some of Tonnies' insights to modern life. In a similar vein to Tonnies, Simmel feared the loss of the community, relating its decline to the rise of the city. As well as Tonnies and Simmel, earlier social commentators such as Marx and Engels and novelists such as Charles Dickens took an equally negative view of the rise of urbanism and its consequent effect on human relations:

> We know well enough that the isolation of the individual – a narrow minded egotism – is everywhere the fundamental principal in modern society.
>
> (Engels 1845: 31)

The work of Louis Wirth (1938) reinforced this pessimistic vision of city life, arguing that an increased population size promotes social differentiation which leads to the establishment of separate neighbourhoods defined by class, ethnicity and other demographics.

What becomes apparent is that these accounts of industrialisation are littered with negative perceptions of urban life as 'impersonal, isolating, alienating' (Worsley 1992: 227). The general consensus would appear to be that community has been thoroughly eroded in urban life. Of course there have been more optimistic approaches to industrialisation, such as Durkheim's (1893) conception of mechanical and organic solidarity. This distinction was primarily based upon differences in the division of labour between pre-industrial and industrial society. Durkheim (1893) argued that organic solidarity was the ideal type for modern advanced societies and that the cause of current social problems was the as yet unperfected, transitional stage between these two modes of solidarity. However, despite this more positive view of urban life the majority of texts appear to resent the progress of the city and the effect this had on more traditional modes of existence. In response to this perceived social evil many commentators sought to highlight the benefits and superiority of the pre-industrial community.

This tradition of yearning for some past life rich in meaningful social relations is one that still persists today. The unfortunate truth is that the body of sociological literature relating to community has failed to distinguish between Willmott's three types of community: territorial, interest and attachment. This view is reiterated by Worsley (1992), who breaks down the ninety-four definitions of community that were outlined in a paper by Hillery (1955) into three categories: community as locality, community as a local social system and community as a type of relationship. These three categories clearly share much in common with Willmott's definition, and the failure of sociologists to distinguish between these three types of community is not lost on Worsley. In addition Worsley suggests that writers have failed to explain why life in a specific area either promotes or destroys relationships:

> For example, rural villages were often assumed to consist of closely knit inhabitants living in happy communion, while in cities there are only isolated, lonely individuals lacking any sense of mutual identity. These assumptions, which purport to identify a unity between locality, local social system and communion, reflect little more than prevailing cultural myths and/or the values of the sociological observer.
>
> (Worsley 1992: 223)

This rural–urban divide has been heavily studied, with early research attempting to demonstrate the existence of 'Gemeinschaft' within rural environments (e.g. Redfield 1947), whilst 'Gesellschaft' was the type of social condition exclusive to urban settings (Wirth 1938). Yet, according to Lee and Newby (1983), more recent findings have suggested a different picture, obscuring this rural–urban distinction by demonstrating the existence of Gemeinschaft within urban villages. Most notable of these have been Young and Willmott (1957) and Hoggart (1957), who both pointed to the existence of Gemeinschaft in both Bethnal Green, London and Hunslet, Leeds. Still other studies began to suggest that the rural idyll of community life was far from always evident (Lewis 1949, Pahl 1965). What these empirical studies demonstrate is that the rural–urban divide is not as clearly distinguished as earlier sociologists would have us believe. Therefore, not only is there significant confusion within the sociological tradition about what constitutes a community, but there is also contradictory research that undermines the notion of the city without communion.

It would therefore appear that the concept of community within sociology has been largely oversimplified, its definition deriving from a wistful, romanticised vision of a bygone era. Clearly, this is not the only perspective, but it has been the one to dominate research and thinking about community. Delanty (2003) points to three conceptions of community that emerged out of nineteenth-century sociology:

1   The discourse of community as irretrievable
2   The discourse of community as recoverable
3   The discourse of community as yet to be achieved.

(Delanty 2003: 19–20)

Of these three conceptions the first two are rooted in the idea that community has been lost as a product of urbanisation, whilst the third represents a more utopian notion, closely associated with the ideas of Karl Marx and a communist society (Marx and Engels 1848).

This notion of traditional community life being preferable to modern urban relationships has had a pervasive effect upon perceptions of how to improve social conditions. For example, Etzioni's (1997) communitarianism advocates the regeneration of shared social and moral values and the New Labour administration pursues its rhetoric of social responsibility and the 'stakeholder' society with vigorous policies designed to encourage participation. The problem is not that politicians and academics have looked to community to help solve some of society's problems, but the manner in which they have utilised the concept. This problem has two main factors. Firstly, there is far too much ambiguity concerning the definition of community and far too much reliance on outdated or common-sense definitions of the term. Secondly, as a result of this ambiguity, and as a result of romanticised visions of the past, there exists an unconscious consensus that believes we can reintroduce social conditions typical of one hundred years ago to combat an entirely new set of social problems in an entirely new set of social conditions.

Yet, theorising community is not only limited to sociology and there have been significant contributions from other disciplines. Chief amongst these is anthropology and the work of Benedict Anderson (1983) and Anthony Cohen (1985). Unlike sociologists, these anthropologist have focused their level of analysis at culture and symbolic meaning rather than the structural conditions of community. Anderson's (1983) work develops the idea of the 'imagined community' and is primarily concerned with outlining a theory of the national community, where people who have never met, and share little in common with regard to social conditions or values, enjoy a common sense of belonging and fellowship. The imagined community is therefore 'imagined' because it is not based on concrete social relation, where individuals are bound together by a kinship, locality or interests. Instead it describes a sense of communion, or belonging, at the nation-state level, whereby a shared sense of nationality unites. This type of imagined community is often manifested at times when nations come together, sharing a common set of causes and attachment:

> The power of the term is to highlight how in a national community there can exist a single common set of feelings and emotions. England rugby fans singing 'Swing Low Sweet Chariot' at Twickenham, or the 'national outpouring of grief' which accompanied the sudden death and funeral of Diana, Princess of Wales, are tangible examples. The 'imagined community' is a central concept in the study of nationalism and national identity.
>
> (Morris and Morton 1998: 74)

This level of analysis is perhaps outside the focus of this book, where most discussion of community exists at the level of subgroups within and across nation-states. Yet, its important contribution is that community need not be constrained to individuals bound by some form of social interaction, however distant, but instead by the power of uniting symbols or culture which infer a sense of similarity or shared character. Hence, imagined communities, whilst conceived as the national community, provide an important revision of how a community is organised beyond the national level. We may all imagine a sense of shared communion beyond those we share our lives with. This can be at the level of the workplace, faith group, class, political affiliation and so on. We imagine that others with whom we share commonalities are members of a wider community with whom we share similarities.

To some extent this dovetails nicely with the work of another anthropologist, A.P. Cohen (1985). A.P. Cohen's work (1982, 1985) is concerned with the theme of belonging and the symbolic community. A.P. Cohen (1985) argues that it is the symbolic power of 'community' that affords meaning to people's sense of belonging. It is the perceptions of individuals that create community, rather than their structural or environmental conditions:

> The quintessential referent of community is that its members make, or believe they make, a similar sense of things either generally or with respect to specific and significant interests, and, further, that they think that that sense may differ from ones made elsewhere. The reality of community in people's experience thus inheres in their attachment or commitment to a common body of symbols
>
> (A.P. Cohen 1985: 16)

Hence, Anthony Cohen's (1985) work on the symbolic construction of community provides yet a further theoretical basis for conceptualising community.

Rather than focus on the structural characteristics of community, he draws on the importance of meaning, derived through both symbols and rituals that provide a common sense of belonging. Intrinsic to this notion of community is boundary, the distinction between those who are part of the community and those who are outside of it. Community suggests that the members share something in common, which distinguishes, or differentiates, them from non-members. In other words, communities are defined not only in terms of similarity between their members, but also by difference between members, and non-members (those who are outsiders, or excluded from the group). For A.P. Cohen (1985) this issue of boundary, or rivalry, between competing communities is the product of industrialisation and urbanisation. He argues that as these processes have undermined the traditional structural boundaries of community the symbolic boundaries have become increasingly important, as they provide new ways of distinguishing between those in the community and those outside of it. In short, modernity has led to a shift in the locus of community, away from the structural and towards the cultural:

> Thus, moving away from the earlier emphasis our discipline placed on structure, we approach community as a phenomenon of culture: as one, therefore, which is meaningfully constructed by people through their symbolic prowess and resources.
>
> (A.P. Cohen 1985: 38)

This does not require community to be invested with either particular physical features or shared values. What it does require is that people perceive themselves to share something in common with others who also unite around shared symbols and ideologies. This can be the nation-state, the football club or the church. What must be remembered is that whilst these symbols may impart meaning and attachment they are not necessarily interpreted or understood in the same way by all members of that community. As A.P. Cohen (1985) warns:

> Age, life, father, purity, gender, death, doctor, are all symbols shared by those who use the same language, or participate in the same symbolic behaviour through which these categories are expressed and marked. But their meanings are not shared in the same way. Each is mediated by the idiosyncratic experience of the individual . . . Symbols do not so much express meaning as give us the capacity to make meaning.
>
> (A.P. Cohen 1985: 14–15)

In other words:

> Different societies, and different communities within the same society, may manifest apparently similar forms – whether these be in religion, kinship, work, politics, economy, recreation or whatever – but this is not to suggest that they have become culturally homogeneous
>
> (A.P. Cohen 1985: 37)

Hence, in this conceptualisation of community it would a gross misrepresentation to present communities as necessarily sharing the same meanings; they simply attach to shared symbols that each member then interprets differently.

This brief tour through the ideas of Anderson (1983) and A.P. Cohen (1985) demonstrates an anthropological tradition that transcends the structural debates so fondly pursued by some the sociologists mentioned above. Their importance is that they add a new dimension to the ways in which community has been theorised and understood. For both Anderson (1983) and A.P. Cohen (1985) community is understood in terms of people's perceptions of belonging and the contours of cultural meaning.

Both the sociological and anthropological work on community demonstrates some of the variations and confusions when theorising the concept. Some of these vagaries have been transferred to the field of crime control, in which community has increasingly become the focus of attention (Crawford 1997). The exact nature of this transference and the type of community being peddled is discussed later in this chapter. The purpose of this discussion has been to illustrate two things. Firstly, that sociological thinking about community is laced with romanticised sentiments that present it either as some form of lost social good or as a form of social relations to which we should aspire. In this sense community comes close to representing an ideal, or utopian, vision of desirable social relations. Secondly, that the concept is contested. There is little agreement on what its characteristics may be or in what conditions it prevails. The two are, of course, linked; the theoretical heritage of how community is understood is wrapped in the author's ideological commitment to a particular type of community life. The anthropological literature, whilst less ideologically infused, has still largely failed to address the shortcomings present in the sociological. To quote A.P. Cohen (1985) once more:

> Over the years it [community] has proved to be highly resistant to satisfactory definition in anthropology and sociology, perhaps for the simple reason that all definitions contain or imply theories, and the theory of community has been very contentious. At its most extreme, the debate has thrown up ideologically opposed propositions which are equally untenable.
>
> (A.P. Cohen 1985: 11)

Yet there are other lessons to be learnt from these theoretical understandings of community. One common theme in the sociological literature would be that the characteristics of community are tied to structural conditions. The onset of industrialisation and urbanisation disrupted structural conditions, which in turn disrupted communities. Another theme, this time from the anthropological literature, is that communities have boundaries, indeed must have boundaries to define themselves, meaning that strong communities will have very well-defined membership which excludes those who do not fit in, and therefore has implications for the political and communitarian commitment to community as the basis for restoring civil society.

Theorising community: the collapse of stability

The communitarian yearning for the lost community is further compromised by a raft of celebrated new perspectives rethinking community in late-, or postmodern society. Whilst it might well be possible to critique Etzioni (1995) for his failure to consider the social processes and structures that shape the nature of social relations in contemporary society, other sociologists have begun to reconceptualise the ways in which community is understood and experienced. Failure to engage with these perspectives is yet another charge to be levelled at the communitarian band-wagon. More fundamentally, these perspectives begin to point towards the conditions of late-modernity that actively preclude and make preposterous Etzioni's (1995) nostalgia for a bygone era of social and moral inclusivity.

Since the late 1980s a growing number of sociological theories have emerged that attempt to rethink how community is both understood and experienced through a postmodern lens. If postmodernity is typified by the breakdown of stability and certainty (Giddens 1990, Bauman 2000), wherein old distinctions of class, race, gender and nation begin to fragment and intermingle, then how does this affect the individual's experience of a sense of belonging? Delanty (2003) outlines a number of perspectives that begin to explore this question. Of key interest in this analysis is the changing nature of society and the birth of new modes of communication, in particular the growth of the internet. The early work in this field by Howard Rheingold (1993) begins to unpick the impact of the internet and email on how social relations increasingly function and are organised. For Rheingold (1993), the internet provides an emancipatory opportunity to form new types of 'virtual communities' that exist on the net, and outside of everyday life. As such, the internet liberates people from their conditions and environment and provides new spaces in which people can interact.

Alongside Rheingold's (1993) early exploration into virtual communities the ideas of Manuel Castells (1996, 2001) and Craig Calhoun (1991, 1992, 1998) have further developed and explored the rise of the information network. For Castells (1996), the internet provides networks of sociability that allow people to effectively 'dip' into new communities from a distance. The internet is thus the forum in which the self can be explored without commitment, though it also provides new ways of maintaining existing networks of family and friends that overcomes many of the traditional geographical and time obstacles to interaction. Castells (1996, 2001) has something in common with Rheingold (1993) insofar as both see the potential of the internet to transform social networks through virtual communities. Yet, in a later work Castells (2001) sees the virtual world as offering only a 'thin' form of community, as he argues that the internet can foster and support existing communities rather than build new ones. Hence, Castells (2001) prefers the notion of networks of sociability rather than virtual community to explain the types of interactions that take place in the virtual world. The phenomena of Friends Reunited, Facebook, Myspace, Twitter and so on all provide compelling examples of how the internet provides new ways of reaffirming existing relationships that would seem to support Castells' thesis.

On a slightly different note, Calhoun (1992) considers mass communications and the media as representing wider social conditions in which the importance of the indirect relationship increasingly governs interactions and exchanges. Calhoun (1991, 1992) therefore perceives the internet as representing wider changes in the way that social interactions occur. Viewed in this way, the internet becomes less able to transform or build new relationships in the way that Rheingold (1993) or Castells (1996) suppose. Instead, Calhoun (1998) is far more cautious, arguing that the internet bolsters communities of similarity where people come together who share aesthetic, life-style or political views and, as such, these are more likely to be virtual communities based around a single shared interest rather networks of people living and sharing their lives in virtual space. For Calhoun (1998) the problem with this is that it is unlikely to create new political and social democracies, but simply to bolster existing ones. Thus, Calhoun (1998) is much more suspicious of the internet, viewing its interactions as reproducing and reifying existing social and cultural groupings.

The era of mass communications and internet technology has opened up new avenues for communication and interaction that create the possibility for communities to exist in different social spaces. This raises questions around whether the internet generates new structures of community life or perpetuates existing social bonds. Either way, what becomes apparent is that geography becomes increasingly redundant for these types of virtual community and that the internet, and social world more generally, increasingly disconnects the individual from the constraints of birth, family or environment, allowing individuals to invest themselves in a complex array of ever-changing social networks. Thus the internet would seem to be both product and producer of the social conditions evident in late-modern or postmodern society. The implications of these conditions and the new technologies of communication that run through them would seem important features for understanding how belonging is experienced in contemporary society.

Understanding these conditions has led to a shift away from the traditional sociology of enlightenment and industrialisation to instead focusing upon deconstructing the intersubjectivities that shape social interactions and the ways in which people generate their sense of belonging with each other. Within these theoretical discourses community, as understood in terms of Gesellschaft and Gemeinschaft, has largely become redundant, replaced instead by an attempt to understand the self.

The rediscovery of the self has long been the remit of postmodern theory. Whilst the enlightenment sought to build universal certainties and cohesive sense of purpose and place, contemporary theorists attempt to understand the nature and construction of the self, or identity, in a world which is increasingly fluid and plural. This world is one in which the mainstream has come to include a far more varied and diverse range of life-styles, cultures and aesthetics. Forms of life that were once very much on the margins are increasingly commonplace and, as such, the self, unhinged from the shackles of tradition, is left buffeted by a cacophony of sights, sounds, life-styles and threats through which it must successfully navigate. Hence, the postmodern world is one where understanding the construction of the self and the other becomes crucial to understanding the character and dilemmas of the social world. As the old social structures of family, class, nation, gender and ethnicity become increasingly less stable, so the construction of the self becomes less stable. As a result the construction of the self becomes increasingly significant because identity is no longer an accident of birth or circumstance but something that must be worked on to provide a sense of meaning and place in an increasingly unpredictable world.

With regard to community, several perspectives have emerged which attempt to consider how and where a sense of belonging is generated and how this sense of belonging is different from the conception outlined by classical sociology. The work of Nancy (1991) and of Blanchot (1988) provides an important sense in which the loss of community can be used to help understand how people experience it. Both Nancy (1991) and Blanchot (1988) argue that community is primarily experienced in the postmodern world as a sense of loss and it is in this context that it should be understood. Nancy (1991) conceptualises the community in terms of communicative relationships with others and argues that, as a result, community can be understood only as personal relations between individuals. For Nancy (1991), any attempt to construct community as an entity in its own right or to recreate some nostalgic notion of community should be viewed with suspicion. Blanchot (1988), on the other hand, postulates that community is unrealisable; glimpsed through the intimacy of friendship but ultimately unobtainable at a societal level. Both Nancy (1991) and Blanchot (1988) therefore endorse a common conception of community that sees it as experienced through the bonds of friendship but unrealisable at either a conceptual or an emotional level in any substantive way.

Emerging from, and alongside, these postmodern renderings of community are the reflexive community of Lash (1994) and the emotional communities of Maffesoli (1996). For Lash (1994), the reflexive community is a product of late-modernity wherein individuals choose which communities to become members of and then consciously use these communities to invent, interpret and modify their identities. For Lash (1994), therefore communities are disembedded from geography, time and tradition and are primarily sites for the cultural configuration of the self. Communities are thus created and defined by their members. In a similar vein Maffesoli (1996) has considered the emotional community which is bound by aesthetic rather than symbolic codes (Delanty 2003). For Maffesoli (1996), emotional communities are types of postmodern 'tribes' where people occasionally come together to share a common theme before dispersing and moving on to the next tribal gathering. This type of community, like Lash's (1994), is de-territorial, insubstantial and unstable. For Maffesoli (1996), these emotional communities emerge in response to the fragmentation of society and the growing heterogeneity of society. Confronted with these conditions, people congregate into tribes wherein they can receive emotional support and protection from a world increasingly hard to interpret and locate themselves within. Thus, Maffesoli's (1996) emotional community is founded purely in terms of its sociability, as opposed to any wider shared or common characteristics. Such communities are inevitably temporary and in constant flux.

These types of perspectives are useful when considering how people experience their lives. Whereas communities were once fixed, immutable and rigid, they are now chosen, changeable and fluid. These types of community theorised are those that pay heed to these fragile and unstable conditions. Drawing together these perspectives suggests that contemporary community can be understood only at a personal level, in terms of the relationships individuals share with one another. The work of Pahl (2000) and Spencer and Pahl (2006) suggests that friendship circles increasingly provide the support and sense of belonging once associated with the traditional community. Instead of community as a form of structure, community becomes a form of culture; an abstract expression of elective social networks that are consciously chosen rather than structurally imposed.

The combination of new technologies such as social networking and late- or postmodernity provides new ways of communicating and new ways of interacting. What becomes apparent is that the traditional community imagined by the classical sociologists is in decline. Yet it does not necessarily follow that social bonds themselves are in decline. New forms of social life emerge in response to the changing conditions people find themselves in. Whilst these may not be recognisably community in the traditional sense, they do nevertheless describe and shape the nature of social bonds in contemporary society.

Membership of these new forms of community may well be transient or partial. People may well become members of multiple groups or routinely move between them. Just as late-modernity is transient, unstable and unpredictable, so too are people's social lives. Yet this does not mean that community does not exist or that social bonds do not remain as important to human beings as they ever were. They are simply changing. Contemporary sociology has managed to acknowledge and keep abreast of much of this change, whilst it would appear that communitarians and their political allies remain bereft of understanding about these new forms of social life and are therefore left harkening back to an older tradition of sociology that dealt with the era of modernity rather than the onset of late-modern or postmodern society.

Curiously, appreciation of this dynamic also seems conspicuously absent from the communitarian ideas of Etzioni (1995). When set against the types of theories touched upon here, Etzioni's formulation of the moral community seems peculiarly anachronistic and out of place. A world where people choose their membership of this or that community; where people have multiple memberships of different communities; where people enter, exit and adapt their community to suit their needs; and where people construct and reconstruct their identities in response to an ever-changing social landscape, would seem one incompatible with the moral authoritarianism that underpins communitarianism.

Community, neighbourhood and crime control

Community has been deployed with crime control debates and research in a variety of ways. One type of community often explored within the crime control arena is one founded on a geographical space that is most commonly associated with the traditional concept of neighbourhood and criminal environment. Within this context the first point to re-emphasise is that a decline in community is often deemed responsible for a corresponding rise in crime (Crawford 1997) although this is more commonly located within a narrative of urban decline in the physical environment or in the decline in economic wealth of a community that leads to high levels of unemployment and a transitory population. There is also a large body of criminological research into the relationship between community disorganisation and anti-social and criminal behaviour. The work of Hope and Hough (1988), Skogan (1990), Bottoms (1992) and others has attempted to illustrate the relationship between environmental phenomenon and crime levels. This involves the careful examination of particular environmental developments and how these can affect the forms of social control that supposedly keep crime in check. Environmental criminology follows in a tradition started by Shaw and McKay (1931, 1942) in the Chicago School and continues with the work of Morris (1957), Newman (1973), Gill (1977), Davidson (1981) and Wilson and Kelling (1982), which looks at neighbourhood and locality to understand crime and the fear of crime. At a diagnostic level the work of environmental criminologists appears to present evidence to support the impact of community disorganisation on levels of criminality. Yet, there is both theoretical and empirical evidence which appears to call this assertion into question.

For example, the work of Hope and Foster (1992) and Foster (1995) in two high crime council housing estates demonstrated that community structures did exist and had a positive influence on the impact of crime in the area, providing local support and resources for victims. This challenges the 'broken windows' thesis of Wilson and Kelling (1982), who argue that a decline in community leads to spiralling crime. Crawford (1997) goes further, by suggesting that these broken windows do not have a uniform effect in every neighbourhood. He argues that communities respond differently to crime and other social problems, depending on the levels of political and social resources available to them. Further, Crawford (1997) makes the salient observation:

> In addition, the logic behind this association between the lack of 'organised' community and crime is that, conversely, more community equals less crime. Community in this context, is cleansed of any negative or criminogenic connotations and endowed with a simplistic and naïve purity of virtue. In some instances 'community', i.e. its communal normative values, itself may be the source of criminogenic tendencies.
>
> (Crawford 1997: 153)

Therefore, community is not always a site for law-abiding behaviour and neither does it exclusively provide social control of the sort that ensures conformity. It can also foster diametrically opposed values that engender criminality and deviation. This highlights another important feature of how community is perceived within crime control strategies. Community is a force for good, a strong community provides the necessary elements of social control that prevent the escalation of crime and also reassures against the fear of victimisation. The empirical evidence for this is, at best, mixed. For example, Walklate's (1998, 2000) research in Salford studied fear and trust within communities and certainly went some way to show that even members of high crime communities feel comparatively safe within their own borders. Yet, they are still high crime communities. Some sense of belonging or mutuality has not meant that crime and anti-social behaviour has been limited. Whilst members of the community trust other members they also express pity for the plight of 'outsiders' entering into their communities:

> It's safe for locals but not for strangers in the area. (Middle-aged male, unemployed, lived in the area for 29 years)
>
> Oldtown is a great area if you are a member of the community, went to the local school and grew up with the local villains, but terrible if you're an outsider. (Elderly female lived in the area 11 years)
>
> I've no real problems because I know the people and the area and grew up with local villains and know local youth. (Middle-aged male, employed, lived in the area for 35 years)
>
> (Walklate 1998: 556)

Whilst these comments suggest that a sense of belonging can reduce the fear of victimisation and limit actual victimisation from other members of the community, they do not suggest that such social conditions actually lead to low levels of criminality, or that this helps with fear of victimisation for those external to the community. This reinforces Crawford's (1997) earlier observation about the capacity of communities to respond differently to incivility and the capacity of communities to harbour, as well as prevent, criminality. The wider implication is one that echoes the ideas of A.P. Cohen (1985), who suggests that for communities to exist they must define boundaries in terms of self and other, the included and the excluded. Even if this manages to provide some sense of security and order-maintenance within communities, the ramifications for those outside of the group are not so positive. Similarly, it would suggest that there may be an equal threat from other communities, who, deciding not to prey on their own members, train their sights elsewhere. Yet, although this presents another obstacle for those who would advocate community as the vehicle for controlling crime, it should come as no surprise to criminologists who have long theorised and researched the existence of deviant subcultures,[1] which could easily be defined as communities using the more anthropological understandings of the concept (A.P. Cohen 1985). Hence, despite the affirmative rhetoric of community generally espoused in crime control debates, it would appear that there is both theoretical and empirical evidence that it can function in less desirable ways, at least with regard to crime control.

In addition to these issues, community is usually conceptualised within the field of crime prevention as a mechanism to prevent threats from external forces (Crawford 1997). This in itself presumes the threat is external, rather than from within the community, and also presumes that there is something alien or frightening about those who are not members of the community. Young (1999) puts this in the context of essentialising the 'other', whereby specific fixed cultural or biological characteristics distinguish the 'other' in ways that are both immutable and highly visible. Within crime prevention this conceptualisation of the other, combined with an ethos of protection against external threats, reinforces the boundaries that segregate the trustworthy and decent from the dangerous and unreliable.

Crawford (1997) has commented that: 'Community has become a policy buzz word' (p. 44). Community crime prevention, community safety, community punishment, community policing, community courts, not to mention probation, restorative justice, family group conferencing, curfew orders, electronic tagging and 'naming and shaming'. All of these approaches, whilst not all recent in conception, have community at the core of their agenda. With this current flurry of activity community justice is fast become the dominant opposing paradigm to the retributive, tough-on-crime language of current rhetoric and policy. With this in mind it becomes all the more important to define and clarify the context in which community is being used. Only by doing this can a clear picture of the effectiveness of such be achieved.

Anthony Bottoms (1995) identifies the importance of community within modern sentencing philosophies:

> modern sentencing change in different countries can be principally understood by reference to three main conceptual developments, which I shall describe as just deserts/human rights, managerialism, and 'the community'.
>
> (Bottoms 1995: 2)

In this discussion Bottoms (1995) divides community issues into three distinct subcategories: community penalties and 'diversion'; justice in and for local communities and groups; devolving decision making to the community. In these subcategories Bottoms documents the growth of community penalties; the call for a more pluralistic approach to sentencing when dealing with special or unique communities (e.g. women who are victimised by serious violent or sexual crimes); the increase in community-based sentencing (victim–offender mediation or family group conferences). Bottoms (1995) begins this discussion by stating the ambiguity surrounding the term community:

> it [community] is the least unified and probably the most vague of the three main concepts discussed in this paper.
>
> (Bottoms 1995: 21)

This issue is endemic within criminological literature and crime control policies. There is a widely held acknowledgement that community is a contested concept, but this is rarely followed by any caution regarding how this difficulty might impact upon any attempt to either understand or evaluate community-based initiatives. Whilst the ambiguity surrounding the meaning and application of community might well be politically advantageous, it is academically dangerous. Simply because the concept is difficult to pin down and can mean different things in different contexts, it does not mean that there should be no attempt at understanding, particularly when there is a wealth of sociological, anthropological and philosophical literature that has sought to do so. Hence there is an urgent need to explore what type of community is currently being advocated within the crime control arena, what assumptions are contained within it and what wider theoretical and empirical evidence is there that either supports or contradicts the communitarian concept of community.

A good example of how this ambiguity might lead to problems in policy can be seen in the development of restorative cautioning by the Thames Valley Police (Hoyle et al 2002). In this approach the normal police caution for juveniles is replaced by a restorative caution. This restorative caution involves a meeting between the offender, the offender's family, the victim and a police officer acting as a mediator. The aim is to give the offender the opportunity to witness the harm caused, apologise and, hopefully, agree to some kind of reparation. Similarly, the victim is given the opportunity to understand the offender's motives, facilitating the victim's recovery from the offence and their reduced fear of crime. The theoretical underpinning to this approach is derived from John Braithwaite's (1989) concept of reintegrative shaming. This notion of reintegrative shaming revolves around the idea that offenders can be integrated back into the mainstream community through the process of positive shaming that condemns behaviour but not the individual. The net result of this is that whilst the individual is shamed, he or she is not stigmatised and labelled deviant but given the opportunity to make amends and apologise. This concept relies heavily on a certain type of community for the process to be successful.[2] Thames Valley Police goes on to define community:

> The community is specific to the circumstances and the individuals involved. The nature of the community is dependent on a common link, an inhabited world, whether this be geographic or personal, for example a school community.
>
> (Thames Valley Police 1997: 25)

At first glance this definition appears perfectly reasonable and has much in common with most definitions of community. Whilst restorative justice is restricted to cautioning, the conceptual difficulties relating to community remain relatively minor. Despite Thames Valley Police's triangle of restorative justice which includes the victim, the offender and the community, restorative cautioning has little community involvement.

It is within this context that problems with the Thames Valley Police's definition of community and the adoption of reintegrative shaming become relevant. Essentially, the main problem with the definition is that it assumes there is some sense of community, a common link, when in fact there may be none or the links may be very different from those imagined or imposed by the police. Further, the suggestion that reintegrative shaming can be employed in the community assumes that the UK, or at least some communities in the UK, is predisposed to act in a positive manner towards offenders. The evidence would seem to suggest that, quite unlike reintegrative shaming, Western societies continue to stigmatise and exclude offenders (Wilkins 1965, Cohen, S. 1971, Young 1971, 1973, Hall et al. 1978). Braithwaite did not use the UK as an example of a reintegrative society but cited Japan, a society with a vastly different set of social conditions from our own. The point is that, because of the conceptual confusion surrounding the characteristics of the community, and because of the subtle social infrastructure that is needed to facilitate reintegrative shaming, restorative justice is in danger of applying community conferencing to localities where it would be inappropriate. This could then easily lead to tensions between the police and the public, caused by a host of unrealistic expectations that could exacerbate, rather than relieve, the crime problem. To conclude, the error is not that of the Thames Valley Police but, rather, a general failure to engage with the concept of community and thus a failure to develop a fuller appreciation and understanding of the nature of contemporary communities.

In the above example the underlying impression is one of a cohesive community presence, organised and focused. There are clear reminders of Willmott's (1987: 2) warning about community conjuring 'warm, almost mystical' images. This is the overriding focus of most criminal justice measures to incorporate community. They are designed either to utilise the community as a force against crime or to regenerate a 'community spirit' to prevent crime. Crawford (1997) points to this circular thinking by outlining the confusion over whether communities are in fact the means to an end or an end in themselves:

> Consequently, 'community' constitutes a means to an end, an end in itself. It is both the vehicle to a better life and the better life. Means and ends have become badly confused. With such circularity, it is hard to recognise and separate off implementation problems associated with community problems, as they constitute as much a failure of theory as of practice.
>
> (Crawford 1997: 152)

Whether this refers to community safety or the rehabilitation of offenders, the error is a 'taken for granted' conception of community and a perception that returning to past models of community structure will provide effective strategies against crime. In an effort to understand this, it is necessary to provide a brief overview of the sociological history of community to demonstrate how this perception has developed.

Within this framework it is not surprising that the concerns of communitarianism (Etzioni 1995, 1997) are also being expressed within the criminal justice system. As crime continues to rise, criminology, as it always has, reflects the dominant trends in society. The communitarian concern with the erosion of relationships and the ideology of individualism has spread to the crime debate. This concern manifests itself in theories that seek to explain why crime continues to rise, and also in measures that seek to ensure that those who have committed crimes are properly reintegrated into society.

Perhaps one of the clearest theoretical perspectives within criminology that applies this communitarian concern with social interactions to crime is relational justice. This perspective seeks to examine the connection between relationships and criminality. Modern society, it is argued, is typified by a number of developments that diminish the number and intensity of relationships we each experience. The increased social mobility has reduced the strength of community ties and inhibited prolonged acquaintances and the development of social networks. Christie Davies (1994) argues that there is a direct correlation between the decline of some types of relationships and the rise in crime. The decline of the 'friendly society' where groups of individuals collaborated to provide welfare and support has slowly been replaced by state intervention, and intimate relations in the workplace have been replaced by anonymous, isolating bureaucratic hierarchies. These trends have been replicated throughout social institutions and have removed many of the moral and social obligations and relations that acted as a control on anti-social behaviour.

Within this field a diverse spectrum of issues are examined, ranging from explanations of crime to mediation schemes to criminal justice reform. Relational justice studies the impact of meaningful relations on the incidence of crime. In a similar vein to communitarianism, relational justice squarely places the blame for many crime problems on the shoulders of the social ethos disseminated during the 1980s:

> Crime and criminal justice are inevitably a product of the society we choose to create. What kind of society do we want? One option is undoubtedly to continue to place the emphasis on unfettered individual freedom. However, this absence of community creates conditions in which crime spreads like an epidemic.
>
> (Schluter 1994: 19)

Relational justice therefore considers intimate relations as a fundamental measure in the prevention of crime. To this end, Bottoms (1994) suggests that the role of relational justice should be the:

> avoidance of injustice and promoting legitimacy and good relationships.
>
> (Bottoms 1994: 53)

Crime is therefore seen as an injury to the victim, their family and the community, rather than just an offence against the state. Relational justice is therefore concerned with repairing relationships damaged by crime.

The broad perspective of relational justice discussed by Burnside and Baker (1994) shares the communitarian concern with the breakdown of community cohesion and blames the increasing levels of anonymity, social mobility and alienation for high crime. This perspective endorses a model of justice which views crime as an offence against individuals and the community rather than the state. As such, it endorses types of sanctions that repair the damage done to relationships by crime and help to rebuild strong social ties in communities. This incorporates strong reintegrative and restorative agendas. Types of criminal justice reform advocated by proponents of this approach include: victim–offender mediation, family group conferencing and reparation.

Given the strong reintegrative component, these ideas draw heavily on Braithwaite's (1989) theory of reintegrative shaming. Braithwaite's theory also endorses a strong form of community life where there are high levels of civic responsibility and social cohesion. Braithwaite explicitly points to a communitarian society as the ideal basis for ensuring reintegrative shaming.

These types of perspectives have filtered into various policies and practices. Whilst it would be incorrect to suggest that they have become part of the mainstream strategy of criminal justice they are becoming increasingly included and involved. Restorative justice is now a comprehensive component of youth offending, with the established option to refer juvenile offenders to restorative conferences. There are also various formal and informal schemes that rely on restorative conferencing. For example, Thames Valley Police piloted restorative cautioning and there have been established victim–offender mediation schemes since the late 1990s. Many of these have operated outside of the formal justice system and rely on volunteers and charities for resources.

The Crime and Disorder Act 1998 placed a formal responsibility on local authorities to develop crime prevention strategies and encouraged a multi-agency approach to crime control. As part of this strategy the anti-social behaviour order was introduced that allowed either the police or the local authority (as provider of housing) to seek prosecution for petty criminal or anti-social behaviour. The courts have a great deal of discretion regarding the type of sanctions imposed, but the importance of this order is that it allows prosecution for non-criminal offences and widens the responsibility for crime control to the local authority. There is within the justifications for this order an acknowledgement of the harm caused to a community by many non-criminal acts such as litter, excessive noise, harassment and abuse. The act of extending the agencies that can instigate proceedings is also intended to increase the ease, access and viability for many residents to make complaints.

The Crime and Disorder Act 1998 also includes various other sanctions that seem to share a concern with reparation and responsibilisation. The most obvious of these is the parenting order, which requires parents to attend parenting classes if their children prove 'troublesome'. Parenting orders require parents to attend counselling or guidance once a week for up to three months. Further conditions such as picking the child up from school can also be enforced. In addition, the reparation order has also been introduced. This order applies to those under 18 and requires that up to 24 hours of work over a period of three months be undertaken. The type of work would be dictated by the victim and could include anything from a written or verbal apology to repairing criminal damage (Home Office 1997). These types of orders have a distinctive focus on the need for individuals other than just the offender to take responsibility for crime control. Parenting orders clearly make parents responsible for their children's offending behaviour and reparation orders make victims (albeit on a voluntary basis) responsible for determining punishment.

In summary, communitarianism, relational justice and reintegrative shaming all share a common theme in that they seek to address a perceived decline in shared community values, community cohesion and community solidarity. They therefore pursue measures that are designed to generate conditions that promote a stronger 'sense' of community. This is somewhat different to earlier notions of community decline that were concerned with the impact of disorganisation and disadvantage on levels of crime. Whereas earlier approaches incorporated some discussion of social inequality, poverty and social deprivation, these more recent approaches have no such focus. They are not interested in economic regeneration or welfare support but in the promotion of responsibilities through the renewal of shared moral consensus. This in no way requires or addresses issues of inequality or social injustice. This is clearly evident in the types of policies that have developed. Restorative justice, anti-social behaviour orders, parenting orders and reparation orders seek to engender responsibility, tolerance and understanding in the offender, the victim and the wider community. Not only is there a purposeful move towards devolved responsibilities (Garland 1996), but also a quite different conception of community decline and a quite different conception of how this should be addressed.

Within the crime control arena it appears that conceptions of community are embedded in its capacity to deliver order maintenance (Crawford 1997). Such notions rely heavily on communities that exert influence over their members to behave in appropriate fashions. Communities are places of conformity and well-ordered civic behaviour. As Walklate (1998) demonstrates, this is clearly not always the case. The temptation is to assume that high crime areas lack some sense of community because they lack the social and economic structures common in the pre-industrial societies that were typified by the likes of Tonnies (1887) and Durkheim (1893). The pursuit of such community structures is thus deemed to be the route out of conditions of high crime and anti-social behaviour. Unfortunately, this is usually in stark contrast to the structural circumstances and wider economic forces that are intrinsically linked to contemporary social relations:

> Efforts at community organizing rarely, if at all, acknowledge, or seek to address, external forces and dynamics which often undermine – especially in high crime areas – those efforts. However, the power of private capital and property interests, resident mobility – particularly changing patterns of tenant allocation in public sector housing (Bottoms and Wiles 1986) – unemployment, social exclusion, and poverty, will all impact upon internal community relations, potentially increasing social and cultural disorganisation.
>
> (Crawford 1997: 152)

Despite this insightful comment, it appears that within crime control debates community is seen as a defence against crime and incivility. Within this perspective communities are the source of social order, their membership united in common values and priorities. Scant attention is paid to the social conditions that produce particular types of social relations. In other words, this notion of community contains little or nothing of the wider concerns about the limits and potential dangers hinted at here. Community is resoundingly endorsed as an effective mechanism for crime control. Yet the type of community on offer is one reminiscent of the pre-industrial, rural community. It therefore shares something in common with the sociological theories outlined earlier: a normative commitment to a nostalgic vision of community.

Conclusion: the community *as* crime control?

The growth of community safety, crime prevention and restorative justice provides a useful point of reference for understanding the ideological and political commitment to communitarian thought within the crime control arena. This commitment entails increased partnership and active participation from the local populace. Similarly, restorative justice attempts to integrate active participation from the community into what are, effectively, sentencing decisions. Thus, in both prevention and the sentencing, appeals to the community are becoming increasingly enshrined in legislation, practice and theory. The explanation for this shift can be understood in relation to the Foucauldian analysis of governmentality discussed in Chapter 3. This analysis suggests that community has emerged in the place of a national welfare doctrine and provides the locus in which government at a distance can take place. Hence, it would appear that this shift has not happened by accident but is driven by increasingly more sophisticated modes of governance where the exercise of power is devolved from the public realm into the private realm. This does not mean that the state has relinquished authority but that it exercises this authority in a new, more discreet, fashion. The focus on community therefore fulfils a function beyond any straightforward crime control activity; it is also the means of governing society (Cohen 1985, Simon 2007).

This is not to suggest that this shift in focus has been categorical, or that the state does not retain core policy-formulation functions or that the state-funded criminal justice agencies do not occupy a privileged place within this process. As both Gilling (2007) and Hughes (2007) have argued, the police and local authorities still retain both the legal responsibility and a central organising role within both community safety and crime and disorder reduction partnerships. Whilst Hughes (2007) and Simon (2007) go on to explore the interaction between these wider geo-politics and crime control techniques, the critique developed over the next two chapters is predominantly concerned not with the techniques of governance but with the values and assumptions contained within them. Hence, unlike Hughes (2007) and Simon (2007), attention shifts away from the crime control arena to social theory and cultural criminology, to build a critique that exposes the dangerous ground on which community as a crime control strategy rests.

What has become apparent is that the community is increasingly being co-opted into both preventative and penal decision making. This shift from government to governance appears to contain two distinctive features that are in need of attention. The first is a normative belief that the community should be involved, and that by doing so more effective crime control can be delivered. This essentially draws on a notion that communities are good, healthy and helpful social institutions whose participation will simultaneously enhance criminal justice processes and bolster shared values. The second is an instrumental function where the creation of responsible subjects delivers improved levels of informal social control. These two elements overlap and help to recreate each other, as responsible subjects are deemed to create strong communities and strong communities engender social responsibilities. The next chapter continues with a discussion of the relationship between this conception of community and contemporary cultural conditions.

Notes

1 See the early work of Tannenbaum (1938), or A.K. Cohen (1955) and the more recent work of Hall and Jefferson (1976), Burke and Sunley (1998), Hobbs (1988) and Hobbs et al. (2003).
2 For example, as previously mentioned, John Braithwaite uses the tightly knit, homogeneous society of Japan as the archetypal example of a re-integrative culture.

References

Anderson, B. (1983) *Imagined Communities*, London: Verso.

Bauman, Z. (2000) *Liquid Modernity*, Cambridge: Polity Press.

Bell, C. and Newby, H. (1971) *Community Studies*, London: Allen and Unwin.

Blanchot, M. (1988) *The Unavowable Community*, Barrytown, NY: Station Hill Press.

Bottoms, A. (1992) Explanations of Crime and Place, in D.J. Evans, N.R. Fyfe and D.T. Herbert (eds) *Crime, Policing and Place: Essays in Environmental Criminology*, London: Routledge.

Bottoms, A. (1994) Avoiding Injustice, Promoting Legitimacy and Relationships, in J. Burnside and N. Baker (eds) *Relational Justice: Repairing the Breach*: Winchester: Waterside Press.

Bottoms, A. (1995) The Philosophy and Politics of Sentencing, in C.M.V. Clarkson and R. Morgan (eds) *The Politics of Sentencing Reform*, Oxford: Clarendon Press.

Braithwaite, J. (1989) *Crime, Shame and Reintegration*, Cambridge: Cambridge University Press.

Burke, R.D. and Sunley, R. (1998) Youth Subcultures in Contemporary Britain, in K. Hazelhurst and C. Hazelhurst (eds) *Gangs and Youth Subcultures: International Explorations*, New Jersey: Transaction Press.

Burnside, J. and Baker, N. (1994) (eds) *Relational Justice: Repairing the Breach*, Winchester: Waterside Press.

Calhoun, C. (1991) Imagined Communities and Indirect Relationships: Large Scale Social Integration and the Transformation of Everyday Life, in P. Bourdieu and J.S. Coleman (eds) *Social Theory for a Changing Society*, Boulder, CO: Westview Press.

Calhoun, C. (1992) The Infrastructure of Modernity: Indirect Relationships, Information Technology, and Social Integration, in H. Haferkamp and N. Smesler (eds) *Social Change and Modernity*, Berkeley: University of California Press.

Calhoun, C. (1998) Community without Propinquity Revisited: Communications, Technology and the Transformation of the Urban Public Sphere, *Sociological Enquiry*, 68 (3): 373–97.

Castells, M. (1996) *The Information Age, 1: The Rise of the Network Society*, Oxford: Blackwell.

Castells, M. (2001) *The Internet Galaxy: Reflections on the Internet, Business and Society*, Oxford: Oxford University Press.

Cohen, A.K. (1955) *Delinquent Boys: The Culture of the Gang*, New York: Free Press.

Cohen, A.P. (ed.) (1982) *Belonging: Identity and Social Organisation in British Rural Cultures*, Manchester: Manchester University Press.

Cohen, A.P. (1985) *The Symbolic Construction of Community*, London: Tavistock.

Crawford, A. (1997*) The Local Governance of Crime, Appeals to Community and Partnership*, Oxford: Clarendon Press.

Crow, G. and Allan, G. (1994) *Community Life: An Introduction to Local Social Relations*, London: Harvester Wheatsheaf.

Davidson, R.N. (1981) *Crime and Environment*, London: Croom Helm.

Davies, C. (1994) Crime and the Rise and Decline of a Relational Society, in J. Burnside and N. Baker (eds) *Relational Justice: Repairing the Breach*, Winchester: Waterside Press.

Delanty, G. (2003) *Community*, London: Routledge.

Durkheim, E. (1893 [1964]) *The Division of Labour in Society*, New York: The Free Press of Glencoe.

Engels, F. (1845 [1958]) *The Condition of the Working Class in England in 1844*, trans. and ed. W.O. Henderson and W.H. Chaloner, Oxford: Basil Blackwell (First published in German in 1845).

Etzioni, A. (1995) *The Spirit of Community: Rights, Responsibilities and the Communitarian Agenda*, Hammersmith: Fontana Press.

Etzioni, A. (1997) *The New Golden Rule: Community and Morality in a Democratic Society*, London: Profile Books.

Foster, J. (1995) Informal Social Control and Community Crime Prevention, *British Journal of Criminology*, 35 (4): 563–83.

Garland, D. (1996) The Limits of the Sovereign State: Strategies of Crime Control in Contemporary Society, *British Journal of Criminology*, 36 (4): 445–71.

Giddens, A. (1990) *The Consequences of Modernity*, Cambridge: Polity Press.

Gill, O. (1977) *Luke Street*, London: Macmillan.

Gilling, D. (2007) *Crime Reduction and Community Safety: Labour and the Politics of Local Crime Control*, Cullompton: Willan.

Hall, S. and Jefferson, T. (eds) (1976) *Resistance through Rituals*, London: Hutchinson.

Hall, S., Critcher, C., Jefferson, T., Clarke, J. and Roberts, B. (1978) *Policing the Crisis: Mugging, the State, and Law and Order*, London: Macmillan.

Hillery, G.A. (1955) Definitions of Community: Areas of Agreement, *Rural Sociology*, 20 (2): 111–23.

Hobbs, D. (1988) *Doing the Business: Entrepreneurship, the Working Class and Detectives in the East End of London*, Oxford: Oxford University Press.

Hobbs, D., Hadfield, P., Lister, S. and Winlow, S. (2003) *Bouncers: Violence and Governance in the Night Time Economy*, Oxford: Oxford University Press.

Hoggart, R. (1957) *The Uses of Literacy*, London: Chatto & Windus.

Hoggett, P. (1997) Contested Communities, in P. Hoggett (ed.) *Contested Communities: Experiences, Struggles, Policies*, Bristol: Policy Press.

Home Office (1997) *No More Excuses: A New Approach to Tackling Youth Crime in England and Wales*, Cmnd 3809, London: HMSO.

Hope, T. and Foster, J. (1992) Conflicting Forces: Changing the Dynamics of Crime and Community on a 'Problem Estate', *British Journal of Criminology*, 32 (4): 488–505.

Hope, T. and Hough, M. (1988) Area, Crime and Incivility: A Profile from the British

Crime Survey, in T. Hope and M. Shaw (eds) *Communities and Crime Reduction*, London: HMSO.

Hoyle, C., Young, R. and Hill, R. (2002) *Proceed with Caution: An Evaluation of the Thames Valley Police Initiative in Restorative Cautioning*, York: Joseph Rowntree Foundation.

Hughes, G. (2007) *The Politics of Crime and Community*, Basingstoke: Palgrave Macmillan.

Lash, S. (1994) Reflexivity and Its Doubles: Structure, Aesthetics, Community, in U. Beck, A. Giddens and S. Lasch (eds) *Reflexive Modernisation: Politics, Tradition and Aesthetics in the Modern Social Order*, Cambridge: Polity Press.

Lee, D. and Newby, H. (1983) *The Problem of Sociology*, London: Hutchinson and Co.

Lewis, O. (1949) *Life in a Mexican Village*, Urbana: University of Illinois Press.

Maffesoli, M. (1996) *The Time of the Tribes: The Decline of Individualism in Mass Society*, London: Sage.

Marx, K. and Engels, F. (1848 [1985]) *The Communist Manifesto*, London: Penguin.

Morris, A. and Morton, G. (1998) *Locality, Community and Nation*, London: Hodder and Stoughton.

Morris, T.P. (1957) *The Criminal Area: A Study in Social Ecology*, London: Routledge and Kegan Paul.

Nancy, J.-L. (1991) *The Inoperative Community*, Minneapolis: University of Minnesota Press.

Newman, O. (1973) *Defensible Space*, London: Architectural Press.

Nisbet, R. (1967) *The Sociological Tradition*, London: Heinemann.

Pahl, R.E. (1965) *Urbs in Rure*, London: Weidenfeld & Nicolson.

Pahl, R. (2000) *On Friendship*, Cambridge: Polity Press.

Redfield, R. (1947) 'The Folk Society', *American Journal of Sociology*, 52 (3): 293–308.

Rheingold, H. (1993) *The Virtual Community: Homesteading on the Electronic Frontier*, Reading, MA: Addison-Wesley.

Schluter, M. (1994) What Is Relational Justice? in J. Burnside and N. Baker (eds) *Relational Justice*, Winchester: Waterside Press.

Shaw, C.R. and McKay, H.D. (1931) *Social Factors in Juvenile Delinquency*, Washington, DC: US Government Printing Office.

Shaw, C.R. and McKay, H.D. (1942) *Juvenile Delinquency in Urban Areas*, Chicago: University of Chicago Press.

Simmel, G. (1950 [1905]) The Metropolis and Mental Life, in K. Wolff (ed.) *The Sociology of Georg Simmel*, New York: The Free Press (First published 1905).

Simon, J. (2007) *Governing through Crime: How the War on Crime Transformed American Democracy and Created a Culture of Fear*, Oxford: Oxford University Press.

Skogan, W.G. (1990) *Disorder and Decline: Crime and the Spiral of Decay in American Neighborhoods*, New York: Free Press.

Spencer, L. and Pahl, R. (2006) *Rethinking Friendship: Hidden Solidarities Today*, Oxford: Princeton University Press.

Stacey, M. (1969) The Myth of Community Studies, *British Journal of Sociology*, 20 (2): 134–47.

Tannenbaum, F. (1938) *Crime and Community*, Boston, MA: Ginn and Company.

Thames Valley Police (1997) *Restorative Justice: Restorative Cautioning – a New Approach*, Oxford: Restorative Justice Consultancy.

Tonnies, F. (1887 [1963]) *Community and Society*, trans. and ed. C.P. Loomis, New York: Harper and Row (First published as *Gemeinschaft und Gesellschaft*, 1887).

Walklate, S. (1998) Crime and Community: Fear or Trust? *British Journal of Sociology*, 49 (4): 550–69.

Walklate, S. (2000) Trust and the Problem of Community in the Inner City, in T. Hope and R. Sparks (eds) *Crime, Risk and Insecurity*, London: Routledge.

Wilkins, L. (1965) Some Sociological Factors in Drug Addiction Control, in B. Rosenberg, I. Bernard and F. Howlen (eds), *Mass Society in Crisis*, New York: Free Press.

Willmott, P. (1986) *Social Networks, Informal Care and Public Policy*, London: Policy Studies Institute.

Willmott, P. (1987) Introduction, in P. Willmott (ed.) *Policing and the Community*, London: Policy Studies Institute.

Wilson, J.Q. and Kelling, G. (1982) Broken Windows, *Atlantic Monthly*, March: 29–38.

Wirth, L. (1938) Urbanism as a Way of Life, *American Journal of Sociology*, 44 (1): 1–24.

Wirth, L. (1964) *On Cities and Social Life*, London: University of Chicago Press.

Wittgenstein, L. (1953) *Philosophical Investigations*, Oxford: Basil Blackwell.

Worsley, P. (1992) *The New Sociology* (3rd rev. edn), London: Penguin Books.

Young, J. (1971) *The Drugtakers: The Social Meaning of Drug Use*, London: McGibbon & Key.

Young, J. (1999) *The Exclusive Society*, London: Sage.

Young, M. and Willmott, P. (1957) *Family and Kinship in East London*, London: Routledge and Kegan Paul.

6 Late-modernity, insecurity and identity

Community, as we have seen, is a contested term, fraught with ambiguities and normative sentiments. Communitarianism (Etzioni 1995, 1997) advances a particular notion of community that relies heavily on both moral cohesion and family relations. Within this perspective, community is conceived as the vehicle for improving social relations and the antidote for a range of social problems. Yet the communitarian ideology progressed by Etzioni (1995, 1997) underplays the nature and character of community structures and arguably fails to engage with contemporary conditions that foster particular forms of social relations. In other words, it is a discourse largely divorced from economic, social and cultural conditions. Power, agency and structure are not evaluated in relation to either community organisation or contemporary forms of living. The concern with this is that, by failing to engage with current social conditions, the communitarian ideology is either potentially unworkable or potentially incompatible with the way people live their lives.

This chapter is therefore concerned to explore what some of the leading sociologists have said about contemporary conditions and to assess their compatibility with the communitarian commitment to a particular form of community life. This entails a systematic review of the sociology of late-modernity and the exclusionary consequences of a communitarian vision at odds with such conditions.

Before embarking on this review it is worth explaining why you will not find some types of research below. First, you will not find any mention of the work of Wacquant (2009) or Whitman (2003), who are both often cited as providing alternative explanations to late-modernity for mass incarceration and degrading punishment. They are not discussed purely because my focus is not about punishment but about a particular dynamic of community revival and its underpinning ideology of traditional or conservative values (rather than neo-liberalism or egalitarianism) that shape this dynamic. This is not to say that their ideas don't overlap with mine, but they seem less directly relevant than late-modernity to questions of shared values and social conditions.

But the same token I have been very careful not to get drawn into the literature on social capital, despite its seeming obvious relevance. At times it has been very tempting to dip into either Putnam (2000) or Bourdieu (1986) and the only reason I have declined to do so is to avoid confusing the focus of my argument by introducing social capital, which is predominantly about the amount and quality of social bonds or social networks that people hold. These are not central to the ideas of this book or my argument, which is about the relationship between morality, community and crime, rather than about social connectedness or isolation and its impact on either civil society or vulnerability. However, it does seem clear to me that this is a further dynamic that cross-cuts the themes I am interested in, albeit along different lines, and I am not suggesting there is not more that could be said about the relationship either between late-modernity and social capital or between criminality and social (or indeed other types of) capital. But that is a whole other can of worms that I have deliberately tried to avoid opening throughout this book and which I shall not include in this chapter for fear of trying to cover more than is coherently manageable.

Modernity, late-modernity and postmodernity

Since the early 1980s there has been a growing literature that suggests we have moved beyond modernity but have not yet arrived at postmodernity. This has led a range of social commentators to try to identify the features of contemporary society that distinguish it from earlier epochs and future visions (e.g. Giddens 1991, Beck 1992, Bauman 2000). This is far from being a complete or systematic analysis of the changes in the social world, containing significant variance in terms of how terms are applied and explained. This limits the explanatory power of terms such as late-modernism or postmodernism to fully explain contemporary social relations; yet, an emerging consensus seems to suggest that we have moved beyond the modern world but have yet to fully arrive at the postmodern. This has led to a bewildering array of new phrases aimed at distinguishing contemporary social conditions from both modernity and postmodernity:

> Others, wishing to mark the distinctiveness of the world these changes have brought into being, but also recognise its continuity with what went before, talk of 'late modernity', 'high modernity', or 'reflexive modernity'. Terms like 'New Times', 'post-Fordism', 'post-welfare', and 'neo-liberalism' also identify the peculiarities of the present.
>
> (Garland 2001: 77)

In this quotation Garland (2001) points to the main terms used to distinguish between different conceptualisations of contemporary social conditions, before opting himself for the phrase 'late modernity'. This, and other terms, seeks to simultaneously point to significant changes in the social, economic, cultural and political spheres whilst also acknowledging the continuation of older traditions that emerged as a result of the modernisation in the late nineteenth and early twentieth centuries.

To complicate matters further, modernism and postmodernism are, at times, distinguished from modernity and postmodernity. Whilst they are sometimes used interchangeably, or without discernible difference, modernism and postmodernism generally refer to the theoretical, cultural and aesthetic representations of either the modern or postmodern eras (Giddens 1991, Thompson 1992). Modernism and postmodernism are therefore the terms used to describe the values and ideologies that inform and help to create modernity and postmodernity, which themselves are terms best used to describe the contours of the social world. Put at its simplest, modernity and postmodernity describe the historical, social, economic and political conditions, whilst modernism and postmodernism are the aesthetic, literary and symbolic representations of those conditions. Perhaps one of the clearest expressions of this distinction can be found in the ideas of Anthony Giddens (1990), who asserts:

> Post-modernism, if it means anything, is best kept to refer to styles or movements within literature, painting, the plastic arts and architecture. It concerns aspects of *aesthetic reflection* upon the nature of modernity . . . Post-modernity refers to something different, at least as I shall define the notion. If we are moving into a phase of post-modernity, this means that the trajectory of social development is taking us away from the institutions of modernity towards a new and distinct type of social order.
>
> (Giddens 1990: 45–6; emphasis in original)

Clearly, the distinction is sometimes blurred or misunderstood. Yet, whatever the vagaries and inconsistencies of such a distinction may be, within this discussion the focus is very definitely upon conditions rather than representations. Whilst this inevitably overlaps in places, the purpose of exploring late modernity in this chapter is to ascertain the specific social and cultural conditions of contemporary society and the consequences of these conditions for the communitarian vision of a new social order.

To provide a clearer picture of what is meant by late-modernity it is useful to briefly review both modernity and postmodernity, as late modernity usually defines itself in reference to these two terms. Modernity is usually associated with the shift from traditional, non-industrial and predominantly rural society to industrialised, urbanised and predominantly capitalist society. Closely linked with the ideas of Karl Marx (1970 [1867]), Emile Durkheim (1964 [1893]) and Max Weber (1904–5), modernity represents the advent of rationality and age of science and truth. According to Kumar (1978), features of modernity include urbanisation, industrialisation, democratisation, secularisation, rationalisation and bureaucratisation. These characteristics are seen as developing from the Middle Ages before reaching fruition at the end of the Enlightenment period with the democratic revolution in France and the capitalist economic revolution in England. At the other end of the scale, postmodernity refers to the social, cultural and ideological conditions that replace those associated with modernity. Unlike modernity, postmodernity asserts the end of the scientific pursuit of rationality with its emphasis on discovering truth and, through it, achieving progress. Instead, postmodernity emphasises fragmentation and fluidity, without absolute values or universal governing laws. Hence, postmodernity is pluralistic, with many competing explanations and understandings of the world. No universal principles should be sought, as all knowledge is contextual, subjective and unfinished:

> the postmodern view of the world [is] as a self-constituting and self-propelling process, determined by nothing but its own momentum, subject to no overall plan – of the 'movement towards the Second Coming', 'universalization of human condition', 'rationalization of human action' or 'civilization of human interaction' type. Postmodernity is marked by a view of the human world as irreducibly and irrevocably pluralistic, split into a multitude of sovereign units and sites of authority, with no horizontal or vertical order, either in actuality or in potency.
>
> (Bauman 1992: 35)

So the path from modernity to postmodernity is a move from the pursuit of answers, of universal truths and human progress to questions, interpretations of truth and the plurality of human meaning. This very crude comparison is perhaps akin to a Weberian (1949) ideal type rather than a comprehensive or systematic description of postmodernity. It would be over-stating the case to suggest that modernity or postmodernity can be so easily defined, particularly as there is significant variation in how the terms have been applied, stretching from the aesthetics of architecture and the arts through to the deconstruction of language and culture (Featherstone 1988, Bauman 1992). Perhaps more accurately, Bauman (1992) refers to postmodernity as a 'mood' or 'state of mind' where the endeavours of modernity (also a state of mind) are overturned, replaced instead with an entirely new set of concerns and ambitions. Postmodernity remains an unfinished discourse without clear boundaries that makes any attempt to argue that we have arrived at a fully fledged state of postmodernity questionable. It is in this gap, this space of uncertainty, that late-modernity finds its footing. Late-modernity is representative of social conditions somewhere between modernity and postmodernity, where the institutions and ideologies of modernity continue to co-exist with new ones. A hybrid, caught somewhere between the two states of mind, with its own distinctive social, economic, cultural and political characteristics.

Arguably the two most significant contributions to late-modernity have come from Anthony Giddens (1990, 1991, 1992) and Ulrich Beck (1992, 1994). Giddens (1992) uses either the term 'high' modernity or 'late' modernity, whilst Beck (1992, 1994) prefers 'reflexive' modernity or 'second' modernity. Both demonstrate a concern with the increasing insecurity and risk associated with mediating existence in contemporary society. The concept of reflexivity plays an important part in this dialogue, as Lash (1994) discusses in detail. Reflexive modernity is a state of mind in which the agent increasingly mediates and navigates through the institutions and values of the social world as well as a more introspective reflection on the self and personal identity. Although Lash (1994) goes on to point to some important differences between Beck's and Giddens' conception of reflexivity, one important theme within both their work is the shift from modernity to reflexive modernity: a world in which individual agents are increasingly more liberated from previous social structures and pressures to determine both action and identity.

This increased reflexivity goes hand in hand with increased vulnerability or, at the very least, an increased perception of vulnerability, which manifests itself in ontological insecurity and anxiety (Giddens 1991) and the forward-looking calculation of risk when making decisions (Beck 1992). Hence, late modernity is an uncomfortable and insecure world, subject to both local and global hazards, at least partially severed from the concrete and comfortable structural certainties of modernity:

> To live in the 'world' produced by high modernity has the feeling of riding a juggernaut. It is not just that more or less continuous and profound processes of change occur; rather, change does not consistently conform either to human expectation or to human control.
>
> (Giddens 1991: 28)

Much more will be said of the ideas of both Beck (1992, 1994) and Giddens (1990, 1991) in the following sections, which aim to consider the specific conditions that have been associated with the late-modern world. Other significant sociological contributions from Bauman (2001b, 2003, 2005a) on the topics of individualisation and consumerism will also be introduced, as they play an important part in mapping the conditions of late-modernity. Hopefully, this section has provided some clarification on how late-modernity is defined, both in its own terms and in relation to modernity and postmodernity. This is a far from complete introduction but, given that many of late-modernity's core features are discussed below, it is hopefully enough to provide an understanding of where the focus of this chapter is within a complicated and fluid discourse about the characteristics of contemporary society. The aim is to point to those specific features of late-modernity that are different or divergent from the earlier, modern stage. Fundamentally, the focus of this chapter is on understanding these features of the social world so that they can be measured against the communitarian philosophy of Amitai Etzioni (1995).

The conditions of late-modernity

Garland (2001) has usefully characterised the conditions of late-modernity with reference to five great social transformations. His first transformation is focused upon changes within the capitalist mode of production and essentially refers to the shift from an industrial to a post-industrial economic system. Garland (2001) argues that since the 1970s there has been a quickening of economic conditions that have resulted in the predominant economic activity moving from industrial production to service provision. This shift is also sometimes referred to as the shift to post-Fordism and describes a profound change not only in economic activity but also in how the labour market is structured. Higher levels of unemployment, less job security and more flexible, short-term and temporary working conditions

led to a more fraught labour market which bears little resemblance to the comparatively stable employment traditions of the manufacturing era.

In his text *The Corrosion of Character*, Richard Sennett (1998) considers these
labour market relations in what he refers to as the new capitalism by exploring
the impact of an insecure labour market upon the employee's sense of place in
the world. For Sennett (1998), these arrangements cause a loss of confidence and
self-understanding that has consequences for the family and wider social relations.
Thus, Sennett (1998) confirms Garland's (2001) description of one of the great
late-modern transformations. Where once there was the manufacturing of goods
there is now the provision of services. Where once there was job security, or at
least job clarity, there is now insecurity and confusion. The transformation of the
mode of production and its corresponding impact on the organisation of the labour
market simultaneously signals a profound change in people's experience of work
and their relationships with others in the workplace.

Garland's (2001) second characterisation of the major economic and social
transformations central to late modernity is located in the structure and organisation of family and household. Beginning in the early to mid-1960s and gathering
pace in the 1980s three key changes to the family structure are discussed. To
begin with, more and more women joined the workforce. At the same time, and
closely associated with this shift in role, there was a decline in fertility as women
opted for career and life-style choices that had hitherto been either economically
or culturally denied to them. Families had fewer children, and later in life, with
mothers rejoining the labour market more swiftly after giving birth than in previous generations. The increase in the numbers of people pursuing a college education from the 1960s onwards is closely linked to having children later in life and
the expansion of professional opportunities for middle-class women. Improved
birth control via the contraceptive pill and changes in accepted cultural boundaries
for how women choose to live their lives impacted upon a wide range of factors,
including: 'expenditure patterns, child-care needs, and time spent in the home to
the average price of family house and the number of cars per household' (Garland
2001: 83).

Alongside this shift in women's life-style was a corresponding shift in the make-
up and composition of the family. In particular the size of the family declined as
more people began to live alone or in small family units. This trend is attributed
to the wider shifts in the pattern of child-birth and family structure. Yet, Garland
(2001) also points to the increase in the number of teenagers going to college and
the number of old people living alone as contributing to this dynamic. Important
to this development are improvements in public and private healthcare, increased
welfare benefits and the above-mentioned flexibility in the labour market, leading
to an increase in the number of part-time and temporary jobs which facilitated
women and students finding increased job opportunities, which in turn helped to
fund independent living.

Finally, the family structure has evolved in response to important changes in
the political, social and cultural landscape. The cultural revolution begun in the
late 1960s saw the rebirth of the feminist movement, which helped to progress

the ideal of female emancipation, thus allowing a wider range of legitimate family arrangements to emerge. Increased tolerance toward divorce and single-parent families, homosexuality and same-sex relationships; choosing to live alone for longer or indefinitely became more socially tolerated and legally available. Thus the family structure is increasingly more fluid, allowing for a diverse set of arrangements around which people can determine their own family life-style. Of course, these conditions have aroused significant ire amongst traditionalists and there have been repeated outcries over the breakdown of the family unit being linked to any number of social ills.

The third transformation detailed by Garland (2001) relates to changes in social ecology and demography. Here, Garland (2001) points to the rehousing projects of the 1960s where, in the USA and UK, inner-city ghettos were demolished, only to be replaced by out-of-town developments which concentrated poor and minority families on the outskirts of towns and cities where there were often fewer local amenities such as shops and transport links. Just as these traditional inner-city ghettos were demolished and communities were uprooted and pushed out of city centres, so were the more affluent middle classes moving from urban to suburban localities. Whilst this shift is better understood in terms of an increased standard of living and the middle classes attempting to secure a better quality of life for themselves, the combination of the largely enforced relocation of the poor and the largely voluntary relocation of the affluent simultaneously depopulated urban inner-city areas and segregated the poor from the affluent. Garland (2001) documents the advent of mass car production and ownership as an important feature in explaining this migratory pattern, in particular the capacity of the car to separate home or community from work environment. Thus, late-modernity is divided between the affluent, who retreat into suburban safety, and the poor, who are corralled into their ghettos and sink estates. This segregation in the late-modern era has in more recent times been talked about in terms of a dual city where rich and poor exist separately but alongside each other (e.g. Castells 1994, Herrnstein and Murray 1994, Bauman 1998, Wacquant 2001). Correspondingly, and unsurprisingly, fear, anxiety and distrust of strangers permeate this socially and economically separated late-modern world (Furedi 1997, Bauman 2001a, 2006).

Closely related to these developments is Garland's (2001) fourth transformation: the emergence of electronic mass media. The widespread ownership of television and radio from the early 1960s brought with it insights and anxieties that were previously unknown to many. Just as mass production and ownership of the automobile meant that people could live or travel from their home or workplace, so television and media meant that people could see further than their own community, region or even nation. Garland (2001) argues that one of the most profound aspects of this development was that people were increasingly exposed to the lives and experiences of other social groups in society. This allowed a greater comparison of the wealth, status and life-styles of groups previously unknown to each other. For Garland (2001), the racial tensions and civil rights campaigns of the 1960s are intimately linked to the comparative knowledge offered by the advent of television and radio. A further impact of this exposure is the increasing awareness of the suffering of others and the threat posed by both natural and man-made phenomena. Whether it is flood, tornado, pollution, disease, warfare or a single child stuck at the bottom of a well, these images are beamed straight into living rooms with their accompanying commentary designed to pull at the heartstrings and connect the audience with the unfolding tragedy. Hence society becomes more afraid of risks that were previously distant, vague and afflicted only unknown, faceless people. This increased awareness of risk and threat, often at levels and on scales that individuals are powerless to prevent, ties well into Ulrich Beck's (1992) thesis on the risk society which, as discussed above, is yet another synonym for late-modern society.

Similarly, the rise of mass electronic communication exposed society to more marketing and advertising. The life-styles of the rich and famous reminded people of what was beyond their grasp and fuelled expectations for material goods and wealth that brought with them the early stages of mass consumption and consumerism so typically associated with late-modernity (Baudrillard 1970, Corrigan 1997, Bauman 2007). Coverage of people, organisations and cultures that were previously distant and unknowable led to both more empathy and more questioning. Television 'conveyed a sense of immediacy and intimacy' (Garland 2001: 86) which revealed far more about celebrities, sporting heroes and politicians. Aside from the impact this had on forms of cultural expression, television and radio peeled back the public persona of both individuals and organisations to make known the failings, contradictions and conceits evident in everyday life. This brought with it increased criticism and questioning of the moral leaders (priests, teachers, politicians) of the day and of the institutions which they represented (church, school, political party). Thus, another condition of late-modernity is born: structural reflexivity (Lash 1994) and its critical consideration and reflection upon the rules and logic of social institutions.

The fifth and final transformation that Garland (2001) considers as fundamental in the journey to late-modernity is what he refers to as the democratisation of social life and culture. This final transformation is perhaps the most interesting with regard to the aim of this chapter. The democratisation of social life and culture essentially refers to the loosening of social hierarchies and moral bonds that had upheld the status quo with regard to both social position and moral consensus. Disadvantaged and marginal social groups demanded greater fairness and opportunity, a formal affirmation of their religions and cultures. Within this context, democratisation refers to the increasing ability of groups to exercise some decision-making power in social institutions such as the school, the workplace or the church. As people became less deferential and more likely to challenge no longer could organisations and businesses be led purely by managerial edict. New forms of internal democracy that gave voice to members and employees emerged across society, and with profound effect upon people's expectations about having their opinion validated. Whilst Garland (2001) states clearly that this change in expectation is a consequence of a change in form, rather than in the amount, of power, he also sees this dynamic as crucial in undermining absolute authority and taken-for-granted social superiority.

This dispersal of authority is closely associated with a similar fragmentation of moral absolutes as confidence in the guardians of morality, such as the church and state, began to slip. Where once society was governed by a strong sense of moral and social stability, late-modernity is a more fluid place. Instead of one truth, there are many, absolutism is replaced with relativism, and life-style and identity are unhinged from the constants of family, community, church or tradition in general. The impact of this moral fragmentation is visible in relation to greater variety in family structures, sexual practices, drug use and political affiliations. As a result, the old party political system no longer adequately reflects or represents a growing minority of life-styles or moral positions. Instead, new forms of social movement or political activism emerge to fill this gap.

Across society, social, cultural and intellectual life was changing. In this late-modern society, established forms of knowledge are suddenly less sure, the scientific pursuit of universal laws is disavowed in favour of pluralism. Postmodernism argues that there is no shared reality, no single rationality or methodology which can explain our existence or nature. Language, culture, history and worldview shape realities which can be understood only in reference to the experience and background of particular groups. Within such conditions moral relativism and a plurality of life-styles prevail. Individuals are increasingly free to determine their own values or ethics, to choose their own life-styles and aesthetics, to move between groups and to use this comparative fluidity to recreate or tailor their identities according to context and desire.

Garland's (2001) overview provides a good beginning for considering both the conditions of late-modernity and, more importantly, the circumstances from which these conditions emerged. The remainder of this chapter is devoted to considering some of the conditions of late-modernity in more detail so that they can then be explored in relation to the communitarian ethic.

Disembedding social relations

Disembedding is a concept most commonly associated with the work of Anthony Giddens (1990, 1991), who uses it to explain the condition of modernity whereby social relations and institutions are 'lifted out' of their local context and restructured 'across indefinite spans of time-space' (Giddens 1990: 21).[1] Without wishing to get drawn into a protracted discussion of Giddens' ideas in his two key texts, *The Consequences of Modernity* and *Modernity and Self-identity*, some explanation of the conditions in which disembedding occurs is required to help us consider its implications for social relations in late-modern society.

Giddens (1990, 1991) argues that disembedding takes place because time and space have become separated from each other in the modern world. In the pre-modern world time was inimitably linked to place, or locale, and was thought about in terms of seasons, harvest, festivals and so on. Time was therefore imprecise, and variable according to locality. Yet, with the invention of the mechanical clock time became measurable, uniform and unhinged from place. Time could be measured by a clock rather than by the turn of a season. Whilst a season or the amount of daylight will vary according to locality, a clock will not. It will measure time independently of locality. As Giddens (1990, 1991) puts it, time is 'emptied out' of place.

Similarly, space can also be separated from place. In the pre-modern world, space and place coincide. Interactions between individuals (the space in which interactions occur) take place in proximity to each other (the place in which interactions occur). Yet, in the modern world the space in which interaction occurs is separated from both place and time:

> The advent of modernity increasingly tears space away from place by fostering relations between 'absent' others, locationally distant from any given situation of face-to-face interaction. In conditions of modernity, place becomes increasingly *phantasmagoric*: that is to say, locales are thoroughly penetrated by and shaped in terms of social influences quite distant from them. What structures the locale is not simply that which is present on the scene; the 'visible form' of the locale conceals the distanciated relations which determine its nature.
>
> (Giddens 1990: 18–19)

Unpacking this complicated statement is instructive when considering the context in which interactions occur in the modern world. When Giddens (1990) uses the word 'phantasmagoric' he means that social interactions are not grounded in specific localities but across vast distances. A combination of transport and media technology alongside the adoption of a universal calendar provides the basis of communication over great distance. Giddens then employs the term 'distanciation' to explain that in effect space and time have become stretched, allowing social interactions to occur outside of, and irrespective of, place (or locale).

It is this stretching between time and space and its independence from place which provides the conditions in which disembedding can occur. For Giddens (1990, 1991) there are two key forms of disembedding mechanisms: symbolic tokens and expert systems. Symbolic tokens are types of interaction or exchange that exist independently and therefore outside of any individual, group or location (Giddens uses the example of money as a type of symbolic token). Expert systems are the interconnected sets of expert knowledge that shape the taken-for-granted world which we inhabit. From the architectural integrity of our houses through to counsellors to help us understand our relationships, we all rely upon these expert systems even if we do not regularly have need to consult them directly. For Giddens (1990, 1991), it is these mechanisms which disembed social relations and spread them out across indefinite time and space. In the sense of these mechanisms time and space have become essentially obsolete.

Giddens (1990, 1991) then goes on to explain that for either of these mechanisms to function, trust must be present. Trust, Giddens argues, is intrinsically linked in the modern world to risk. Without some awareness of risk we do not trust. We therefore trust in our symbolic tokens and expert systems to the extent that we believe they protect us from risk. For example, we put our trust in money insofar as we believe that others will honour equally the value of the token, just as we put our trust in the electrician that he will install new wiring in our homes without electrocuting us. Trust is therefore akin to faith. We do not know that our symbolic tokens will be honoured or that are experts are competent – we simply must trust them. A breakdown in such trust would therefore threaten the very foundation of the social world we inhabit. A good example of this would be the recent financial crisis in the banking system, the bankruptcy of several major banking institutions and breakdown of lending and borrowing trust between the banks themselves. The potential for outright anarchy, should trust in our currency or financial institutions collapse, is breath taking. No credit, payment of wages or purchase transactions could occur – the very basis of labour and exchange could crumble. Trust is therefore a prerequisite for disembedding.

Alongside these disembedding mechanisms Giddens (1990) discusses the reflexive appropriation of knowledge. By this he means that the modern world is characterised by a continuous process of reflection upon new and unforeseen forms of knowledge that assault our social practices. Modernity is hence characterised by an on-going process of reflection which continuously shapes and redefines the contours of social practices and institutions. The process of reflection is thus one of the defining features of modernity. Unlike pre-modern societies, where reflexivity can be understood in terms of thinking about how new knowledge impacts upon traditional ways of life, in modernity:

> reflexivity takes on a different character. It is introduced into the very basis of system reproduction, such that thought and action are constantly refracted back upon one another.
>
> (Giddens 1990: 38)

This means that the modern world is a world where even knowledge is uncertain. At the very same time that knowledge is reflected upon and thus appropriated, it is likely to be revised still further and yet new forms of knowledge emerge. Hence knowledge no longer offers the promise of stability, or certainty. Giddens (1990) likens this condition to 'being aboard a careering juggernaut' (p. 53) where social practices and institutions in the modern world are unstable, disembodied and unpredictable.

To summarise, Giddens (1990, 1991) is arguing that one of the defining characteristics of the modern world is that social interactions have become separated from either geographical location or any individual or group quality. Interactions now take place in, and across, spaces that simply cannot be measured by either time or distance, but they can be understood in terms of abstract mechanisms which are based on a shared trust that provides the basis for meaningful interactions with unknown strangers in remote locations. Misztal (1996) effectively summarises Giddens' (1990) theoretical stance on the nature of trust by linking it to the need that individuals have to create identity in a world where identity is no longer provided:

Modern institutions are grounded in 'reflexivity' and modern individuals, without the guidance of traditional authority, must self-reflexively construct their identities. Consequently, the conditions of trust in pre-modern and modern societies are totally different, with the former based on personal trust secured by kinship, community, religion and tradition, and the latter resting on trust in abstract systems.

(Misztal 1996: 89)

Disembedding can therefore be understood in terms of technological advancements (the clock, the computer) and the associated recalibration of social processes to accommodate changes in the ways in which we inhabit social spaces. Trust is the 'glue' which allows us to navigate our way through these social spaces. Yet Giddens (1990, 1991) is careful to remind us that we still have bonds of intimacy that remain at the local level. In particular, friendships and sexual partners remain physically proximate in the disembedded world. For Giddens (1990), intimacy is also transformed in modernity. Unlike in the pre-modern world, where trust is located through community and kinship networks, it must be worked at, or earned, in the modern world. Hence, the basis of intimacy, or personal trust, in the modern world is mutual openness and self-disclosure. Intimate relationships are therefore formed through a process of self-enquiry or self-reflection that is then shared with another. This is part of the search for self-identity which is bound up with the process of self-reflection in the late-modern world. This search for self-identity is closely linked with decline of community and kinship networks as the identities and roles prescribed for us by these social institutions are stripped away in the modern world, leaving people with the complicated task of determining their own identity.

The character of intimacy is therefore transformed as a consequence of a disembedded and increasingly global society that is nevertheless still routinely traversed on a day-to-day basis in physical localities. In response to this, dynamic intimacy becomes part of the search for self-actualisation and identity; a way of exerting one's sense of presence or purpose in a world which constantly shifts around us. Intimacy therefore becomes a form of defence against the intrusion of the vagaries and challenges of an external and threatening world. Giddens (1991, 1992) characterises this intimacy in terms of a 'pure relationship':

A pure relationship is one in which external criteria have become dissolved: the relationship exists solely for whatever rewards that relationship as such can deliver. In the context of the pure relationship, trust can be mobilised only by a process of mutual disclosure. Trust, in other words, can by definition no longer be anchored in criteria outside of the relationship itself – such as criteria of kinship, social duty or traditional obligation. Like self identity, with which it is closely intertwined, the pure relationship has to be reflexively controlled over the long term, against the backdrop of external transitions and transformations.

(Giddens 1991: 6)

Intimate social relations are therefore inextricably linked to the wider social conditions that define modernity. Emotional intimacy, or openness and sincerity between friends or lovers, can be understood as providing both internal and external forms of authenticity. The people with whom we are intimate help to shape identity and the ability to connect more widely with the abstract notion of trust, thus enabling us to function in the modern social world.

This short overview of some of Giddens' (1990, 1991, 1992) key thoughts regarding the nature and conditions of the modern, or late-modern, world begins to demonstrate two crucial problems with the communitarian approach (Etzioni 1995, 1997). Firstly, Etzioni (1995, 1997) would have us believe that certain social ills, like crime, are the consequence of a political doctrine that asserts the primacy of individual rights and denigrates civic responsibilities. Yet, it would appear that there are economic, technological, political and intellectual explanations for the way in which our social world has developed. Social conditions cannot be understood simply in terms of a moral breakdown in society, but in terms of more fundamental changes that alter the very basis of how we exist. Re-establishing traditional communities or traditional morality therefore requires more than an articulation of values or an exhortation to take responsibility. It requires a wholesale return to the past, a rolling back of technological advancement and intellectual life. The cat is out of the bag. It cannot be put back. Communitarianism as conceived as a wider political ideology or the basis of a crime control strategy is thus doomed to inevitable failure, as it has entirely failed to recognise or address the character and conditions of the social relations it so desperately wishes to see changed.

Secondly, it would also appear that communitarianism is guilty of a fundamental category error insofar as the cause of what it defines as social ills is the collapse of community. Even if it is true that community as a social institution has collapsed, this is better understood as a symptom of the structural conditions ascribed to the onset and development of modernity rather than the cause of the problem itself. Hence, communitarianism is essentially looking at the wrong thing; similar to a medical doctor suggesting a lung cancer patient can be cured if they stop smoking.

Finally, it is less than clear that community has collapsed. Perhaps traditional community life may no longer be as evident as it once was, but new forms of social bonds develop independently of either geography or biography. These new forms of community need to be understood in different ways, in terms both of their constitution and of the terms on which people belong to them. To summarise, community, as the basis of social bonds, may not have collapsed, but merely changed or evolved. Perhaps these new forms of social bonds have not always been appreciated, or perhaps not always been seen as normatively desirable, but this in itself does not correspond with the collapse of community. These themes are considered more fully in Chapter 7, whilst the rest of this chapter continues to explore some of the key features of late-modern society and what these suggest about the validity of the communitarian thesis.

Anthony Giddens, identity and ontological insecurity

Another common theme in the literature on late-modernity is its impact upon identity and the individual's sense of security (Giddens 1991, Bauman 2000, 2005b).

As a topic of intellectual enquiry, identity has a rich and varied literature which includes psychoanalytic, psychological, philosophical and historical debate (see du Gay et al. 2000 or Hall and du Gay 1996). Within the confines of this discussion it is the relationship between the conditions of late-modernity and the construction of identity that is relevant. The purpose of this is to continue charting the contours of late-modernity to help build a critique of Etzioni's (1995) communitarianism. Jenkins (1996) distinguishes between social identity and identity to illustrate this difference, and whilst this is a somewhat tenuous distinction it is meant to broadly delineate between psychological and philosophical debates about the creation of individual identity, usually understood in terms of the 'self', or the 'I', and sociological debates about the identification of similarity and difference between individuals and groups.

Social identity refers to characteristics or features that people use to understand their own or other people's social groups. For example, ethnic identity, sexual identity or national identity would be examples of social identity. Social identity is therefore socially constructed, a product of how people are seen, described and categorised in society. Jenkins (1996) defines this sociological articulation of identity as follows:

- 'Identity' denotes the ways in which individuals and collectivities are distinguished in their relations with other individuals and collectivities.
- 'Identification' is the systematic establishment and signification, between individuals, between collectivities, and between individuals and collectivities, of relationships of similarity and difference.
- Taken – as they can only be – together, similarity and difference are the dynamic principles of identification, and are at the heart of the human world.

(Jenkins 1996: 18)

This definition of identity provides a useful framework for reviewing what a range of commentators have had to say about the nature of identity in late-modern society. The focus is therefore to consider how the structure and order of society shapes the production of identity.

Continuing on from the above discussion of disembedding social relations, Giddens' (1990, 1991) work develops with what he refers to as 'self-identity'. Giddens (1991) argues that one of the main characteristics of late-modernity is self-reflexivity, a condition whereby individuals continuously consider and reconsider their sense of self-identity. This, Giddens (1991) explains, is linked to the process of disembedding, which has unencumbered the human race from the social institutions of tradition that predetermined identity. In pre-modern society, the institutions of family, community or church effectively proscribed identity. Yet, in late-modernity this proscription is all but gone; each person, now unencumbered from the shackles of tradition, is now able to choose, change and reflect on the nature of their own identity:

The narrative of self-identity has to be shaped, altered and reflexively sustained in relation to rapidly changing circumstances of social life, on a local and global scale. The individual must integrate information deriving from a diversity of mediated experiences with local involvements in such a way as to connect future projects with past experiences in a reasonably coherent fashion. Only if the person is able to develop an inner authenticity – a framework of basic trust by means of which the lifespan can be understood as a unity against the backdrop of the shifting social events – can this be attained. A reflexively ordered narrative of self-identity provides the means of giving coherence to the finite lifespan, given changing external circumstances.

(Giddens 1991: 215)

This continuous process of self-reflection is a consequence of living in a 'post-traditional' society (Giddens 1994) where insecurity and risk become on-going causes of anxiety. For Giddens (1991) these are essentially psychic and existential anxieties that he describes as ontological insecurities whereby a person becomes unhinged from biographical reference points which allow them to construct a narrative for themselves that provides them with a sense of emotional or psychic stability in an unpredictable and constantly changing world.

Giddens (1991) maps out some of these 'dilemmas of the self' where each person must navigate between the emancipatory qualities of late-modernity and the fragmented, uncertain and potentially meaningless search for self in an increasingly unregulated world. For Giddens (1991), maintaining self-identity is therefore bound up with the trust in expert systems and symbolic tokens outlined earlier in this chapter. Uncertainty and anxiety (or ontological insecurity) are overcome only by self-reflexively developing an authentic self-identity in which individuals strive to overcome their inner psychic blocks that prevent a person from 'being true to themselves'. Hence, the basis of ontological security in late-modern society is the capacity to existentially determine one's place in an uncertain and undefined world. This is achieved by devising a self-identity that is simultaneously 'true to oneself' and able to adapt to whatever new jolt the 'juggernaut' of late-modernity is likely to cause. This seems like a very fine line to tread, but at its heart this analysis is part of Giddens' (1984) wider project to reconcile agency with structure. Hence the conditions of late-modernity lead individuals to continuously create, recreate and reflect on their self-identity in a world that is itself reflexively ordered and liable to unpredictable change. The late-modern world is therefore a world in which the ability to personally construct and maintain an identity is crucial to survival. Otherwise insecurity and anxiety are all that late-modernity has to offer.

Ulrich Beck, the risk society and individualisation

Giddens (1991) is not entirely alone in this analysis of late-modernity. In a similar vein, Ulrich Beck (1992) considers the intrinsic nature of insecurity in late-modernity in what he refers to as both reflexive modernity and the risk society.

For Beck (1992), reflexive modernity describes the increasing ability that people have to self-confront, and therefore transform, the social conditions in which they exist. For Beck (1992) this reflexivity ushers in a new stage of modernity which brings with it a reordering of social institutions based on the distribution and management of risks. For Beck (1992) these circumstances are a naturally occurring product of the advancement of modernisation. They are not linked to any particular political or economic transformation; they are simply the next stage in the modernity project:

> The concept of risk is directly bound to the concept of reflexive modernization. *Risk* may be defined as a *systematic way of dealing with the hazards and insecurities induced and introduced by modernization itself.* Risks, as opposed to older dangers, are consequences which relate to the threatening force of modernization and to its globalisation of doubt.
>
> (Beck 1992: 21; emphasis in original)

Hence the risk society is a place where insecurity has become all-pervasive. Further, risk is produced by the process of modernisation. As the human race makes advances in knowledge it creates both new technologies and hitherto unknown risks. For example, the splitting of the atom or introduction of genetically modified foods bring with them risks that lead to economic and political debate about the threat of potentially uncontrollable risks. Thus the social institutions and political landscape of late-modernity are recalibrated around the distribution and management of risks such as these.

For Beck (1992), the risk society leads to the transformation of three interrelated arenas of social life. Firstly, late-modernity leads to the gradual dissipation of the natural and cultural resources of industrial society. Secondly, late-modern society produces risks that threaten the notion of safety; which in turn leads to the assumptions of science, business or law being called into question. Thirdly, Beck (1992, 1994) argues that collective sources of meaning such as class consciousness or political ideology begin to break down as people become disenchanted with them.

This leads to what Beck (1992, 1994) characterises as the 'individualisation process', which he uses in two distinctive ways. Firstly, he distinguishes individualisation from the type imagined by some of the classical sociologists (e.g. Simmel, Durkheim, Marx) who saw industrialisation as releasing people from the traditional bonds of religious and feudal society, by arguing that individualisation in late-modernity is release from industrial society into 'the turbulence of a global risk society' (Beck 1994: 7). Yet Beck (1994) argues that this occurs against the backdrop of an expanding welfare state which imposes a highly individualised notion of entitlement with regard to education, healthcare, employment and so on. Whereas traditional and modern society still allowed for collective or, at least, family responses to crises, late-modernity increasingly demands highly individualised decision making that by-passes the possibility of collective decision making. As Beck (1994) puts it:

Social rights are individual rights. Families cannot lay claim to them, only individuals, more exactly working individuals (or those who are unemployed but willing to work). Participation in the material protections and benefits of the welfare state presupposes labour participation in the majority of cases.

(Beck 1994: 15)

Beck (1994) is very clear in saying that he does not intend the process of individualisation to refer to increasing 'atomization, isolation, loneliness, the end of all kinds of society, or unconnectedness' (p. 13). Instead, individualisation is used is a similar fashion to Giddens (1990, 1991), who considers the process of disembedding and re-embedding as individuals attempting to produce and manage their biographies (or self-identities). For Beck (1992), this process of individualisation is therefore a product of the general conditions of industrial society and the welfare state that have developed since the 1960s. Thus, individualisation is not a personal choice, a free decision, but a consequence of modernity. Like Giddens (1990, 1991), it is the reflexive creation of a biography that constitutes individualisation. This creation provides a self-referential narrative from which each individual can constitute their individuality in an uncertain and inherently 'risky' late-modern world. Biographies are therefore reflexive, meaning that individuals increasingly choose their identities. Yet Beck (1992) sees these choices as conditional upon a number of constraints and dependencies that lead to contradictions in the individualisation process. In particular, the shaping of individualisation through the market and patterns of consumption makes the process of individualisation subject to: ' *external control* and *standardization* that was unknown in the enclaves of familial and feudal subcultures' (Beck 1992: 132; emphasis in original).

Thus the process of individualisation is governed by consumption within a fully developed market that extends into all aspects of social and economic life in the late-modern world. This combination of individualisation and market leads to what Beck (1992) refers to as standardisation, where all forms of reflexive biography are ultimately dependent upon the market for their nourishment. For Beck (1992), this denotes a new form of societal control where the creation of identity is shaped by social and economic institutions that are ultimately located in the marketplace. This new form of relationship creates the conditions in which forms of previously unseen risks rise to the surface. Whereas institutional decisions were once seen as a matter of fate, the reflexive biographer will seek to adapt and innovate in the face of decisions that affront the individual's on-going project of identity creation. These risks are located in the arena of identity, whereby the decisions and structures of institutions (or systems) that negatively affect an individual are internalised in terms of personal failure or feelings of guilt. Hence, the negative impact of institutional decisions can be understood in terms of risk management, the need for individuals to continuously reflexively monitor their biography in an on-going effort to mediate the risks presented to their sense of identity:

As a consequence the floodgates are opened wide for the subjectivization and individualisation of risks and contradictions produced by institutions and society. The institutional conditions that determine individuals are no longer just events and conditions that happen to them, but *also consequences of the decisions they themselves have made*, which they must view and treat as such.

(Beck 1992: 136; emphasis in original)

Both Giddens (1990, 1991) and Beck (1992, 1994) are fundamentally concerned with insecurity in the late-modern world (Lash 1994). For both authors this insecurity is a consequence of structural conditions that emerge out of modernity and that alter the basis in which social institutions function and social relations occur. The construction of 'reflexive biographies' is used by both Giddens and Beck to denote the complicated path that individuals must tread to create identity in this insecure and unpredictable world. It is the creation and maintenance of an existentially confident persona that prevents anxiety, in the form either of ontological insecurity or of unmanageable risks. Giddens and Beck are therefore both concerned with structural reflexivity, though Giddens (1991, 1992) goes on to develop his ideas in relation to self-reflexivity (Lash 1994). Before considering some problems with this type of reflexive sociology it is worth drawing on a final theorist, Zygmunt Bauman, to further explore the themes of individualisation, consumerism and uncertainty in late-modern society.

Zygmunt Bauman, the consumer society and dystopia

Zygmunt Bauman (2000) builds on the earlier work of both Anthony Giddens (1990, 1991, 1992) and Ulrich Beck (1992, 1994) to further explore the conditions of late-modernity. Coming from a broadly neo-Marxist perspective, Bauman has written prolifically on the topic of 'liquid modernity' and the 'individualised society'. For Bauman (2000), liquid modernity is his rendering of late-modernity, a place in which the certainties of both pre-modern and modern society are done away with and replaced with a new, lighter and fluid set of arrangements. Bauman (2000) therefore sees the rise of modernity as the replacement of one set of solid social and economic conditions belonging to traditional society (religion, monarchy, community) with another set of solid social economic traditions (rationality, secularisation, democracy, industrialisation). Thus, modernity is characterised by Bauman (2000) as heavy capitalism. It is an industrial society grounded in the market forces of labour, production and the factory. As such, it is highly regulated, predictable, repetitive and orderly. By contrast, liquid modernity has none of these characteristics; it is post-industrial society, grounded on nothing except the pre-eminence of an unregulated and flexible market where mass consumption has replaced all forms of regulation and order with a compulsive, market-driven desire to consume. Liquid modernity is therefore light capitalism, unanchored, free-floating and directionless.

the present day situation emerged out of the radical melting of the fetters and manacles rightly or wrongly suspected of limiting the individual freedom to choose and act. *Rigidity of order is the artefact and sediment of the human agents' freedom.* That rigidity is the overall product of 'releasing the brakes': of deregulation, liberalization, 'flexibilization', increased fluidity, unbridling the financial, real estate and labour markets, easing the tax burden, etc.

(Bauman 2000: 5; emphasis in original)

In this sense Bauman is in broad agreement with Giddens (1990, 1991) and Beck (1992) that late-modernity is a post-traditional society in which the certainties and securities of the modern world have been torn away, leaving society nakedly exposed to a barrage of unpredictable threats. These threats are then managed by individuals reflexively creating and continuously adapting their identities in response to constantly changing circumstances at both the local and global level (Bauman 1997, 1998).

This on-going quest for identity is inextricably both a product and consequence of individualisation. Yet, for Bauman (2001b) the quest for identity is qualitatively different in late or liquid modernity than in modernity. This distinction is important, as it helps to locate both Bauman's (2005a, 2007) belief that we live in a consumer society, and that degradation of collective meaning and action. Bauman (2001b) argues that in the pre-modern world a person was given an identity by virtue of their birth right and the solid institutions and traditions into which they were delivered. In modernity, identity is no longer given, but taken. Drawing on notions of disembedding that resonate strongly with Giddens (1990, 1991), Bauman (2001b) posits that, once separated from tradition, the determination of identity becomes a lifelong pilgrimage to strive for an identity, where the aim is how to achieve a chosen identity. Yet, in the liquid modern world, Bauman (2001b) likens the quest for identity to that of a vagabond rather than a pilgrim. No longer is identity a lifelong quest, but a transitory and constantly changing set of queries about what direction to take, where a particular road may lead, and where next. In other words, the quest for identity in liquid modernity is not really a quest at all. There is no holy grail, no end in sight and no goal. Each day demands a new quest in the full and certain knowledge that this will be transplanted by yet another, unknown, pursuit tomorrow:

the quandary tormenting men and women at the turn of the century is not so much how to obtain the identities of their choice and how to have them recognised by people around – but *which* identity to choose and how to keep alert and vigilant so that another choice can be made in case the previously chosen identity is withdrawn from the market or stripped of its seductive powers. The main, the most nerve-wracking worry is not how to find a place inside a solid frame of social class or category, and – having found it – how to guard it and avoid eviction; what makes one worry is the suspicion that the hard-won frame will soon be torn apart or melted.

(Bauman 2001b: 147; emphasis in original)

Indeed, for Bauman (2000) the only remaining certainty appears to be uncertainty, and it is this final, flimsy bedrock upon which late-modern social relations rest. Yet these social relations have been emptied of collective endeavour and public political concerns for aspiring to the good society. Just as identity has been robbed of its direction, so has society. Liquid modernity is without shape and, lacking any discernible shape, lacks any context for public life or collective activity.

It is in this climate that Bauman (2005a, 2005b, 2007) argues consumer society emerges. For Bauman (2005a), the consumer society is one where the primary engagement of its members is as consumers. Consumer society is a place where wanting, longing and desire replace labour and production. Consumer society is therefore a characteristic of liquid modernity, whereas producer society is located in modernity. Bauman explains this transformation in terms of the ceaseless, furtive search for identity. This is complemented by the individualised and disordered social conditions that typify liquid modernity. Thus the shift to a consumer society is explained in terms of individuals constantly shopping around for this or that new item to help create or recreate some aspect of identity or life-style that is fundamental to the individual's sense of self in the liquid modern world.

Whilst this inevitably includes shopping in the traditional sense, it increasingly means consuming other aspects of a particular life-style. Yet the trappings of life-style are apt to go out of fashion, meaning that they need replacing with something newer:

> models fluctuate according to fashion. Any sense of complacency is the enemy of production and consumption and to keep its wheels moving forward requires that the consumer attitude is relentless in its desires. Were we to keep products as long as they served their ostensible uses, market activity would soon grind to a halt. The phenomenon of fashion prevents this from happening. Things are discarded and replaced not because they have lost their usefulness, but because they went out of fashion.
>
> (Bauman and May 2001: 155)

The consumer society is therefore one of constant shopping where individuals seek to define their inner identity through a continuous process of purchasing and discarding whatever fashionable life-style seems currently in or out of vogue. Bauman (2000) likens this to an addiction where consumerism is fuelled by an entirely unreal fantasy, or wish, that strives to meets the fleeting and spontaneous desires of the individual to realise some dimension of their inner self. Drawing on Christopher Lasch's (1979, 1985) work on the relationship between mass consumption and narcissism, Bauman (2001b) argues that the ability to consume life-styles becomes integral to the individual's sense of freedom. In this context, consumer society is founded on the principle of choice (Bauman 2005a, 2007), the ability to choose and discard both material and social goods. Yet this choice is dependent on the market. The market is the sole provider of goods to be consumed. Advertisements, marketing strategies, shiny retail goods, the school your children go to or the bars you drink in are all presented in terms of life-style choice available for the consumer's delectation. Christopher Lasch (1985) perhaps best expresses how this dependency engenders an infantile narcissism which is both producer and product of the individualised consumer society:

> The consumer experiences his surroundings as a kind of extension of the breast, alternatively gratifying and frustrating. He finds it hard to conceive of the world except in connection with his fantasies. Partly because the propaganda surrounding commodities advertises them so seductively as wish-fulfilments, but also because commodity production by its very nature replaces the world of durable objects with disposable products designed for immediate obsolescence, the consumer confronts the world as a reflection of his wishes and fears.
>
> (Lasch 1985: 34)

Bauman (2007) clearly articulates a similar point of view regarding the transient, impulse-driven and excessive qualities of the consumer society. It is a society governed by ever-changing desires that require constant, yet ultimately unsatisfying, gratification. Shopping, or consumption, becomes the basis on which individuals attempt to express and define their identities. Freedom to choose is exalted as the pinnacle of liberation and self-determination. Social relations are therefore structured around this never-ending carnival of consumption. Neo-tribes (Bauman and May 2001) emerge as proxies for community and belonging, yet the only similarity is the consumption of life-styles that can just as easily be discarded or adapted by 'changing one's dress, refurbishing one's flat and spending one's free time at different places' (Bauman and May 2001 156).

Whereas the dystopian imaginings of the twentieth century (Huxley 1932, Orwell 1949) saw the subjugation of humankind as a consequence of advanced strategies of technological control mastered in the hands of insidious totalitarian regimes, Bauman (2000) argues that liquid modernity provides a very different type of dystopia, one where there is a frightening lack of clarity about the direction in which individuals and society should be travelling. This type of society, argues Bauman (2000), is anomic, a place without norms, where only fear and doubt persist. In essence, the lack of order, of regulation, of collective meaning and endeavour leads to a devastating freedom which, far from liberating the human race, subordinates it to the whimsy and caprice of a mindless and meaningless existence:

> What has been cut apart cannot be glued back together. Abandon all hope of totality, future as well as past, you who enter this world of fluid modernity.
>
> (Bauman 2000: 22)

Bauman (2000) is clearly not a fan of liquid or late-modernity. Coming from a Marxist perspective, he sees individualisation and consumerism as the victory of the market over collective action and public political life. His agonisingly depressing description of late-modernity has at its heart a sense of despair that these conditions cannot be changed. The social bonds required for collective political action no longer even exist. Every solid feature of modernity against which collectivities might rise up has been replaced by an ungraspable and fluid set of conditions in which each individual spends their time narcissistically trying to both write and outwardly convey an identity that demonstrates their uniqueness in a world that is increasingly devoid of any other benchmarks that might give some sense of security or purchase.

Points of divergence and convergence within discourses on late-modernity

Anthony Giddens (1990), Ulrich Beck (1992) and Zygmunt Bauman (2000) have all written extensively and in great detail about the nature and conditions of late-modernity. Of course there are many others who have also talked about these conditions or who have made important contributions to the analytical tools used by these three scholars. Yet this sociological triumvirate perhaps provides the most compelling and well-known accounts of late-modernity. Notwithstanding the various different phrases they have coined to describe late-modernity, all three of their analyses share certain core features that are of value when critiquing Etzioni's (1995) communitarianism. Yet, before continuing with this it is worth pointing to a few key differences and one or two problems with their collective ideas on late-modernity.

Firstly, the three of them are interested in different aspects of late-modernity, reflecting both their intellectual and ideological predilections. Giddens' (1990, 1991, 1992) discussion of late-modernity is part of his on-going project to understand and reconcile the relationship between structure and agency (Giddens 1984). His focus therefore develops from the relationship between the individual and social institutions to the relationship between individuals in late-modern society. Given this context, Giddens (1984, 1990) is arguably ambivalent about late-modernity, conceiving it as both constraining and enabling. Giddens (1984, 1990) is therefore less concerned with making normative claims and more concerned with analysing the character of social relations in late modernity.

Beck (1992) shares some of Giddens' (1990, 1991) concerns insofar as he too is interested to explain and analyse the individual's relationship with social institutions, but for him, the object of analyses is the reordering of social institutions and social relations around the management of risk. Hence, Beck (1992) progresses his notion of the risk society, in which both social institutions and social relations have been recalibrated around the distribution and management of risks. Hence, both Giddens (1991) and Beck (1992) share a common concern to explore the implications of individualisation and insecurity for social relations. Both concur about a reflexive project of the self, but Beck (1992) takes this reflexive project further than Giddens (1991), arguing that individuals must see themselves as centre of all action, treating both their personal relationships and their relationships with social institutions as controllable resources, or face the penalty of permanent disadvantage. Further, Lash (1994) argues that, despite their similarities, reflexivity for Giddens (1990, 1991) means placing trust in expert systems, whilst for

Beck (1992) reflexivity means the ability to critically consider, and therefore distance oneself from expert systems. In other words, reflexive modernity for Giddens (1990, 1991) is based on trust in expert systems, whilst for Beck (1992) it is based on distrust.

Finally, Bauman (2000) approaches late-modernity with by far the most pessimistic outlook. This is perhaps unsurprising, given his Marxist leanings, but it also has implications for his own point of analysis. Bauman (2000) sees late-modernity as the era of 'light capitalism' and shares Giddens' (1990) and Beck's (1992) focus on individualisation and insecurity but is more firmly located in the role of the market as the vehicle for both encouraging and perpetuating these conditions. Whilst both Bauman (2000) and Beck (1992) share an interest in how individuals become dependent on the market to assert their identity, Beck (1992) sees the avoidance of risk as the basis for social change, whilst Bauman (2000) foresees only a bankruptcy of collective meaning and action. Hence, Beck (1992) sees late-modernity as containing the ingredients for new forms of political action, whilst Bauman (2000) sees it as final nail in the coffin of class consciousness and progressive politics.

Apart from these differences of approach and focus, each author has also been criticised for historicism, artificially manufacturing unique characteristics to distinguish between historical epochs (Jenkins 2008). Similarly, it can be argued that the case for late-modernity has been overstated, whilst still others might take issue with the normative implications of a particular author's approach (e.g. Hall et al 2008). Yet, regardless of the specific nuances and values of each author, few take issue with the common set of themes that consistently appear in all of their accounts of late-modernity.

Box 6.1 The characteristics of late-modernity

Insecurity: a pervasive sense of threat, or risk, that emerges out of the breakdown of modernity and the Enlightenment project. Reason, science and knowledge all now proffer dangers as well as insights.

Uncertainty: the future is unknowable. Transience and unpredictability infect the social world, leading to anxiety.

Reflexivity: individuals and institutions become engaged in a continuous process of critical confrontation that both questions and transforms social conditions in an effort to overcome insecurity and uncertainty.

Identity: the basis for exerting control over an increasingly volatile social world is to reflexively create and adapt a personal biography that allows individuals to develop an individuality (or life-style) that provides a sense of security and confidence.

Consumerism: the excessive and mass consumption of goods and identity (or life-style) through the marketplace. These are routinely discarded and replaced in pursuit of an ever-changing fantasy that is governed by fashion.

Individualisation: the inward and private process of identity creation replaces collectivities. The individual now becomes the centre of all social relations and action.

Late-modernity and communitarianism as irreconcilable

The above themes represent the distilled features of late-modernity that are consistently outlined by the Giddens (1990, 1991), Beck (1992) and Bauman (2000) and infrequently contradicted by others. Together they paint a picture of a society in which collective forms of social action and meaning are being eroded. It is against this backdrop that the rise of communitarianism can be understood. As traditional forms of civic society dissipate, it is therefore unsurprising that a rallying call should be heard for their return. As Bauman (2000) rather neatly puts it:

> communitarianism is a *rational* response to the genuine crisis of 'public space' – and so of politics, that human activity for which public space is the natural home ground.
>
> (Bauman 2000: 108; emphasis in original)

Communitarianism is therefore an entirely understandable reaction to the conditions of late-modernity. Unfortunately, it is also entirely misguided. Why? Because the structural conditions of late-modernity outlined here are entirely incompatible with the communitarian call for a civic renewal based on shared morality and civic responsibility. As Bauman (2000) argues:

> The prospects of individualized actors being 're-embedded' in the republican body of citizenship are dim. What prompts them onto the public stage is not so much the search for common causes and for the ways to negotiate the meaning of the common good and the principles of life in common, as the desperate need for 'networking'.
>
> (Bauman 2000: 37)

Here Bauman (2000) essentially asserts the futility of the communitarian logic. Even should there be some attempt at reinvesting in community life, it would be for reasons that have little or nothing to do with developing shared bonds of mutuality. As Bauman goes on to say, 'individualization is here to stay' (2000: 37). Beck (1994) echoes this sentiment with:

This litany of lost community remains two-faced and morally ambivalent as long as the mechanics of individualization remain intact, and no one really calls them seriously into question, nor wants to nor is able to.

(Beck 1994: 16)

Late-modernity is therefore the era of the individual. Mass consumption and consumerism allow people to purchase and therefore choose their own identities. Moral relativism provides the social freedom to self-select life-style and viewpoint. Social mobility provides the space in which to move through the world without being constrained to membership of a single group or its expectations. Unbounded individualism, with all its potential freedom and excesses, is the direction in which late-modernity travels. Whilst this may be very liberating for some it is also potentially frightening or exclusionary for others. Typically the poorest in society are left unable to avail themselves of the products or life-styles on display on their television sets (Bauman and May 2001); whilst others, still bound to more traditional outlooks, fear moral relativism and see the vast array of social ills surrounding them as a product of this moral breakdown.

It is from this fear that Etzioni's (1995) communitarianism is born. His concern that individual rights have outweighed collective responsibilities is at the heart of his communitarian doctrine. For Etzioni (1995), late-modernity and its individualism is the root cause of many contemporary social ills. His solution is to rebuild shared moral values via the institution of the community. Yet this solution ignores the fact that the conditions of late-modernity are structurally located and permeate throughout the cultural fabric of the social world. The freedom of individualism cannot be understood purely in terms of a political imbalance, as Etzioni (1995) suggests, but needs to be thought about as conditional upon the social, economic and intellectual changes sketched out here. For Etzioni (1995) and the communitarians, the belief is that there has been a breakdown in family, community and civil society. Their response is that what is needed is a 'change of heart':

Without stronger moral voices, public authorities are overburdened and markets don't work. Without moral commitments, people act without consideration for one another. In recent years too many of us have been reluctant to lay claim on one another. It is a mistaken notion that just because we desire to be free from governmental controls we should also be free from responsibilities to the commons, indifferent to the community.

(Etzioni 1995: 247)

Even assuming that Etzioni (1995) is right about the breakdown of shared morality, the fundamental problem with this perspective, irrespective of whether it is applied to criminality, or more generally to incivility and community decline, is that it fails to understand that this has come about because of very specific changes in the economic and social world, which in turn have been brought about by new technologies, ways of thinking and the ordering of social life. The supposed moral breakdown caused by these conditions cannot simply be overturned by saying: 'do it differently' or 'please care more about one another'.

It is true that the communitarians point to the family, community and government as the social institutions for achieving change, but they are conceived in a particular way, as the vehicles for delivering a moral consensus, which they no longer can be because of the very conditions that led to their transformations in the first place. This sounds rather fatalistic. It is not that social change should not or cannot be achieved in general but that, as a social movement, communitarianism is looking in the wrong direction. Moral breakdown (again, still working with this assumption) is not the cause of the problem, it is a consequence of the sorts of transformations outlined at the beginning of this chapter. Addressing moral breakdown by trying to rebuild a moral consensus is therefore tantamount to a misdiagnosis. The error is to confuse cause with effect. Moral breakdown is not the cause of society's ills, and to suggest that it is not only fails to appreciate the nature of contemporary social conditions but is also largely tautologous insofar as the explanation of the problem looks suspiciously like the problem itself (i.e. immoral behaviour is caused by low morality). The problem with this is that because Etzioni's (1995) communitarianism doesn't really address the wider sociological explanations for social change his entire doctrine begins to look rather out of place and incompatible with the economic and social conditions of late-modernity. A modernist quest for structure in a fluid, late-modern world. Square pegs into round holes, if you will. Thus, efforts to create or recreate social bonds that rely upon social conditions no longer applicable quickly begin to look both repressive and potentially oppressive.

Communitarianism is therefore wildly out of kilter with social conditions. Guilty of the worst form of sociological ignorance and naivety, communitarianism is founded on an ideological concern to see a return to civic society without ever really grasping why such social conditions might have declined in the first place. As has been demonstrated, the society in which we live is predicated upon a vast array of social, economic, technological and cultural conditions. It is difficult to imagine how these conditions could even accommodate the basis for a political transformation of the communitarian type, let alone what such a transformation might entail.

Etzioni's (1995) communitarianism is therefore reminiscent of a male mid-life crisis where, in an effort to regain a lost sense of virility, a 50-year-old will buy a sports car or have an affair with a 25-year-old. Yet, life has moved on and it was neither car nor woman that provided virility, but a life and world filled with expectation and opportunity. Like the misguided male, the communitarians make the same mistake: a historical abbreviation in which they seek to excavate the features from the past that they associate with a better time, and bring them into the present. Yet they have also forgotten that these features (community, shared morality and tradition) are a product of the social conditions of their time and make sense only within the logic of those conditions. By examining late-modernity it becomes clear that, one, these traits have declined in society for a reason, and two, they have no place and make no sense within it.

The conditions of late-modernity inevitably bring with them their own set of problems. Answers to these problems are to be found in the careful examination of these conditions so that appropriate solutions can be found. To regenerate the type of community, shared morality and traditional life that Etzioni (1995) and the communitarians see as the antidote to the social ills that they believe beset us requires far more than an exhortation to a new political credo. For the communitarian solution to work, it would require a social, economic and cultural transformation on a scale hitherto unknown and incomprehensible. This would indeed be a utopian dream on a scale unimaginable.

Conclusion: a requiem for community?

Chapter 5 sought to explore a range of theoretical and empirical perspectives about community and the problems associated with Etzioni's (1995, 1997) particular conception of communitarianism. This chapter has sought to consider in detail the conditions of late-modernity in an effort to critique both the viability and appropriateness of the communitarian agenda in late-modern society. What has emerged is a set of social conditions entirely at odds with the communitarian vision. Exploration of these conditions perhaps goes some way to explaining the emergence of communitarianism and its recent political popularity on both sides of the Atlantic, but it also highlights the sociological shortcomings of the communitarian perspective.

At one level it would appear that community in late-modernity is dead and buried. Individualisation has won the day and mutuality and collective endeavour have become the casualties of insecurity and consumerism. Maybe this is the case, maybe it is not. But what is certainly not the case is that social bonds no longer persist. Given this, the next chapter will begin to consider some of the perspectives outlined in this chapter for thinking about the relationship between identity, insecurity and criminality in late-modern society. It will be demonstrated that, when viewed through this lens, crime is better understood in terms of the individual's search for identity. Quite apart from crime being a consequence of immorality, it is in fact an expressive act that emerges in response to the tensions and dilemmas inherent in the cultural conditions of late-modernity. The implications of this for how justice and punishment function as forms of cultural and expressive action themselves will then be explored, before concluding that the penal philosophies that govern how we explain and justify punishment need reconsidering if we are to ever break free from the political deadlock that has given rise to the culture of high crime societies (Garland 2000).

Note

1 Giddens' discussion of disembedding is focused on 'modernity', meaning that period that begins with the Industrial Revolution and the expansion of the capitalist economy. This period extends from the beginning of the Enlightenment period in the mid to late seventeenth century and continues through to the present. Yet, these conditions of modernity remain constant into the period that Giddens refers to as 'high modernity',

which is characterised by the end of the Enlightenment project, insofar as science and reason no longer represent safety and understanding, but also by fear and trepidation as science increasingly makes us aware of a host risks that were either previously unknown or non-existent.

References

Baudrillard, J. (1970 [1998]) *The Consumer Society: Myths and Structures*, London: Sage.

Bauman, Z. (1992) *Intimations of Postmodernity*, London: Routledge.

Bauman, Z. (1997) *Postmodernity and Its Discontents*, Cambridge: Polity Press.

Bauman, Z. (1998) *Globalisation*, Cambridge: Polity Press.

Bauman, Z. (2000) *Liquid Modernity*, Cambridge: Polity Press.

Bauman, Z. (2001a) *Community: Seeking Safety in an Insecure World*, Cambridge: Polity Press.

Bauman, Z. (2001b) *The Individualised Society*, Cambridge: Polity Press.

Bauman, Z. (2003) *Liquid Love*, Cambridge: Polity Press.

Bauman, Z. (2005a) *Work, Consumerism and the New Poor*, Maidenhead: Open University Press.

Bauman, Z. (2005b) *Liquid Life*, Cambridge: Polity Press.

Bauman, Z. (2006) *Liquid Fear*, Cambridge: Polity Press.

Bauman, Z. (2007) *Consuming Life*, Cambridge: Polity Press.

Bauman, Z. and May, T. (2001) *Thinking Sociologically*, Oxford: Blackwell Publishers.

Beck, U. (1992) *Risk Society: Towards a New Modernity*, London: Sage.

Beck, U. (1994) The Reinvention of Politics: Towards a Theory of Reflexive Modernisation, in U. Beck, A. Giddens and S. Lash (eds) *Reflexive Modernisation: Politics, Tradition and Aesthetics in the Modern Social Order*, Cambridge: Polity Press.

Bourdieu, P. (1986) The Forms of Capital, in J. Richardson (ed.) *Handbook of Theory and Research for the Sociology of Education*, New York: Greenwood.

Castells, M. (1994) European Cities, the Informational Society, and the Global Economy, *New Left Review*, 204 (March–April): 19–35.

Corrigan, P. (1997) *The Sociology of Consumption*, London: Sage.

Du Gay, P., Evans, J. and Redman, P. (2000) *Identity: A Reader*, London: Sage.

Durkheim, E. (1964 [1893]) *The Division of Labour in Society*, New York: The Free Press.

Etzioni, A. (1995) *The Spirit of Community: Rights, Responsibilities and the Communitarian Agenda*, Hammersmith: Fontana Press.

Etzioni, A. (1997) *The New Golden Rule: Community and Morality in a Democratic Society*, London: Profile.

Featherstone, M. (1988) In Pursuit of the Postmodern, in *Postmodernism*, special double edition of *Theory, Culture and Society*.

Furedi, F. (1997) *Culture of Fear: Risk-taking and the Morality of Low Expectation*, London: Cassell.

Garland, D. (2000) The Culture of High Crime Societies: Some Preconditions of Recent 'Law and Order' Policies, *British Journal of Criminology*, 40 (3): 347–75.

Garland, D. (2001) *The Culture of Control: Crime and Social Order in Contemporary Society*, Oxford: Oxford University Press.

Giddens, A. (1984) *The Constitution of Society*, Cambridge: Polity Press.

Giddens, A. (1990) *The Consequences of Modernity*, Cambridge: Polity Press.

Giddens, A. (1991) *Modernity and Self Identity: Self and Society in the Late Modern Age*, Cambridge: Polity Press.

Giddens, A. (1992) *The Transformation of Intimacy*, Cambridge: Polity Press.

Giddens, A. (1994) Living in a Post-traditional Society, in U. Beck, A. Giddens and S. Lasch (eds) *Reflexive Modernisation: Politics, Tradition and Aesthetics in the Modern Social Order*, Cambridge: Polity Press.

Hall, S. and du Gay, P. (1996) *Questions of Cultural Identity*, London: Sage.

Hall, S., Winlow, S. and Ancrum, C. (2008) *Criminal Identities and Consumer Culture: Crime, Exclusion and the New Culture of Narcissism*, Cullompton: Willan.

Herrnstein, R. and Murray, C. (1994) *The Bell Curve*, New York: Free Press.

Huxley, A. (1932 [1994]) *Brave New World*, Glasgow: Flamingo.

Jenkins, R. (1996) *Social Identity*, London: Routledge.

Jenkins, R. (2008) *Social Identity (Key Ideas)* (3rd edn), London: Routledge.

Kumar, K. (1978) *Prophecy and Progress: The Sociology of Industrial and Post-Industrial Society*, Harmondsworth: Penguin Books.

Lasch, C. (1979) *The Culture of Narcissism: American Life in an Age of Diminishing Expectations*, New York: W. W. Norton & Company Inc.

Lasch, C. (1985) *The Minimal Self: Psychic Survival in Troubled Times*, London: Pan Books.

Lash, S. (1994) Reflexivity and its Doubles: Structure, Aesthetics, Community, in U. Beck, A. Giddens and S. Lasch (eds) *Reflexive Modernisation: Politics, Tradition and Aesthetics in the Modern Social Order*, Cambridge: Polity Press.

Marx, K. (1970 [1867]) *Capital, 1*, London: Lawrence and Wishart.

Misztal, B.A. (1996) *Trust in Modern Societies*, Cambridge: Polity Press.

Orwell, G. (1949 [2000]) *Nineteen Eighty-Four*, London: Penguin Classics.

Putnam, R. (2000) *Bowling Alone: The Collapse and Revival of American Community*, London: Simon and Schuster Paperbacks.

Sennett, R. (1998) *The Corrosion of Character*, London: Norton.

Thompson, K. (1992) Social Pluralism and Post-modernity, in S. Hall, D. Held and T. McGrew (eds) *Modernity and Its Futures*, Trowbridge: Polity Press in association with the Open University.

Wacquant, L. (2001) Deadly Symbiosis: When Ghetto and Prison Meet and Merge, *Punishment and Society*, 3 (1): 95–134.

Wacquant, L. (2009) *Punishing the Poor: The Neoliberal Government of Social Insecurity*, London: Duke University Press.

Weber, M. (1904–5 [1976]) *The Protestant Ethic and the Spirit of Capitalism*, London: Allen and Unwin.

Weber, M. (1949) Objectivity in Social Science and Social Policy, in E.A. Shils and H.A. Finch (eds) *The Methodology of the Social Sciences*, New York: The Free Press.

Whitman, J.Q. (2003) *Harsh Punishment: Criminal Punishment and the Widening Divide between America and Europe*, Oxford: Oxford University Press.

7   Community, or intimacy?

> Standard men and women; in uniform batches. The whole of a small factory staffed with the products of a single bokanovskified egg. 'Ninety-six identical twins working ninety-six identical machines!' The voice was almost tremulous with enthusiasm. 'You really know where you are. For the first time in history.' He quoted the planetary motto. 'Community, Identity, Stability.' Grand words.
>
> (Huxley 1932: 5)

These words are spoken by the Director of the Central London Hatchery in the opening pages of Aldous Huxley's classic novel *Brave New World*. This world is a place where people are grown rather than born; a place where there is no suffering or inconvenience; a place where human existence is ordered and shaped around the needs of society. This is a topsy-turvy tale in which Huxley aims to comment on all that he sees as repellent and perverse in 1920s America. His science-fiction vision of the future presents a satirical 'utopia' in which all aspects of our emotional, social and physical existence have been effectively sterilised. From the family and sexuality through to anger and hunger, all of our needs and desires are synthetically met through a system of biological, psychological and pharmacological technologies. The needs of the community are pre-eminent and community is achieved through social stability, which in turn is achieved by conditioning human beings to their preordained function.

Set apart from this nightmarish utopia are the 'savage reservations' where people live according to the traditions, religions, deprivations and desires of the old world. The savages that populate these highly fenced reservations are juxtaposed with the sterile order of the new world. Old age, disease, religion, family, sex and violence are rife in the savage reservation, whilst unknown in the futuristic World State. The savage reservation is a place of diverse language, belief, life-style and opportunity. Conversely, London is a place of drug-induced happiness, conformity and obeisance to caste and community. Huxley's exploration of this world is shown through the eyes of those who are either unable or unwilling to conform to the required social order of the World State. What emerges is a distasteful image of a soulless society that has deemed difference and desire as at odds with social order and public tranquillity. The appeal of the dangerous and visceral savage reservation, with all its fraughtness and vulgarity, emerges in sharp contrast to the fragile and paradoxically unsustainable social stability so prized and essential to the brave new world.

Whilst Huxley is far from alone in presenting dystopian and totalitarian images of the future (see Orwell's *Nineteen Eighty-four* (1949) or Moore and Lloyd's *V for Vendetta* (1990)), his cautionary tale encapsulates an on-going tension between social conformity and personal freedom. Within the context of this book this tension manifests itself between the moralising and ultimately constraining community and the disembedded social and cultural conditions that foster an environment where individuals have to navigate their way through a complicated range of life-style and value choices. Aside from the apparent contradiction between communitarianism and late-modernity, it is also far from clear how community can offer up the good society. Unlike Huxley, the critique that has been mounted against communitarianism in the previous two chapters is not based on an esoteric debate about the rights and wrongs of freedom versus security. This would require a normative commitment to either one or the other that would do nothing more than reduce the critique to a statement of political values. Instead, a two-pronged attack begins by unpicking the somewhat shaky ground on which communitarians base their claims about the virtue of community to create the good society and then continues with an exegesis of three key commentaries about late-modern life and its incompatibility with communitarian goals.

It would, of course, be facile in the extreme to suggest that there is not a normative commitment behind this analysis, but the analysis itself is based on flaws in the communitarian argument that lead it to be ultimately self-defeating as an approach to controlling crime or addressing other perceived social ills. Self-defeating because communitarians have either ignored, or missed, the essence of Huxley's warning. Community presupposes boundary. There are those within the community and there are those without. In the fictional brave new world these boundaries are both deliberate and overt, clearly demarcating the space between the prevailing community of the World State and the corralled savages in their reservations. Even when community is conceived on a global scale it still has its outcasts, those who do not, or cannot, fit in. Hence community is innately dualistic, distinguishing between the self and the other. In short, community is defined in terms both of similarity to those in the community and of difference from those without. The stronger the sense of community, the stronger the sense of both affinity and differentiation. Thus the question must be asked: if communitarians wish to rebuild communities around a shared moral consensus, who will be outcast from community? The answer appears straightforward enough: those who do not agree with whatever the moral consensus is. On the basis of the communitarian writings of Etzioni and others it would seem that fundamental to this moral consensus will be a commitment to behave in non-criminal, socially responsible ways. In other words, the people most likely to be excluded from the moral community are those who are deemed most in need of it.

At this point the communitarians might complain that they have been misrepresented. Theirs is a broad church, designed to be inclusive and tolerant, not at all the sort of place in which people are rejected for being different. This would be what Selznick (1994) would refer to as communion, not community:

> The quest for commune is for communion rather than community. Communion is psychic unity, whereas community embraces a range of activities and associations. Because it is narrowly based on psychic unity, the commune is an inherently unstable social form. If it desires more stability, the commune must become a community.
>
> (Selznick 1994: 367)

Undeniably, the communitarians are at pains to demonstrate that community must entertain a range of life-styles and debates about what constitutes leading the 'good life'. Yet the fundamental tension remains; if there is to be a moral consensus, if the problems of society lie in the permissiveness begun in the 1960s, then some forms of life-style or behaviour must be outlawed if the tidal wave of amorality is to be reversed. Which forms, and who decides and what happens to those who are judged immoral has never really been clear in the communitarian discourse. Without such clarity the concern must remain that reinvesting social relations with a morally prescriptive consensus will have little effect beyond further isolating and excluding those already living on the edge of, or outside of, the mainstream. On what terms is communion avoided? What happens to the criminal, the single mother, the sexually promiscuous, the drug taker, the avant-garde, the loud, the rebellious and the dissenting? How do they avoid becoming outcast others?

This tension remains unanswered by the moral authoritarian communitarians. But, if truth be told, it is a problem not just for communitarians but for anyone seeking to invest some notion of community with the task of building a better world. For it is not just a communitarian problem but a feature of community itself. What, then, is the answer to this conundrum? This chapter is given over to addressing this issue. Not by seeking some more palatable or progressive (whatever that might mean) conception of community, but by rejecting it utterly, drawing inspiration from the late-modern lens outlined in the previous chapter to think about how identity, insecurity and intimacy might become more suitable vehicles for understanding and responding to criminality.

High walls and frightened rabbits: crime, fear and segregation

As we have seen in previous chapters, the rise in crime and anti-social behaviour is often associated with the decline of community. Alongside these ecological theories of crime Garland (2000) has talked about the culture of high crime societies in which crime issues become hugely emotive and highly politicised. In this climate the symbolic importance of the crime victim rises to the fore and commercial interests begin to market security measures that have the effect of increasing the fear of victimisation still further. According to Garland (2000), this begins to create the cultural conditions in which the threat of victimisation leads to a withdrawal from public space and a population transition from the inner city to suburban gated communities. It is arguably this dynamic which provides a fertile soil for the intellectual and political claims outlined in the previous chapters, that rebuilding communities will provide the antidote to the fear and social division brought about by crime.

In support of such claims there is also now an acknowledged body of literature which has sought to explore the contemporary urban landscape with reference to crime and the fear of crime (for example, Davis 1990, Young 1999, 2007, Caldeira 2000). One of the key findings of this literature is that urban spaces have become increasingly segregated, leading to a breakdown of social cohesion and public spaces. Whilst there is disagreement over the exact nature of these divisions and how they can be best explained, there does appear to be a general consensus that there are growing divisions within urban spaces.

Viewed collectively, this literature suggests that the late-modern urban experience is one of fragmented social relations where the fear of crime and other types of threatening behaviour has built seemingly insurmountable urban barriers that manifest themselves in terms of both the design of urban spaces and the social, economic and cultural distance between social groups. Hayward (2004) argues that the gated community becomes a key symbol by which individuals distinguish themselves and their worth from others. This is driven by the fear of the criminal 'other', combined with an urban migration out of the inner city which then creates the conditions in which segregation occurs. In a similar vein, Teresa Caldeira's ambitious ethnography of São Paulo points to crime and the fear of crime as organising themes for both city life and social status:

> To live behind walls and fences in the everyday experience of Paulistanos, and the elements associated with security constitute a language through which people of every class express not only fear and the need for protection but also social mobility, distinction and taste. While this language has many class dialects, it also has some general features that cut across all social classes. For all social groups today, security is an element through which they think of their place in society and materially create their social space.
>
> (Caldeira 2000: 291)

São Paulo provides an excellent example of the extreme segregation between different social classes and their ability to defend themselves against either the perceived or the very real threat of violence and criminality. Caldeira's ethnography draws a picture of São Paulo where a combination of city planning and an ever-present sense of menace lead to incredibly sharply drawn lines between the fortified enclaves in which the affluent cocoon themselves and the ramshackle, shanty-style favelas and *cortiços* where the poorest exist. In this sense she draws a clear comparison between the increasingly inward-looking development of fortified enclaves in São Paulo and the growth of gated or fortress communities in Los Angeles (Davis 1990, Blakely and Snyder 1997).

Both Davis (1990) and Caldeira (2000) provide compelling discussions of the trend towards the privatisation of public space. For Davis this is seen as a consequence of self-interest and fear as whole districts try desperately to fend off the external threat of violence and theft. Davis' (1990) analysis of a Los Angeles riven by the unbridled forces of fear and consumption is neatly summarised by Hayward (2004):

> This market-led 'destruction of public space' has seen a propertied elite demanding 'social and spatial insulation' from the rank and file, and an unruly and disenfranchised underclass left to fight it out in under-funded and socially excluded crime-ridden ghettos. Los Angeles, Davis argues, is a city transformed by middle-class paranoia into something reminiscent of a medieval citadel complete with architectural ramparts.
>
> (Hayward 2004: 115)

In a similar vein, Caldeira's (2000) ethnography reveals the inhospitable nature of São Paulo's public spaces:

> In a city of walls and enclaves such as São Paulo, public space has undergone a deep transformation. Experienced as dangerous, framed by fences and walls, fractured by the new voids and enclaves, privatized with chains closing off streets, armed guards, and guardhouses, public space is increasingly abandoned by the well-to-do. As the spaces for the rich are enclosed and turned inward, the remaining space is left to those who cannot afford to go in. Because the enlarged, private worlds of the better-off are organised on the principles of homogeneity and exclusion of others, they are by principle the opposite of the modern public space.
>
> (Caldeira 2000: 309)

For Caldeira (2000) this privatisation of public space has happened in both the affluent and the deprived parts of São Paulo. Whilst the avenues of the wealthy are cordoned off under the watchful eye of private security, so the sidewalks and pavements of the favelas become enclaves that only their inhabitants can traverse confidently. Public space and, in Caldeira's (2000) view, an important component of public life in the city is denied to almost all of its citizens. Streets and squares become symbolic boundaries that are infused with territorial meanings that generate suspicion and inhibit social interaction amongst different social groups:

> The idea of going for a walk, of naturally passing among strangers, the act of strolling through the crowd that symbolises the modern experience of the city, are all compromised in the city of walls. People feel restricted in their movements, afraid, and controlled; they go out less at night, walk less on the street, and avoid the 'forbidden zones' that loom larger and larger in every resident's mental map of the city, especially the elite. Encounters in public space become increasingly tense, even violent, because they are framed by people's fears and stereotypes. Tension, separation, discrimination, and suspicion are the new hallmarks of public life.
>
> (Caldeira 2000: 297)

In this sense Caldeira's (2000) work resonates with Sennett's (1974) insightful commentary, *The Fall of Public Man*.[1] For Sennett (1974), city planners have sought to build communities within the urban setting and, as such, present community against the city. This demarcation of community segregates people from each other and inhibits the ability of citizens to come to know one another. Drawing on the example of the Forest Hill dispute in New York, Sennett (1974) paints a disturbing picture of atomised communities at war, turning inwards and away from each other. For Sennett (1974), the fall of public man is linked to the boundaries or barricades that are built both physically around a location (the gated community) and mentally in terms of withdrawal from the outside world (individualisation).

Sennett's (1974) articulation of this impulse provides a warning which is central to this discussion. The quest for community has become a nostalgic attempt to recreate the conditions of traditional, pre-industrial, life. Yet this is not because such times are seen as intrinsically better or more desirable but because it becomes the symbol of a life which was free from the pervasive divisiveness of modernity. As such the search for community becomes both sanctified and reified. Yet the very process of seeking community creates obstacles to meaningful public life and ends with the reverse effect from the intended; creating more, not fewer, barriers.

São Paulo is one of the most violent cities in the world and its segregation could therefore be understood as an extreme example of what Castells (1991) has referred to as 'dual cities'. This dualism refers to a separation of space within the city. On the one hand, there are the business, shopping and tourist areas with their restaurants, hotels and gentrified executive penthouses, and on the other, the grubby ghetto with its squalid housing, ingrained deprivation and prevailing sense of threat. Young (2007) has been quick to take issue with this rather neat presentation of segregation presented by Castells (1991) and it may well be that the distinction has been rather too sharply drawn in many cases. Yet, although Young (2007) questions this sense of boundary he nevertheless endorses the sense of division presented by Castells (1991), Young's (2007) differentiation between border and division rests on the difference between physical space and social division. He argues that the physical boundaries are frequently bridged, as it is the poor who provide many of the menial jobs required to service the affluent world. Yet the broad notion of distinction between the included majority and the excluded minority remains a theme with Young's work (1999, 2007), and whilst his distinction might not be so clearly drawn geographically it nevertheless endorses the wider perspective of city life in which there is a growing demarcation between the 'haves' and the 'have nots'.

For Bauman (2005a, 2007) this distinction is drawn around a person's consumer status. The poor are 'flawed consumers' who cannot, as a result of their poverty, meaningfully engage with the consumer society. Given that human value in the consumer society is interpreted in terms of the ability to consume, the poor are effectively outcast:

> They are failed consumers, walking symbols of the disasters awaiting fallen consumers, and of the ultimate destiny of anyone failing to acquit herself or himself in the consumer's duties. All in all, they are the 'end is nigh' or the

'memento mori' sandwich men walking the streets to alert or frighten the bona fide consumers. They are the yarn of which nightmares are woven – or, as the official version would rather have it, they are ugly, yet greedy weeds, which add nothing to the harmonious beauty of the garden but make the plants famished by sucking out and devouring a lot of the feed.

(Bauman 2007: 124)

This aspect of Bauman's commentary on late-modernity is discussed in the previous chapter and is in many ways a product of Bauman's political leanings. Yet, whilst this might explain both the over-statement and pessimism in his thinking, the impact of the market and the growth of the consumer society are hard to deny. A more balanced exposition of this society and its logic can be found in Hayward (2004), who adroitly navigates between the unrequited wants and desires (Katz 1988) that are intrinsic to the consumer society and the ontological insecurity (Giddens 1990, 1991, Young 1999) that is a condition of late-modernity. In doing so he begins to question the efficacy of the segregation so potently described by Davis (1990), Young (1999) and Bauman (2005a).

For Hayward (2004), the logic of rampant consumerism cannot be so neatly understood in terms of either physical or social segregation. Unlike Young (1999) and Bauman (2005a, 2007), who see the flawed consumer as simply excluded, Hayward (2004) argues that the excluded terrain to which they are consigned can be viewed as a potential site of resistance in which counter-cultures to the consumer hegemony might be found. For Hayward (2004), therefore, whilst the urban geography of the city might indeed be drawn in terms of a consumer logic that distinguishes between the affluent and the deprived, this distinction cannot be understood in terms of a modernist nostalgia which bemoans the loss of place and its association with the politics of class struggle. Hayward (2004) argues that this tradition of sociology and criminology can explain only the past, and what has passed, rather than the present and what is going on. Rooted in the sociology of tradition and its corresponding nostalgic sense of loss, this sociology fails to engage with the conditions of late-modernity and the associated themes of insecurity and identity which help to shape and explain both urban behaviour and urban space.

Regardless of the nuances of explanation, it is clear that these perspectives are rooted in the late-modern conditions that shape social relations. Alongside these social commentaries there are a number of influential sociological and criminological texts that seek to explore and explain fear and insecurity (Hope and Sparks 2000, O'Malley 2004, Bauman 2006, Furedi 2006, Ericson 2007). A brief survey of these texts reveals a complex interplay between anxiety, insecurity and the fear of crime. What becomes apparent is that the fear of crime is predicated not purely on the risk of victimisation but also upon the conditions of late-modernity that create a wider sense of insecurity and risk. These conditions frame a governmental response that becomes increasingly focused on the management of risk (Feeley and Simon 1992), which in turn leads to a still greater sense of insecurity that then generates a new market in private security technologies (e.g. locks, alarms,

cameras, security guards and so on). This does little more than place overt reminders of the threat of victimisation in the physical environment which simultaneously sustain both the level of fear and the security market (Green 2008).

This resonates with Caldeira's (2000) description of urban and architectural
conditions in São Paulo, where lines of segregation are clearly drawn around an
ever-present sense of threat. In this city it appears to be not the insecurity of late-
modernity but the reality and harshness of pervasive violence that provide the
themes around which urban life is organised. Yet Caldeira's (2000) explanation of
fear and segregation is rooted in Brazil's history of colonisation and its subsequent
effect on democratisation, economic conditions and civil rights. In other words,
the social and cultural forces affecting São Paulo and Los Angeles in the early
1990s are not necessarily the same. Caldeira (2000) makes this point herself, arguing that São Paulo and Los Angeles have important differences in their urban land-
scapes. Los Angeles, she argues, has witnessed a far greater emptying of public
space, whilst its fortifications are far milder than those in São Paulo. Yet, despite
these important differences, she points to the underlying social and cultural forces
that are common to both cities:

> In both São Paulo and Los Angeles, therefore, we can detect opposing social
> processes, some promoting tolerance of difference and the melting of bound-
> aries, and some promoting segregation, inequality, and the policing of bound-
> aries. In fact, we have in these cities political democracy with urban walls;
> democratic procedures used to promote segregation, as in NIMBY move-
> ments; and multiculturalism and syncretic formations with apartheid zones,
> promoted by segregated enclaves. These opposing processes are not unrelated
> but rather tensely connected. They express the contradictory tendencies that
> characterise both societies. Both are going through significant transforma-
> tions. Both have been unsettled by the opening and blurring of boundaries
> (migration and economic restructuring in Los Angeles and democratization
> and economic crisis and restructuring in São Paulo).
>
> (Caldeira 2000: 334)

It is precisely because of these similarities that Caldeira (2000) makes the
comparison between São Paulo and Los Angeles. Her analysis concludes that,
despite their different historical and cultural experiences and despite the differences in crime rates between the two cities, both exhibit similar trends with
regard to fear and segregation. Whilst the roots of this segregation might differ,
Caldeira (2000) is very clear that both can be explained in terms of the social
and cultural forces at work beyond the borders of each city. These she locates
in wider changes to the political, social, technological (in terms of media in
particular) and market forces that she sees as intimately related to the urban
geography emerging in many cities across the world. For Caldeira (2000), the
convergence of these concerns has profound implications for the character of
urban life. In a statement that clearly echoes Sennett's (1974) earlier work, Caldeira (2000) comments:

Among the conditions necessary for democracy is that people acknowledge those from different social groups to be co-citizens, having similar rights despite their differences. However, cities segregated by walls and enclaves foster the sense that different groups belong to separate universes and have irreconcilable claims. Cities of walls do not strengthen citizenship but rather contribute to its corrosion.

(Caldeira 2000: 334)

Thus, neither fear nor segregation can be explained purely in reference to high crime. They require an understanding of the convergence of local and global circumstances that shape social, economic and cultural responses to high crime. According to Garland (2000), fear and segregation in the UK or USA can be understood only in terms of the conditions of late-modernity. The research and commentary discussed here suggests that whilst crime may be an organising theme around which urban and social boundaries are drawn, it is not in fact high crime per se that leads to fear and segregation but the *culture* of late-modernity combined with high crime.

This discussion is crucial to understanding why the intellectual and political pull of moral authoritarian communitarianism is based on a superficial and ultimately flawed understanding of the dynamics of fear and segregation. The mistake has been to understand fear and segregation purely in terms of high crime, rather than the culture of high crime. Because of this mistake appeals to the moral community are politically attractive because they are based on an abbreviated appreciation of the socially divisive impact of high crime and the fear of it. This misreading leads to a dangerous vicious cycle which can only further exacerbate fear and segregation in society (Figure 7.1).

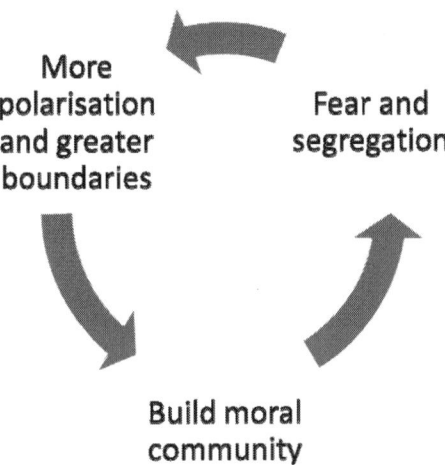

Figure 7.1 The vicious cycle of communitarianism

Because of this mistake the communitarian logic appears sound. Crime is immoral. High crime is caused by a decline of morality. Rebuilding morality is therefore required. Community embodies togetherness and is therefore the appropriate social institution from which to combat immorality and crime. Underpinning this is an emotional pull towards community, as it seems to also provide the basis for resisting the increasing fragmentation and segregation of the social world. Yet this is a conflation of issues that ignores the significance of late-modernity in framing the cultural reaction to high crime. Consequently, communitarianism offers a flawed solution that, far from helping to control crime, will only increase the fear and segregation that flows from the culture of high crime societies.

Thin theories of criminality: declining community and rising immorality

If viewed through a late-modern lens, moral authoritarian communitarianism of the sort advocated by Etzioni (1995) is a doomed endeavour. Moreover, crime control strategies that are predicated on a moralising sentiment that seeks to invest communities with moral authority and oversight will not work because criminality cannot be explained by a net loss in the amount of morality. Instead, crime needs to be thought about in terms of the key features of late-modern society. Distilled in the previous chapter, these features include growing insecurity and uncertainty; reflexivity and identity; consumerism and individualisation. Communitarianism has little to offer in relation to these themes beyond a crude and ultimately flawed suggestion that high crime is to do with the breakdown of morality and community. Whilst it is certainly the case that late-modern society is a place where social institutions like community have become disembedded (Giddens 1990) from their traditional anchors, this phenomenon needs to be understood with reference to the conditions that led to this disembedding and how it affects the lived realities of the people who exist in such conditions.

Morality and community are of course part of the fabric of society, and changes in their constitution can therefore be meaningful in terms of how we understand human behaviour. But the contention here is that neither plays an important part in understanding criminality. Not because they are unimportant themes in themselves but because the characteristics of both are, in fact, products of the contours of late-modernity. As a result, neither provides an adequate starting point for understanding the character of contemporary social life or how this shapes criminality.

Before continuing, two further points are worth making. Firstly, criminals are not devoid of community (see for example Crawford 1997, Walklate 1998, 2000, Young 2001) and, whilst early sociological research (Shaw and McKay 1942) makes connections between community decline and high crime, it also sees socially disorganised neighbourhoods as able to transmit criminal values, which presupposes the existence of some form of community life in which such values should flourish. Whilst this may not be the type of community rooted in the sociological imagination of 1930s and 1940s America, the emerging literature on subcultural theory and environmental criminology seems to be premised on the existence of closely knit groups sharing common goals and a sense of mutual purpose. These are neither socially disorganised nor criminally disinclined. Interestingly, it is precisely this historical emphasis on an American past built on a strong community life that moral authoritarianism bases much of its claims upon. This would seem to be in spite of the research undertaken in Chicago which strongly suggests that strong community can be anything but conformist. Yet this image of an inclusive past is so compelling that it is also found in Young's (1999) analysis of the *Exclusive Society*, in which he appears to suppose an era of modernity in which social conditions were of the sort so hankered after by Etzioni (1995). Yet Young (1999) is by no means endorsing communitarianism and he is clear to demonstrate that, sociologically speaking, the horse has bolted and the stable door is closed. There can be no return to the inclusionary world of modernity. However, Young (1999) has also attracted criticism for failing to account for the authoritarian and exclusionary elements of modernity (Yar and Penna 2004, Hall et al 2008) which marginalised groups by gender, religion, sexuality and ethnicity. The message is once again writ large: a bygone era of strong community and inclusionary citizenship is fictional. Even if such a place ever did exist, it contained its own exclusionary forces and fostered its own criminal culture.

Secondly, the supposedly self-evident relationship between criminality and immorality is far from clear. At one level crime is, of course, immoral. Theft and violence do contravene moral boundaries, and unless these acts are undertaken as wilful political action or deliberately provoked by actions or circumstances that would themselves be considered immoral, then such behaviour is deemed wrongful. Of course these are a couple of rather big caveats and, depending on political and theoretical position, most criminality can be seen as reaction to adverse social and political conditions.[2] Yet, even if crime is uncritically viewed as immoral this does not mean that the explanation of crime can be understood simply in terms of immoral people doing bad things because they are immoral. In other words, the association of crime with immorality might well be clear (if somewhat tautologous) but this in no way helps us to understand what leads a person to behave in immoral ways.

There have been various psychological studies that have attempted to locate the causes of criminality in some form of underdeveloped morality or personality deficit (for example, Kohlberg 1964, 1978, Eysenck 1977), but these forms of explanation have been heavily criticised for reductionism and their flawed pseudo-scientific methodologies that cannot accommodate the complex array of meanings, symbols and interpretations that human beings routinely use to make sense of the social world (Taylor et al. 1973). Even without this powerful critique such explanations lack currency. Criminals are not usually indiscriminately criminal towards everyone. They will avoid certain types of crime and certain types of victim and spend a large proportion of their life abiding by the same rules as everybody else (Matza 1964). If immorality is the explanation of criminality, then it would need to provide some explanation of not only this dynamic, but also why crime rates fluctuate across time and location and how changes in the criminal law (for example, making seatbelts compulsory or lowering the age of sexual consent for homosexuals) then affect the immoral criminals (does the seatbelt-wearing fraudster rebelliously unbuckle, or do gay men start sleeping with 12-year-olds just to maintain their deviant impulses?). Similarly, Karstedt and Farrall (2006) have explored the extent to which the law-abiding majority are in fact not at all law-abiding and frequently take opportunities to engage in both immoral and illegal behaviour. Activities such as:

> jumping red lights; not paying TV licence fees; making false insurance claims; claiming for refunds one is not entitled to; requesting and paying 'cash in hand' in order to avoid taxes; claiming benefits and subsidies that one is not entitled to.
>
> (Karstedt and Farrall 2006: 1011)

Such behaviours, argue Karstedt and Farrall (2006), are routinely commonplace for many people who would consider themselves (and generally be considered) upstanding citizens. They do not commit the sorts of crimes that are generally the cause of much public and political concern but are, nevertheless, morally dubious at best. As such, this suggests that an explanation of criminality rooted in the moral immaturity of the individual presents difficulties in terms of understanding what governs why an individual should break one rule and not another.

Clearly, the commission of a criminal act is inevitably governed by a complicated set of variables on which there is a wealth of both theoretical and empirical material.[3] Doubtless it is a combination of needs, opportunity, background and so forth that helps to shape what particular criminal act a person commits. These structural and environmental factors are what most theories of crime and deviance use to explain criminality. These theories flow from a sociological positivism that sees human behaviour as predetermined by social conditions. In the case of criminality it is inequalities or social reactions to crime that usually form the basis of explanation.

What this brief discussion, hopefully, demonstrates is that explanations of criminality cannot be located either in the decline of community or in tautologous explanations of immorality. There are a multitude of crimes and a multitude of factors which explain why a particular person might commit a particular crime at a particular time. Research which attempts to explore these specifics is inevitably drawn into a positivist language and logic which explains criminality in reference to social structure and environment. This can provide a compelling indictment of social and personal injustices (Hayward 2004) and can also provide important strategies for helping to either prevent crime or reduce reoffending. Yet, it also imposes an almost inescapable distinction between the criminal and the non-criminal. This is a distinction that this discussion has so far treated unproblematically.

Criminality is behaviour which breaches the criminal code, and a criminal is someone who intentionally and purposefully breaks the law (the principle of *mens rea*). This definition obliges explanations of criminality to be in response and reference to the criminal code. In other words, the starting place for enquiry is what are the laws and how do we explain why people break them. This perspective leads to the reification of crime and criminality as discrete categories that can be understood in self-referential terms. Crime and criminality are therefore afforded a special status as both the points of reference and the objects of enquiry. What this means is that because the legal system defines certain behaviour to be criminal, then the scope of criminological enquiry is shaped and focused by this definition. The problem with this is that it presumes that there is something unique about either criminality or criminals that ought to be researched. What this tends to preclude is an explanation of criminality that transcends such a narrow focus or which considers criminality in the context of some other perspective.

Yet criminality can be seen in a broader context. As Hayward and Young (2004) state, 'Crime is an act of rule-breaking. It involves an attitude to rules, an assessment of their justness and appropriateness, and a motivation to break them' (p. 266). Rule-breaking is thus a feature intrinsic to criminality. Yet it is not specific to criminality and also applies to a range of other 'transgressions' which involve rule-breaking. For example, adultery, promiscuity and some sexual fetishes involve non-criminal forms of rule-breaking. Similarly, lying, deceitfulness, selfishness, laziness and so forth might also be considered forms of rule-breaking insofar as the deliberate indulgence of these tendencies is at odds with accepted social norms. As such, criminality is just another form of rule-breaking. Whilst the consequences of, and responses to, criminality might be very different from other types of rule-breaking, the act of rule-breaking is itself no different to any other. It may be that there are a wide range of social, cultural and economic conditions that explain which rule will be broken but, when it is viewed in this way, a wider question about the motivation to rule-break emerges. As Hayward and Young (2004) postulate:

> It is not, as in positivism, a situation where the actor is mechanistically propelled towards desiderata and on the way happens to cross the rules; it is not, as in rational choice theory, a scenario where the actor merely seeks the holes in the net of social control and ducks and dives his way through them. Rather, in cultural criminology, the act of transgression itself has attractions – it is through rule-breaking that subcultural problems attempt solution.
>
> (Hayward and Young 2004: 266)

In other words, the act of rule-breaking is invested with meaning and therefore becomes the object of enquiry. The particular form that the rule-breaking takes becomes a secondary and largely independent question. In this sense the act of rule-breaking can be understood in terms of the sensations and experiences associated with the choice to rule-break itself. Whilst structural conditions may constrain and direct available options or choices, the crucial choice over whether to rule-break or not is always open (providing that there are more rules to break and the means to do so), and it is therefore this choice that carries meaning.

Thus a distinction between structure and agency is discernable. Whilst structure may inhibit or constrain which rule is to be transgressed, the decision to transgress it is governed by an act of will, or agency (Crewe 2009). So, whilst sociological positivism remains useful in understanding the relationship between structural conditions and behaviour, it has never been able to explain why some individuals choose to rule-break and others do not. This decision is an act of agency that is not predetermined by environment but chosen by individuals in reference to their own internal, or existential desires. Such choices are by no means limited to criminality but form an intrinsic part of human behaviour that requires understanding in terms of the cultural conditions in which rule-breaking occurs. These are the concerns of an emerging cultural criminology, articulated by Ferrell et al. (2008) as:

> the circumstances of fluidity and reflexivity – an everyday world where meaning circulates and spirals, experience comes and goes, and images and emotions flow between individuals, situations, and global communities: a world of immigration, impermanence, and 'instant living' where transience trumps durability. In this world, transgression – the crossing of borders, the violation of taboos, the rupture of certainties – is the stuff of the mass marketer, the digital musician, the migrant worker . . . and the criminal. In its very uncertainty, transgression becomes a shifting common ground for everyday experience.
>
> (Ferrell et al. 2008: 174)

Thus, it would appear that one of the main aims of a cultural criminology is to explore the relationship between cultural conditions and why people rule-break. Given the failure of moral authoritarian communitarianism to account for the cultural conditions associated with late-modernity, it would seem that cultural criminology can perhaps offer a more suitable insight into how criminality can be understood in relation to these conditions. Drawing on the conceptual framework of late-modernity outlined in the previous chapter, a model of rule-breaking that attempts to consider the work of Giddens (1991) alongside that of Katz (1988) and Lyng (1990) will be undertaken to explore the cultural and sensorial qualities that make rule-breaking appealing in late-modernity.

Authenticity and risk-taking: towards a theory of rule-breaking

Late-modernity is characterised by high levels of uncertainty and insecurity that are a consequence of the decline of traditional community and kinship networks and the separation of social institutions from both place and time. Without these anchors the world becomes an increasingly unpredictable and risky place in which psychic and existential anxieties pervade. This ontological insecurity is managed through a continuous process of reflexive creation and recreation of self-identity which then allows the individual to connect to the past and present by constructing an authentic self-identity that is true to oneself whilst also being able to adapt to an ever-changing social world. Thus one of the core features of late-modernity is ontological insecurity and the on-going task of building a self-identity that provides a measure of control and composure in conditions that constantly buffet the self in the eddies of a social and cultural malaise that is simultaneously liberating and deeply threatening (Giddens 1990, 1991).

How is this authentic self generated? For Giddens (1991), one of the main consequences of late-modernity is the basis on which trust is established in a world where community and kinship networks are in decline. In such a world Giddens (1991) argues that personal trust is achieved by developing intimate relationships with friends and lovers. In an environment increasingly devoid of stable social institutions, trust is achieved through mutual openness and self-disclosure rather than pre-existing social networks. Intimacy is therefore achieved through an ongoing process of self-enquiry and self-discovery with other people. This is the basis of what Giddens (1991) refers to as the pure relationship, developed in relation to internalised emotional desires and personal connections. This pure relationship forms an important part of the search for an authentic self-identity, as it provides defence against external threats and the capacity to connect with abstract notions of trust which are essential to survival in the late-modern world. Authenticity is therefore derived through emotional honesty and openness with other people. These purely emotional and very intimate connections become central to the search for ontological security.

Thus emotional openness becomes the basis for connecting with others in an increasingly fluid and reflexive world. Evidence of this phenomenon can be gleaned across the social world. As Morgan and Averill (2008) argue:

> Whereas once, for example, people typically derived identity from clear cut religious and class expectations, now people more often define who they are in relation to 'inner' needs and capacities, looking inward for markers of 'authentic being' that may let them know themselves.
>
> (Morgan and Averill 2008: 158)

Similarly, Furedi (2004) discusses emotions and authenticity in the therapy culture of late-modern society and Aslama and Pantti (2008) outline the popularity of reality television in relation to the on-going search to authentically know oneself. Greer (2004) explores the relationship between media reportage and coverage and the emotional outpourings of grief when a child goes missing or is murdered. Highly reminiscent of the public reaction to the death of Princess Diana, Greer (2004) argues that it is the conditions of late-modernity that create the emotional urge for people to come together to publicly share their grief:

> Amid widespread ontological insecurity, individual life histories are structured, shaped, and made sense of within the frames of reference provided, to a significant degree, by mass media, to the extent that a sense of shared (popular) culture generates 'imagined community'.
>
> (Greer 2004: 110)

Emotions and emotionalism are increasingly vested in a wide range of social interactions that are as transient as they are powerful. From intoxicating romance to wailing grief through to blinding rage, the social world is increasingly invested with a level of emotional outpouring hitherto unknown. Whether it's sat on the sofa with Oprah, histrionics in the Big Brother house or tabloid campaigns to 'out the pedo', emotions have become very public. If authenticity is achieved by emotional openness, such displays can be understood as part of a cultural practice of reaching out to others; the louder and stronger the emotion, the greater the need for self-identity and security.

With all the fragile insecurities of late-modernity, emotion becomes one of the few remaining benchmarks of genuineness. The stronger, the purer, the more 'from the heart' the emotion is, the more profound the sincerity and the greater the authenticity of the individual. Yet, late-modernity is also a place in which features of Baudrillard's (1970, 1983, 1994) hyperreality become increasingly evident. Not only do the media augment and transmit these emotional outbursts; reality itself has become irrelevant, replaced instead by a rampant consumerism which provides and interprets reality through the signs and symbols it uses to advertise its preferred images. Hence, even emotions become hyperreal. The disjunction between hyperreality and authenticity further exacerbates the yearning desires that characterise the consumer society. Giddens' (1991) search for the pure rela-tionship to authenticate the self is at war with Baudrillard's (1970, 1983, 1994) hyperreality and its associated instabilities. Put simply, hyperreality precludes authenticity; late-modernity demands it.

In such conditions emotions become exaggerated in a desperate attempt to reach out to others and authenticate the self. Emotionalism achieves the status of a trust currency from which people compete to demonstrate the openness and suitabil-ity as either friend or partner. Legions of psychoanalysts earn huge fees helping individuals to connect with their inner self and broadcasting and print media are saturated with edifying and educational tales of emotional adversity and romantic pursuits. The resultant strain between the need for authenticity and the inability to achieve it then becomes the motor that drives consumer society's unrequited desire for continuous consumption. Ironically, the quest for authenticity and the pure relationship creates the conditions for a consumer culture that markets prod-ucts and life-styles that play to, and thus generate, the exact same anxieties that the pursuit of authenticity was supposed to alleviate in the first place. This creates a self-perpetuating cycle of consumption which fuels both life-politics (Giddens 1991) and the creation of neo-tribes (Maffesoli 1996, Bauman and May 2001) that become the outward expression of the reflexive creation and recreation of self-identity. Thus the process of creating self-identity either greedily consumes the latest offering that popular culture has to offer it or co-opts its fads or forms to new ends that then provide the necessary cultural reinterpretation to then be assimilated by the consumer society (Ferrell et al. 2008).

Hayward's (2004) analysis of consumer culture and the city provides a clear account of how crime and consumerism are linked together through the emotional satisfactions derived from planning and committing crime. Hayward (2004) links these emotions to the ontological insecurities of late-modernity and the associ-ated urge for self-actualisation. Consumer culture, he argues, is at the heart of understanding the impulses to commit crime and other forms of transgression. Drawing on the work of Katz (1988) and Young (1999), Hayward (2004) seeks to articulate an approach to understanding crime which explores the emotional seduction and repulsions of crime with the wider social and cultural conditions in which these emotions are expressed. As such, Hayward's (2004) study can be read as an attempt to provide an explanation of criminality that draws together agency and structure through emotion and culture. Katz (1988) provides the initial inspiration for this marriage with his fascinating exploration into the sensual thrills of criminal transgressions. Arguing that more traditional criminological explanations have left the explanation of the individual's emotional experiences of crime in the background, Katz (1988) proffers an approach that seeks to foreground the emotional appeal of criminality. In an effort to both situate and explain these emotions in their wider cultural context, Hayward (2004) draws on Young's (1999) influential study of the relationship between exclusion, crime and late-modernity. At its heart, Hayward's (2004) synthesis is concerned to provide the beginnings of an explanation of crime that explains the emotional pull of criminal transgressions in terms of the ontological insecurity associated with the conditions of late-modernity and the consumer culture that, paradoxically, fuels both insatiable desires and the incitement to crime that are driven by the never-ending hunt for identity and self-actualisation.

The search for identity and authenticity becomes both a creative and organising force in late-modernity. Authenticity foregrounds the emotional importance of particular actions as it contextualises the cultural significance of the on-going construction and reconstruction of identity and its concomitant ontological security. With regard to crime, the importance of this emotional appeal and its associated life-styles is seized upon by Katz (1988) in his phenomenological study of the moral and sensual attractions of crime:

> Seen in the form of snapshots taken from the outside, the hardman seems to be a collection of impulsive outpourings of hostile feelings – anger, aggressive instincts, and sadistic inclinations. But after a series of frustrated robberies, lost fights, betrayals by intimates, arrests, and prison sentences, one always has a multitude of reasons for *not* responding from the guts. Just because they are done against the background of reasonable grounds for deterrence, the hardman's aggressive moves carry, in their sensual vibrance – in the heavy awe and felt charge they bring to scenes – the ringing significance of their transcendent project.
>
> (Katz 1988: 235; emphasis in original)

This example of the armed robber's continued criminality in the face of overwhelming reasons to desist neatly encapsulates the power of emotions in allowing people to transcend the mundane, the chaotic and the frightening moments of everyday life. In a later text, Katz (1999) maps out how the study of emotions can provide understanding of not only how people react to specific and fleeting moments but how emotions are illustrative of the life narratives that shape identity and a sense of self:

Emotions do not *introduce* feelings and themes of transcendence into social action, they highlight them. Better, emotions are metamorphoses of themes of transcendence. Emotions give dramatically new and emphatically visible forms to the narrative themes that had been less visibly present in social life. The relationship between socially situated emotions and their less visible origins can be traced, but, because emotions are revelations through processes of transformation, they can be traced only with great difficulty. In a way, the understanding that emotions are in tension with reason, self-reflection, or thought exactly misrepresents what emotions are. Emotions are ways of turning back on the self, ways of reflexively amplifying and giving added resonance to the transcendent meanings of situated action.

(Katz 1999: 322; emphasis in original)

What this demonstrates is the importance of emotions in providing both the basis and insight into how people seek to authenticate themselves by transcending, or lifting themselves out of and above, an uncertain and insecure late-modern world. Emotions are therefore not only the basis and currency of authenticity, they are also important in understanding the cultural meanings of action. For Katz (1988), the emotional appeals of rule-breaking are just one example of understanding the role that emotions play in explaining action. But, located within the social theory of Giddens (1991), emotions become the last human resource upon which a person can rely in the day-to-day navigation of risks and relationships in late-modernity.

A closely aligned perspective that provides further insight into this dynamic is the work of Stephen Lyng, who has been interested to explore why people voluntarily engage in high-risk activities (1990, 2004, 2005, Lyng et al. 2009). Lyng (1990) develops the concept of edgework to describe the phenomenon of 'negotiating the boundary between chaos and order' (p. 855). To do this, Lyng (1990) provides a synthesis of Marx and Mead's theories to develop a dialectic of constraint and spontaneity in which edgework can be understood. This dialectic is premised on the assertion shared by Marx and Mead that spontaneous and free action can be achieved only under conditions of constraint.[4] In the context of edgework Lyng (1990) argues that late-modernity[5] has created social conditions that effectively deny the individual of the capacity to exert meaningful control over their existence:

The paramount reality for the individual under these conditions then is a loss of ego. In the absence of a fully developed social self (involving not only 'generalized attitudes' but also a broad range of social and economic roles), the ego fails to develop fully. The predominant sensation for the individual is one of being pushed through daily life by unidentifiable forces that rob one of true individual choice. This experience can be conceptualised as 'oversocialization'.

(Lyng 1990: 870)

In these conditions, Lyng (1990) argues, individuals do not always remain passively 'oversocialised' but develop strategies to overcome their alienation. This, he contends, takes the form of searching for the self, which can take various shapes such as consumer-orientated narcissism (Lasch 1979) or leisure activity that involves elements of both risk and skill. It is in this context that Lyng (1990) argues edgework can be understood as a response to the conditions of late-modernity. Using examples of edgework such as skydiving, rock climbing, drug use and motor-cycle racing, Lyng (1990) paints a picture of people engaged in highly skilled but also highly dangerous activities that are about putting oneself at the edge of chaos and then exerting one's survival skills to overcome the impending pandemonium. Thus, edgework is a very calculated risk rather than a gamble, wherein the goal is a 'controlled sense of loss of control' (Hayward 2004) that takes the individual to the teetering edge of possibilities. Stripped bare of social and cultural constraints, all that is left is the 'residual self' that is then capable of unconstrained spontaneous and creative action. It is in these moments that the individual achieves a heightened state of emotional clarity that celebrates the self's ascendancy:

> Chief among these sensations are the feelings of self-determination and self-actualization reported by people involved in all types of edgework. Although the notion of self-actualization has long been regarded with some suspicion by hard-nosed social scientists, the present framework provides a conceptual basis of this idea. Simply put, people feel self-actualised when they experience a sense of direct personal authorship in their actions, when their behaviour is not coerced by the normative or structural constraints of their social environment.
>
> (Lyng 1990: 878)

More recently, Lyng (2004, 2005, Lyng et al. 2009) has extended his concept of edgework to consider embodied, or corporeal, aspects of edgework as well as its application to criminality. Ferrell (1996, 2005), in particular, has applied the notion of edgework to criminality by considering the adrenalin rush of emotions often associated with committing an offence and the subsequent relationship between aggressive policing and the refinement of the skills and strategies used by criminals to evade detection and capture. Hence, edgework involves a deliberate choice to engage in highly risky activity as a means of exerting one's sense of self over one's circumstances. This choice is underpinned by careful training and management of the environment so that the individual is able to fulfil their sense of mastery of both the immediate conditions in which they have placed themselves and the conditions in which they more generally live their lives.

It is in this context that Lyng's (1990) edgework begins to overlap with both Katz (1988) and Giddens (1991). As has already been discussed, Katz (1988) is interested in exploring the emotional sensations involved in criminality and, more generally, the capacity of emotions to liberate the self from the mundane. The intense emotional 'highs' experienced by edgeworkers resonate with the emotional sensations that Katz (1988) describes in relation to various types of criminality. Similarly, the equation of emotional intensity with the construction of self in the oversocialised and alienating conditions of late-modernity fits snugly alongside the importance Giddens (1991) places on intimacy in the search for ontological security and self-actualisation in an insecure and uncertain world.

Thought of together, the combination of Giddens (1991) and Lyng (1990) begins to suggest a useful framework for considering how criminality, under the wider auspices of rule-breaking, can be understood in late-modernity. Rule-breaking is any type of behaviour that transgresses a legal, social, cultural or moral norm. Regardless of which rule is broken, the act of breaking is invested with meaning. When considered in relation to the conditions of late-modernity this meaning can be conceptualised in terms of the on-going search for identity and self-actualisation in an insecure and uncertain world fraught with risks and anxieties. The cultural context which frames this search is provided by Giddens (1991), who describes the process of disembedding in which emotions and intimacy become increasingly important to social bonds. Media and public displays of emotion are increasingly valorised in popular culture as the hallmarks of authenticity. The toxic combination of this need for intimacy and unbridled consumerism creates unrealisable desires that constantly change as new fads and fashions emerge onto the market. In this climate, rule-breaking becomes increasingly attractive as it provides opportunities for self-actualisation through the intense emotions and risks associated with it. Katz (1988) provides a further clue to this dynamic with his study of emotion and style in criminal subculture. Finally, Lyng's (1990) notion of edgework offers an explanation for rule-breaking that allows the self to emotionally transcend the anxiety-ridden and alienating conditions of late-modernity.

What this, hopefully, starts to demonstrate is that criminality is not a unique or distinctive form of activity[6] and is therefore better understood as just one form of rule-breaking behaviour. This explanation of such behaviour has attempted to consider both the social and cultural conditions of late-modernity and how they begin to prioritise emotions and intimacy as the basis for establishing relationships. At the other end of the spectrum, inspiration has been taken from Katz (1988), Lyng (1990) and cultural criminology more generally for thinking about how individuals might experience and choose to rule-break, and the emotional and sensory appeals of such transgressions. Hayward (2004) attempts a similar tentative project with regard to the relationship between consumer culture and late-modernity. This is not a dissimilar project to the one attempted here. Whilst Hayward (2004) focuses on exclusion and consumerism, the focus here has been to concentrate on authenticity and risk-taking. Yet both are overlapping and mutually reinforcing projects that have at their heart a concern to explore the relationship between structure and agency insofar as they provide insight into crime and rule-breaking behaviour.

For Hayward (2004), this project emerges out of an attempt to map the contours of the urban experience in the consumer society, whilst this discussion is aimed at providing a wholesale denial of the political and ideological moralising of Etzioni (1995) and New Labour. As such, it is worth remembering that this model of rule-breaking emerges out of conditions of late-modernity used to critique communitarianism in the previous chapter. With this in mind one, final point is worth briefly mentioning. Rule-breaking, viewed from the perspective of authenticity and risk-taking articulated here, suggests another danger inherent in New Labour and communitarian moralising. This danger mirrors the vicious cycle of communitarianism outlined earlier in this chapter and suggests another unpleasant sequence whereby increased moral censorship leads to even more rules that alienate and marginalise even more life-style choices; which in turn leads to even more oversocialisation. Following the logic of risk-taking outlined by Lyng (1990), this then leads to increased risk-taking behaviour in an effort to self-actualise in a society that is not only insecure and uncertain but increasingly authoritarian and intrusive.

None of this discussion should be taken to mean that criminality is somehow being excused or romanticised just because its explanation is not to be found in immorality. The purpose of this discussion is in fact precisely the opposite. Moral authoritarianism is socially corrosive and intellectually flawed. It is therefore a dangerous logic on which to base crime control strategies. The very real and very horrible traumas inflicted on crime victims are not to be ignored or underestimated. With this in mind it is now worth turning to criminal justice. Following the logic used to develop this model of rule-breaking it will now be considered how suitable our present system of justice is for responding to crime in late-modernity.

Maladapted justice: the cultural and emotional framing of punishment

The theory outlined above attempts to consider criminality as an expressive act of rule-breaking that can be understood as a way of gaining some sense of control in conditions of uncertainty and insecurity. The purpose of developing this model has not been to present anything like a 'general theory of crime', at least, not in the traditional criminological sense of suggesting that one type of circumstance (poverty) causes a type of behaviour (crime); but, rather, to outline the cultural conditions that make rule-breaking, or transgression, appealing. What has become clear is that the conditions of late-modernity can be mapped onto the emotional appeals of rule-breaking. This provides a useful framework for understanding such appeals that, hopefully, puts to rest the communitarian and New Labour rhetoric that high crime can be understood in terms of moral decline.

Yet, if it is reasonable to view criminality through the lens of late-modernity, should not punishment be considered in the same way? For, as Garland and Young (1983) contend:

> We would conceive of penality as a specific *institutional site* which is traversed by a series of different social relations. Political, ideological, economic, legal and other social relations do not merely 'influence' or 'shape' or 'put pressure upon' penality – they *operate through it* and are materially inscribed in its practices. Penality is thus an over-determined site which relays

and condenses a whole series of social relations within the specific terms of its own practices.

(Garland and Young 1983: 21; emphasis in original)

If this is true, then penality and punishment can also reasonably be expected to both assimilate and produce the conditions of late-modernity. Specifically, punishment should reflect the emotional and consumerist conditions that seem wedded to the late-modern conditions of uncertainty and insecurity. Loader and de Haan (2002) have pointed to a number of ways in which emotions have become more central to the delivery of justice, concluding that emotions have become 'inescapably implicated in both the "volatile and contradictory" nature of late-modern penality' (Loader and de Haan 2002: 247).

Garland (2000) provides a succinct overview of the culture of high crime societies in which he points to the social changes associated with late-modernity as a way of understanding the new emotionalism found in penality. To this end he points to a number of significant trends that help to explain this emotionalism. Chief amongst these is the increasingly cultural salience of the symbolic victim, the impact of which he describes in his polemic on the culture of control:

> The victim is every victim, she could be you or related to you. This personalizing trope, repeated endlessly on television news and documentaries, represents the crime victim as the real life, 'it could-be-you' metonym for the problem of personal security. And in so doing, it shifts the debate away from the instrumental reasoning of crime control analysis towards the visceral emotions of identification and righteous indignation. Once this shift has been effected, the terms of the debate are transformed and 'facts' become 'less persuasive than the moral authority of grief'. If the centre-piece of penal-welfarism was the (expert projection of) the individual offender and his or her needs, the centre of contemporary penal discourse is (a political projection of) the individual victim and his or her feelings.

(Garland 2001: 144)

This builds on Garland's (1996) earlier work that considers the way in which the state adapts to its perceived inability to control the spiralling crime rate. Garland (1996) argues that one of these adaptations is based on the state's denial of the failure of punitive strategies to control crime by invoking increasingly severe language and punishment, which it uses to camouflage its powerlessness to bring about positive change. Linked to this is the development of the 'criminology of other', where criminals are alien, dangerous and different. This is in direct contradiction to the adaptive strategies that represent the 'criminology of self', where the offender is like us, a rational, free-thinking individual.

Garland concludes that these two paradigms ignore the 'welfarist' criminology that concerned itself with disadvantage and inequality and sought to address these social injustices. As a result, we are left with two diametrically opposed perspectives that undermine each other and promulgate insecurity and exclusion.

The symbolic power of victimisation is intrinsically connected to media representations of crime and justice that portray both real and fictional accounts of when the criminal justice system fails victims and which invasively thrusts crime and its awful consequences into the homes and consciences of everyone. For Garland (2000, 2001), these expressive and emotive conditions are strongly associated with the conditions of late-modernity from which they arise.

In a similar vein, Karstedt (2002) explores what she refers to as the emotionalisation of the law. Like Garland (2000), she also sees this trend as in keeping with the conditions of late-modernity and explains emotionalisation in terms of authentic assertions of self-identity that underscore individual autonomy and self-representation. Karstedt (2002) considers the impact of these conditions on the way in which the penal process functions. Whilst she acknowledges the emotional context in which crime and criminal justice has always occurred, she argues that since the mid-1990s there has been a noticeable increase in the emotional content of public discourses about crime and the introduction of punishments that 'are explicitly based on – or designed to arouse – emotions' (Karstedt 2002: 301). Drawing Garland (2000) and Karstedt (2002) together, a picture of the cultural conditions that heighten the symbolic power of the victim and introduce emotionalism in the penal process emerges. It is therefore perhaps unsurprising that virtually all of the arenas in which emotionalism has crept into penal policy have been predominantly victim centred. Victim impact statements, restorative justice, vulnerable witness and victim contingencies in court and Victim's Champions[7] all resonate strongly with both the increasing symbolic significance afforded to crime victims and the direction in which our cultural sympathies lie.

Alongside Garland (2000) and Karstedt (2002), others have also sought to consider the increased salience afforded to emotions in criminal justice. For example, Laster and O'Malley (1996) discuss the advent of what they refer to as 'sensitive new-age laws', where they argue that the conditions of late-modernity have inculcated both technocratic and emotional tendencies in the penal process. Laster and O'Malley (1996) argue that, despite the apparent contradictory nature of these two trends, they are best understood as both emerging from the social, economic and political conditions of late-modernity. This accords well with Garland's (1996) criminologies of the self and other, and the rational offender versus sadistic monster dialectic that, he argues, emerges from the state's adaptations to its failure to control the crime rate. Hence they conclude that claims that either technocratic or emotional justice are emerging as the dominant trend are misplaced; both are in fact emerging simultaneously and in response to the tensions and contradictions inherent is wider social conditions. Freiberg (2001) has argued that crime prevention will fail to succeed, regardless of how technically successful it becomes, unless it manages to 'tap into the deeper psycho-social forces which have driven the recent wave of popular punitiveness and which underlie the criminal justice system generally' (p. 266). Whilst his suggestions for how crime prevention might achieve this are less than convincing, his general point resonates with those of Garland (2000) and Karstedt (2002). Crime and punishment have become terrains far more heavily invested with emotional content than was previously known.

Within this context, Karstedt (2002) cites the return of shame and its associated restorative processes as an exemplar of this trend, before considering the appropriateness and suitability of such strategies for penal legitimacy. She argues that emotions are rational responses to the unfairness and injustice of criminality, and that feelings of anger, disgust, shame, compassion and so forth reflect our individual and shared moral values. From her wider analysis of emotion theory she concludes:

> Legal institutions are not based on a small number of basic emotions, but on different and contradictory ones. Processes of punishment are linked to feelings of disgust as well as being embedded in emotions of sympathy. Any efforts to bring one of these to the forefront, and make it the foundation of criminal justice procedures, will necessarily ignore the range of moral sentiments which are involved in the individual as well as the collective.
>
> (Karstedt 2002: 312)

These concluding remarks from Karstedt (2002) provide the basis from which punishment can begin to be viewed as culturally and emotionally maladapted. Drawing together the influential thought of both Garland (2000) and Karstedt (2002), a clear relationship between late-modernity and the expressive significance accorded to crime and punishment becomes evident. Yet a perplexing bifurcation can be witnessed between increasingly punitive and vitriolic public sentiments about crime (Bottoms 1995, Tonry 2004) and the increasingly technocratic approach to the administration and management of crime and its associated risks (Feeley and Simon 1992). The exception to this appears to be the emergence of restorative and victim-centred initiatives, which seem to have cornered the emotional market with their focus upon anger, shame, remorse, inclusion and forgiveness (Loader and de Haan 2002). These apparently contradictory directions resonate with Laster and O'Malley's (1996) assertion that legal processes have become increasingly technocratic and emotional. Yet it would appear that, with regard to punishment, this emotionalism is predominantly directed towards certain types of emotion that are designed to achieve certain instrumental goals, specifically those of remorse, reintegration and forgiveness.

What this suggests is that whilst crime and punishment have become culturally loaded with emotional meaning, the penal process has allowed only for a particular form of emotional participation – namely, one built around shame and forgiveness. This presents a dangerous divergence between public discourse and penal policy which threatens the system's integrity (legitimacy) and its capacity to meaningfully respond to the late-modern context in which criminality occurs (expressive). For Karstedt (2002), this over-emphasis on shame seems to set a dangerous precedent whereby one emotion is set above the rest.

The upshot of this is that the expressive qualities so valorised in late-modern society have been tethered to particular outcomes in the penal process. If criminality can be understood as a form of expression that provides the basis for authentic self-actualisation, then why should punishment not become the forum through which society in general, and victims in particular, are able to similarly authentically self-actualise? For this to happen, freedom must be given for people to express themselves openly. Thus, in some senses the success of restorative justice inhibits the legitimate expression of emotions or sensibilities that are out of kilter with restorative goals. Vengeance, retribution, disgust and hatred are repressed within the restorative focus on reconciliation and restoration (Green 2011).

Whilst it is clearly legitimate for participants in a wide variety of restorative settings to express their anger and frustrations over the harm caused to them, the process is designed to transcend these feelings and reach a stage of understanding and forgiveness. Of course this doesn't seem like an undesirable outcome in itself, but it does constitute a type of moralising sentiment that has something in common with the moral authoritarian communitarianism critiqued in this work. There is an expectation upon those involved in restorative justice to reach a desired outcome that is premised upon a normative commitment to reconciliation and restoration. In other words, if you want to take part you're expected to at least outwardly conform to these values. You are in fact being told how to behave. Herein lies the nub of the problem. The self-actualising qualities invested in expressive acts will not be understood as authentic by those involved in restorative justice if, as Bennett (2007) contends, they are either required or expected to express themselves in particular ways. This would in fact be the very antithesis of authentic expression. Thus the emotionalism so sought for its qualities of authenticity is effectively neutered by the normative goals of restorative justice. This perhaps helps to further explain Daly's (2003) research in the restorative field, which suggests that many victims are unsatisfied about the sincerity of offender apologies or other forms of material or symbolic reparation.

It is in this sense that justice is maladapted. It is *emotionally* maladapted. Emotions have been reintroduced into how 'we do' justice and punishment; but only some emotions and only in the pursuit of certain goals. This in turn undermines the authenticity of any emotional expression, as it is generated from a biased process rather than genuine feelings. To be clear, it is not that remorse, shame or forgiveness are unworthy sentiments but that, unless freely expressed, they cannot provide the authentic representation of self that has become so integral in late-modern society. Unless expressions of defiance, pride or vengeance (or any other emotion for that matter) are equally valid, then participants are robbed of the opportunity to genuinely decide on what they feel or how to express themselves. To exclude or minimise certain emotional responses is therefore both emotionally repressive and counter-productive if the goal is to rebalance the scales of justice. If emotions are to be reintroduced into the penal system, then they must be given full vent if they are to be meaningful in terms of both authenticity and recovery from the consequences of crime. To put it in therapeutic terms, there are no right or wrong emotions, there are just emotions.

About two hundred years ago we stopped punishing people in public. The spectacle of punishment was taken indoors and behind the prison walls. Part of the reason behind this was the threat to the legitimacy of the emerging nation-state. If the crowd publicly expressed their dissatisfaction with the punishment because it was either too lenient or not severe enough, this could be interpreted as a challenge to the authority and integrity of the state. This focus on the crowd is extended and developed by Gatrell (1994) in his penetrating historical analysis of the abolition of the death penalty. For Gatrell (1994), the end of public execution can be understood in terms of the emergence of squeamish sensibilities in the early nineteenth century that turned people's heads away from the visceral and appalling spectacle of death and began to view feelings of curiosity and interest in such deaths as mawkish and disreputable (McGowen 2000). In the context of this discussion this is a useful insight built on a meticulous historical analysis that explains the crowd's experience and emotional reaction to the spectacle of death. For Gatrell (1994), the feelings and sentiments evoked by public execution were profound and worthy of both respect and attention. To ignore such emotions is to 'misunderstand the operation of the penality in the past as well as to underestimate the political and cultural force it exerts in the present time' (McGowen 2000: 13).

This warning chimes with conditions of late-modern society which have propelled public and political interest about crime and punishment to hitherto unknown levels. Fear and anger about crime run high and emotions find new resonance across society and within penal policy (Karstedt 2002). Yet, like our forebears, we remain suspicious and wary of the public's sentiments. In the context of the Enlightenment tradition and its concomitant critique of the brutalising and disproportionate 'bloody code' of corporeal and capital punishment, the subjective and unreliable involvement of the crowd was replaced with objective principles and external criteria by which punishment should be administered.

Today, public participation appears to have been reintroduced into criminal justice. The scaffold has been metaphorically rebuilt and the crowd reassembled. But, rather than take the chance that they might cheer or boo at the wrong moment, someone is at the front with a large board telling everyone when to clap. The crowd must be educated to behave in the appropriate fashion to deliver the desired response.[8] In the culture of high crime, society's politicians and journalists do their best to demonstrate their solidarity with crime victims by showing how tough they are on criminals. In the realm of penal policy emotions are reintroduced but in a very managed and controlled fashion. Punishment is thus caught between two opposing forces, both of which derive from the conditions of late-modernity. On the one hand, is popular punitiveness (Bottoms 1995), and on the other, an impotent emotionalism that has its roots in the normative values of liberal elites. Yet these values are misplaced. Justice has become harsher, more intolerant and more degrading. Burgess's (1962) *Clockwork Orange* looms large as an object lesson; the tormented Alex, the victim of his enforced conditioning and its unintentional ruination of his love of Beethoven's 9th Symphony.

If emotions are to be allowed a say in how justice is done, then they must be liberated from expectation and demand. This does not mean that punishment should be entirely governed by how people feel about crime, but they must be allowed to express themselves honestly and without interference. Otherwise, the punitive braying of politicians and the media is left without release and the sanitisation of emotional content becomes increasingly culturally unattractive. In this context such opportunities are construed as insincere or soft options, designed by those perceived or written-off as out-of-touch, woolly liberals who don't have to deal with the harshness of day-to-day life. In such a way punishment can be considered as maladapted. Emotionally stunted and culturally unappealing public and political sensibilities are left with nowhere to go except increasing punitiveness. Fear of mob rule and the vitriolic urges of the ignorant prevent the opportunity of genuine emotional engagement. Yet, without accepting this risk, emotion in justice will remain inhibitory and repressive rather than liberating and transformatory.

Conclusion: the logic of emotion

In the previous two chapters the sociological shortcomings of communitarianism were considered at length. In terms of both its conception and understanding of community and its compatibility with late-modernity, Etzioni's (1995) communitarianism has been shown as flawed. This raises profound questions about the applicability of communitarian thinking for understanding and responding to crime. This chapter has therefore sought to consider these sociological limitations in relation to crime in late-modern society. Beginning with a close examination of how crime and the urban life are experienced, it becomes apparent that criminality must be understood not only in terms of its extent and consequences but also in terms of the social and cultural conditions in which it occurs. Because of communitarianism's failure to engage with theories of late-modernity it is remarkably short-sighted in its theoretical understanding of crime and criminality. This short-sightedness is then transferred into the political domain, where community-building strategies and moral exhortation are deployed in attempts to do something about crime.

It is in this sense that community is rejected. Not community in general, not community as people understand or experience it, but community as proposed by academics and politicians. It is rejected for several reasons. Firstly, because there are intrinsic problems in the nature of community that pose unanswered questions about its capacity to deliver either a more moral or a more inclusive society. Secondly, because the particular type of moral community being proposed is based on a severely limited sociological perspective that is out of kilter with social and cultural conditions. Thirdly, because of this it provides only the thinnest of circular explanations for crime that does not convince when held up against either its own logic or the evidence of others.

As a consequence of this critique an attempt has been made to consider an explanation of criminality that does pay full attention to the social and cultural conditions in which all action occurs. Drawing on an emergent cultural criminology that locates explanations of crime in reference to both late-modernity and expressive action, a model of rule-breaking has been developed that attempts to unite the structural conditions that lead to the emotionalisation of public life with the sensorial appeals of risk-taking. Viewed from this perspective, criminality can be understood as a reaction to the uncertain and insecure conditions of late-modernity that lead to an increasing emphasis on emotional openness and intimate moments as the basis for establishing social bonds. Criminality can thus be conceived as part of the late-modern condition in which the construction and reconstruction of self-identity becomes central to the conditions of existence.

It is in this sense that intimacy is embraced. Criminality can be viewed as expressive. It can be seen as part of a wider late-modern quest for self-actualisation and authenticity. Similarly, there is some evidence that this intimacy is finding its way into the penal process. Yet these emotions are managed, and co-opted to instrumental goals of shaming and forgiveness. This curtailment of emotions has been criticised on two levels. Firstly, its limited capacity to afford victims, and society more widely, the same self-actualising and authenticating emotional experiences associated with rule-breaking. And secondly, its inability to offer a meaningful outlet for emotions that could both aid the recovery of individuals and provide cathartic opportunities for society's more widely held fears and anxieties about crime.

The logical consequences of this critique are twofold. The first is that to preserve the principles on which punishment and the penal process rest, emotionalism should be removed from penal decision making. This is appealing on a number of levels, not least because it protects some well-established legal principles that provide procedural safeguards against the tyranny of the state. The second is that punishment and the penal process should embrace emotionalism, accepting that it serves important individual and cultural therapeutic needs. This then entails finding a balance between the formal and expressive aspects of criminal justice. Yet, thinking about justice in this way invites a perspective that places rational and procedural concerns against irrational, emotional and expressive concerns. As both Katz (1999) and Karstedt (2002) have contended, emotions are in fact rational responses that both help to interpret and highlight social circumstances. Yar (2009) develops this point further, arguing that 'criminologists have misunderstood the nature of emotions . . . they can in fact be seen as reasonable (and hence rational) subjective response to objective experiences' (p. 2). He concludes that cultural criminology's critique of positivist, rational choice and administrative criminology has reinforced an established criminological status quo that sets rationality in opposition to emotionality.

If, as Yar (2009) contends, emotions are rational, then this suggests that they can play a meaningful and constructive part in the penal process. One of the greatest concerns must be that the fear and anger of a punitive public would lead to a mob-rule mentality that produces excessive and illiberal punishments. Yet, whilst this is a very real fear it is by no means a foregone conclusion. For example, research by Roberts and Hough (2005) has shown that if people know the context in which penal decisions are made they often become less harsh in their opinions about sentencing. Perhaps allowing people a bigger say in how decisions are made can provide greater insight and expressive opportunity. Then again, perhaps the space to merely express whatever one is feeling is enough (Tyler 1988, Wemmers 2002). Christie's (1977) famous essay on conflicts as property outlines the case for returning the ownership and responsibility for crime to individuals. This argument has been appropriated by the restorative justice movement but maybe the answer lies in a recalibration of restorative processes that allows for a more open-ended dialogue. Clearly, there is need for significant further investigation and contemplation of these issues but the entrance of emotionality into the penal process has opened the door to such questions. Whilst this may be fraught with dangers, it is increasingly apparent that the emphasis on particular emotions is unlikely to appease the punitive appetites of society; appetites that have for too long been suppressed and which, arguably, need to be indulged if they are to be satiated. If emotionalism is to achieve any meaningful outcome the rough must be taken with the smooth. Vengeance and forgiveness. Anger and compassion. Love and hatred.

This chapter began with a quotation from the opening pages of Huxley's *Brave New World* that expressed the sterile aspirations of a society built on the back of stable community. This seemed to rather neatly introduce the dangers inherent in an overweening moral consensus. This same text also engages in a debate between the Mustapha Mond, the World-Controller and John, a Savage. In this debate they discuss the merits of life in the World State and life in the Reservation; the comfort and security of one versus the visceral appeal of the other. The dilemma presented in this conversation is between competing and seemingly irreconcilable desires for both security and freedom. It is this tension that exists at the heart of how we perceive and respond to crime. How much of one or the other are we prepared to sacrifice and what will this sacrifice mean for the quality of our lives? I can therefore think of no better way of ending this chapter than with this thought-provoking passage from *Brave New World*:

'Violent Passion Surrogate. Regularly once a month. We flood the whole system with adrenin. It's the complete physiological equivalent of fear and rage. All the tonic effects of murdering Desdemona and being murdered by Othello, without any of the inconveniences.'

'But I like the inconveniences.'

'We don't,' said the Controller. 'We prefer to do things comfortably.'

'But I don't want comfort. I want God. I want poetry, I want real danger, I want freedom, I want goodness. I want sin.'

'In fact,' said Mustapha Mond, 'you're claiming the right to be unhappy.'

'All right, then,' said the Savage defiantly, 'I'm claiming the right to be unhappy.'

'Not to mention the right to grow old and ugly and impotent; the right to have syphilis and cancer; the right to have too little to eat; the right to be lousy; the right to live in constant apprehension of what may happen tomorrow; the right to catch typhoid; the right to be tortured by unspeakable pains of every kind.'

There was a long silence.

'I claim them all,' said the Savage at last.

Mustapha Mond shrugged his shoulders. 'You're welcome,' he said.

(Huxley 1932: 218–19)

Notes

1 Also, in a similar vein, Jacobs (1962) *The Death and Life of Great American Cities*, London: Cape.
2 From radical and Marxist perspectives in particular. See Quinney (1969, 1973, 1977), Taylor et al. (1973), Chambliss and Mankoff (1976), Hall et al. (1978) for examples of such perspectives and their comments on both criminal motivation and the political economy in which the criminal code is generated.
3 Citing examples of this work seems rather fruitless, but good overviews of much of this research can be found in Vold et al. (2002), Downes and Rock (2007), Maguire et al. (2012) and many others.
4 For Marx, this constraint exists in relation to labour. In the capitalist system man's alienation from his labour is both constraining and dehumanising, whilst in non-capitalist, or communist, society labour is constraining but also spontaneous and creative. For Mead, spontaneous and creative behaviour occurs in the internal dialectical relationship between the 'I' (which is the individual act in response to an interpreted circumstance) and the 'me' (which is the constrained self, or 'voice of society').
5 Which he refers to as post-industrial in 1990, but later shifts to late-modern (Lyng et al. 2009).
6 Except insofar as it breaches the criminal code.
7 In the form of Sara Payne in England and Wales. Sara Payne is the mother of the kidnapped and murdered child Sarah Payne, who became the basis of tabloid claims for a British version of the US 'Megan's Law' whereby a public sex offender register is kept.
8 Which connects with the notion of Foucauldian governmentality and the shaping of decisions from a distance discussed in Chapter 3.

References

Aslama, M. and Pantti, M. (2008) Talking Alone: Reality TV, Emotions and Authenticity, in M. Greco and P. Stenner (eds), *Emotions: A Social Science Reader*, London: Routledge.
Baudrillard, J. (1970 [1998]) *The Consumer Society: Myths and Structures*, London: Sage.
Baudrillard, J. (1983) *Simulation*, New York: Semiotext(e).
Baudrillard, J. (1994) *Simulcra and Simulation*, Ann Arbor, MI: University of Michigan Press.
Bauman, Z. (2005a) *Work, Consumerism and the New Poor*, Maidenhead: Open University Press.
Bauman, Z. (2006) *Liquid Fear*, Cambridge: Polity Press.
Bauman, Z. (2007) *Consuming Life*, Cambridge: Polity Press.
Bauman, Z. and May, T. (2001) *Thinking Sociologically*, Oxford: Blackwell Publishers.
Bennett, C. (2007) Satisfying the Needs and Interests of Victims, in G. Johnstone and D.W. Van Ness (eds) *Handbook of Restorative Justice*, Cullompton: Willan.
Blakely, E.J. and Snyder, M.G. (1997) *'Fortress America': Gated Communities in the United States*, Washington, DC: Brookings Institute Press.
Bottoms, A. (1995) The Philosophy and Politics of Sentencing, in C.M.V. Clarkson and R. Morgan (eds) *The Politics of Sentencing Reform*, Oxford: Clarendon Press.
Burgess, A. (1962 [2000]) *A Clockwork Orange*, Harmondsworth: Penguin Books.
Caldeira, T.P.R. (2000) *City of Walls: Crime, Segregation and Citizenship in São Paulo*, London: University of California Press.
Castells, M. (1991) *The Informational City*, Oxford: Blackwell.

Chambliss, W.J. and Mankoff, M. (1976) *Whose Law? What Order?* London: John Wiley and Sons.

Christie, N. (1977) Conflicts as Property, *British Journal of Criminology*, 17 (1): 1–15.

Crawford, A. (1997) *The Local Governance of Crime: Appeals to Community and Partnership*, Oxford: Clarendon Press.

Crewe, D. (2009) Will to Self-consummation, and Will to Crime: A Study in Criminal Motivation, in R. Lippens and D. Crewe (eds) *Existentialist Criminology*, London: Routledge Cavendish.

Daly, K. (2003) Mind the Gap: Restorative Justice in Theory and Practice, in A. von Hirsch, J. Roberts, A.E. Bottoms, K. Roach and M. Schiff (eds) *Restorative Justice and Penal Justice: Competing or Reconcilable Paradigms?*, Oxford: Hart.

Davis, M. (1990) *City of Quartz: Excavating the Future in Los Angeles*, London: Vintage.

Downes, D. and Rock, P. (2007) *Understanding Deviance: A Guide to the Sociology of Crime and Rule-breaking* (5th edn), Oxford: Oxford University Press.

Ericson, R.V. (2007) *Crime in an Insecure World*, Cambridge: Polity Press.

Etzioni, A. (1995) *The Spirit of Community: Rights, Responsibilities and the Communitarian Agenda*, Hammersmith: Fontana Press.

Eysenck, H. (1977) *Crime and Personality* (3rd edn), London: Routledge.

Feeley, M. and Simon, J. (1992) The New Penology: Notes on the Emerging Strategy of Corrections and Its Implications, *Criminology*, 30 (4): 452–74.

Ferrell, J. (1996) *Crimes of Style*, Boston: Northeastern University Press.

Ferrell, J. (2005) The Only Possible Adventure: Edgework and Anarchy, in S. Lyng (ed.) *Edgework*, New York: Routledge.

Ferrell, J., Hayward, K. and Young, J. (2008) *Cultural Criminology*, London: Sage.

Freiberg, A. (2001) Affective versus Effective Justice: Instrumentalism and Emotionalism in Criminal Justice, *Punishment and Society*, 3 (2): 265–78.

Furedi, F. (2004) *Therapy Culture: Cultivating Vulnerability in an Uncertain Age*, London: Routledge.

Furedi, F. (2006) *The Culture of Fear Revisited*, London: Continuum.

Garland, D. (1996) The Limits of the Sovereign State, *British Journal of Criminology*, 36 (4): 445–71.

Garland, D. (2000) The Culture of High Crime Societies: Some Preconditions of Recent 'Law and Order' Policies, *British Journal of Criminology*, 40 (3): 347–75.

Garland, D. (2001) *The Culture of Control: Crime and Social Order in Contemporary Society*, Oxford: Oxford University Press.

Garland, D. and Young, P. (1983) Towards a Social Analysis of Penality, in D. Garland and P. Young (eds) *The Power to Punish: Contemporary Penality and Social Analysis*, London: Heinemann Educational Books.

Gatrell, V.A.C. (1994) *The Hanging Tree: Execution and the English People 1770–1868*, Oxford: Oxford University Press.

Giddens, A. (1990) *The Consequences of Modernity*, Cambridge: Polity Press.

Giddens, A. (1991) *Modernity and Self Identity: Self and Society in the Late Modern Age*, Cambridge: Polity Press.

Green, S. (2008) Crime, Victimisation and Vulnerability, in S. Walklate (ed.) *Handbook of Victims and Victimology*, Collumpton: Willan.

Green, S. (2011) Vengeance and Furies: Existential Dilemmas in Penal Decision-making, in J. Hardie-Bick and R. Lippens (eds) *Crime, Governance and Existential Predicaments*, Basingstoke: Palgrave Macmillan.

Greer, C. (2004) Crime, Media and Community: Grief and Virtual Engagement in Late

Modernity, in J. Ferrell, K. Hayward, W. Morrison and M. Presdee (eds) *Cultural Criminology Unleased*, London: Glasshouse Press.

Hall, S., Winlow, S. and Ancrum, C. (2008) *Criminal Identities and Consumer Culture: Crime, Exclusion and the New Culture of Narcissism*, Cullompton: Willan.

Hall, S., Critcher, C., Jefferson, T., Clarke, J. and Roberts, B. (1978) *Policing the Crisis: Mugging, the State and Law and Order*, London: Macmillan.

Hayward, K.J. (2004) *City Limits: Crime, Consumer Culture and the Urban Experience*, London: Glasshouse.

Hayward, K.J. and Young, J. (2004) Cultural Criminology: Some Notes on the Script, *Theoretical Criminology*, 8 (3): 259–73.

Hope, T. and Sparks, R. (eds) (2000) *Crime, Risk and Insecurity*, London: Routledge.

Huxley, A. (1932 [1994]) *Brave New World*, Glasgow: Flamingo.

Jacobs, J. (1962) *The Death and Life of Great American Cities*, London: Cape.

Karstedt, S. (2002) Emotions and Criminal Justice, *Theoretical Criminology*, 6 (3): 299–317.

Karstedt, S. and Farrall, S. (2006) The Moral Economy of Everyday Crime: Markets, Consumers and Citizens, *British Journal of Criminology*, 46 (6): 971–5.

Katz, J. (1988) *Seductions of Crime: Moral and Sensual Attractions in Doing Evil*, New York: Basic Books.

Katz, J. (1999) *How Emotions Work*, London: University of Chicago Press.

Kohlberg, L. (1964) Development of Moral Character and Moral Ideology, in M. Hoffman and L. Hoffman (eds) *Review of Child Development Research*, 1: 383–431, New York: Russell Sage Foundation.

Kohlberg, L. (1978) Revisions in the Theory and Practice of Mental Development, in W. Damon (ed.), *New Directions in Child Development and Moral Development*, San Francisco, CA: Jossey-Bass.

Lasch, C. (1979) *The Culture of Narcissism: American Life in an Age of Diminishing Expectations*, New York: W. W. Norton & Company Inc.

Laster, K and O'Malley, P. (1996) Sensitive New-Age Laws: The Reassertion of Emotionality in Law, *International Journal of the Sociology of Law*, 24 (1): 21–40.

Loader, I. and de Haan (2002) On Emotions of Crime, Punishment and Social Control, *Theoretical Criminology*, 6 (3): 243–53.

Lyng, S. (1990) Edgework: A Social Psychological Analysis of Voluntary Risk Taking, *The American Journal of Sociology*, 95 (4): 851–86.

Lyng, S. (2004) Crime, Edgework and Corporeal Transaction, *Theoretical Criminology*, 8 (3): 359–75.

Lyng, S. (ed.) (2005) *Edgework*, New York: Routledge.

Lyng, S., Matthews, R. and Millar, W.J. (2009) Existentialism, Edgework, and the Contingent Body: Exploring the Criminological Implications of Ultimate Fighting, in R. Lippens and D. Crewe (eds) *Existentialist Criminology*, London: Routledge Cavendish.

Maffesoli, M. (1996) *The Time of the Tribes: The Decline of Individualism in Mass Society*, London: Sage.

Maguire, M., Morgan, R. and Reiner, R. (eds) (2012) *The Oxford Handbook of Criminology* (5th edn), Oxford: Oxford University Press.

Matza, D. (1964) *Delinquency and Drift*, London: John Wiley.

McGowen, R. (2000) Revisiting the Hanging Tree, *British Journal of Criminology*, 40 (1): 1–13.

Moore, A. and Lloyd, D. (1990) *V for Vendetta*, New York: Vertigo.

Morgan, C. and Averill, J.R. (2008) True Feelings, the Self, and Authenticity: A Psychosocial Perspective, in M. Greco and P. Stenner (eds), *Emotions: A Social Science Reader*, London: Routledge.

O'Malley, P. (2004) *Risk, Uncertainty and Government*, London: Glasshouse.

Orwell, G. (1949 / 2000) *Nineteen Eighty-Four*, London: Penguin Classics.

Quinney, R. (ed.) (1969) *Crime and Justice in Society*, Boston: Little Brown and Company.

Quinney, R. (1973) *Critique of Legal Order: Crime Control in Capitalist Society*, Boston, MA: Little Brown and Company.

Quinney, R. (1977) *Class, State and Crim* e, London: Longman.

Roberts, J.V. and Hough, M. (2005) *Understanding Public Attitudes to Criminal Justice*, Berkshire: Open University Press.

Selznick, P. (1994) *The Moral Commonwealth: Social Theory and the Promise of Community*, London: University of California Press.

Sennett, R. (1974) *The Fall of Public Man*, London: Penguin.

Shaw, C. and McKay, H. (1942) *Juvenile Delinquency and Urban Areas*, Chicago: University of Chicago Press.

Taylor, I., Walton, P. and Young, J. (1973) *The New Criminology: For a Social Theory of deviance*, London: Routledge.

Tonry, M. (2004) *Punishment and Politics: Evidence and Emulation in the Making of English Crime Control Policy*, Cullompton: Willan.

Tyler, T.R. (1988) What Is Procedural Justice? Criteria Used by Citizens to Assess the Fairness of Legal Procedures, *Law and Society Review*, 22 (1): 32–51.

Vold, G.B., Bernard, T.J. and Snipes, J.B. (2002) *Theoretical Criminology* (5th edn) New York: Oxford University Press.

Walklate, S. (1998) Crime and Community: Fear or Trust? *British Journal of Sociology*, 49 (4): 550–69.

Walklate, S. (2000) Trust and the Problem of Community in the Inner-city, in T. Hope and R. Sparks (eds) *Crime, Risk and Insecurity*, London: Routledge.

Wemmers, J. (2002) Restorative Justice: The Choice between Bilateral Decision-making Power and Third Party Intervention, in B. Williams (ed.) *Reparation and Victim-Focused Social Work*, London: Jessica Kingsley Publishers.

Yar, M. (2009) Neither Scylla nor Charybdis: Transcending the Criminological Dualism between Rationality and the Emotions, *Internet Journal of Criminology* (www.internet-journalofcriminology.com/ijcarticles.html).

Yar, M. and Penna, S. (2004) Between Positivism and Post-modernity: Critical Reflections on Jock Young's The Exclusive Society, *British Journal of Criminology*, 44 (4): 533–49.

Young, J. (1999) *The Exclusive Society*, London: Sage.

Young, J. (2001) 'Identity, Community and Social Exclusion', in R. Matthews and J. Pitts (eds) *Crime, Disorder and Community Safety*, London: Routledge

Young, J. (2007) *The Vertigo of Late-modernity*, London: Sage.

Conclusion

Community is obviously not a bad thing *per se*. The purpose of this book has not been to criticise or complain about the 'traditional' community or those settings where it still exists. But there is a world of difference between the village community that continues to offer support and comfort to its members and a politically driven, morally prescribed and crime controlling community that is thrust upon those who neither choose nor acknowledge the types of life-style or values on offer.

The village may well retain some sense of the traditional community. People are more likely to have grown up and remained in the same geographical area and are therefore much more likely to share similar characteristics than their urban counterparts. Yet village life, despite all of it is comforts and support, is not for everyone. Some villagers leave for the big city and sometimes those 'comers-in' that move from the city to the village do not always find welcome from the villagers. People who look different, live differently, believe different things or simply don't come from the area can easily be viewed with suspicion or even be shunned. In other words, the traditional community is, by its very nature, incapable of accommodating the variety and difference that is both characterised and prized by the inhabitants of late-modern society.

It is this tension between the traditional and the late-modern which seems lost on both politicians and communitarians. The traditional community cannot and does not offer the variety or freedom that an ever-changing and increasingly diverse late-modern culture demands. New forms of non-traditional community have emerged from the social and cultural conditions of late-modernity, but these appear to have been largely ignored by both the communitarians and the politicians.

Failure to acknowledge changes in the cultural conditions and social relations is a failure to acknowledge the conditions in which criminal acts are given meaning and how society responds to them. This leads to a type of sociological shorthand that gives rise to insidious perspectives about how to reduce crime or improve society more generally. As a result, an impoverished understanding of community and crime has prospered in recent years.

This book has sought to provide an original critique of the communitarian (Etzioni 1995) values that have informed contemporary political values. The last three chapters therefore concentrate on a diverse range of published opinion and research that explores this relationship. The aim of this is to demonstrate the futility of the communitarian logic for crime control strategies. Unlike a range of other social commentaries (e.g. Hughes 1996, Levitas 1998, Little 2002) that have taken issue with Etzioni's (1995) moral authoritarian politics, this book has attempted to interrogate his ideas in relation to their relevance and applicability to contemporary social and cultural conditions.

Chapters 4 and 5 began this task by considering the range of perspectives on the nature and character of community and how well these perspectives fit within the communitarian conception of community. The range of potential contradictions within communitarian thinking about community begins to surface in these chapters. In particular, recent sociological research into how community is experienced and how social bonds have evolved in line with both technological developments and underlying cultural conditions provides the initial clue that communitarianism has misunderstood the dynamics of social relations in contemporary society. Much of the more recent sociological discussion of community draws heavily on ideas of either late-modernity or post-modernity, and Chapter 6 sought to develop this theme by considering the ideas of Giddens (1991), Beck (1992) and Bauman (2000), in an effort to distil the key ingredients of the late-modernity book.

The purpose of this analysis was to measure the communitarian explanation of social problems and its proposed solution to them against the prevailing sociological consensus about how and why these conditions have emerged. What becomes apparent from this analysis is that the communitarian explanation only makes sense at the most superficial of levels. Whilst the conditions of late-modernity may well resonate with the communitarian claim that both community and morality have declined, what is equally apparent is that this cannot be simply explained in terms of a warped political imbalance between rights and responsibilities. Instead, the late-modernity literature points to a more fundamental explanation for these changes that has its roots in social, economic and cultural change. These changes are a consequence of technological advancement, new patterns of employment and consumption, globalisation and life-style choices.

The implications of this for Etzioni's (1995) communitarianism are profound. The communitarian agenda of rebuilding strong communities requires far more than a common assertion of shared values and responsibilities, but the wholesale undoing of an infinitely complex array of social, technological and economic changes that have shaped the nature of contemporary cultural conditions and social relations. When measured against this, the communitarian vision begins to appear a combination of the fanciful and the unworkable. This is the grounds on which this book argues that the communitarian agenda is futile.

Chapter 7 returned to the crime control arena and attempted to map out the implications of this argument for explanations of criminality, and suggested strategies for dealing with it. The argument progressed is that because of the sociological misconceptions inherent in communitarianism there are potential dangers in trying to implement its vision. Chief amongst these is the danger that communitarianism will create greater social divisions and higher levels of fear. Alongside this there is a very real danger that trying to reimpose a moral or social conformity will serve only to alienate and marginalise an increasing number of social groups who cannot or will not convert to a new moral order. This further suggests that, instead of reducing crime and the fear of crime, communitarianism will only aggravate these problems still further. The vicious cycle of communitarianism thus emerges from yet another contradiction within the communitarian schema, namely its failure to adequately account for the cultural conditions in which crime and the fear of crime occur. Thus the futility of the communitarian vision and the dangers inherent within its flawed understanding of both social bonds and crime are illustrated.

This leads into a wider discussion of the underpinning political perspective that crime can be understood in terms of either community decline or growing immorality. These positions are discussed and critiqued and an alternative explanation based around the cultural anxieties induced by late-modernity is proffered. Flowing from this analysis is an attempt to present a culturally nuanced explanation of criminality that looks at rule-breaking behaviour as a strategy for responding to the conditions and anxieties of late-modernity. Drawing for inspiration on Giddens' (1991) work on identity and Lyng's (1990) discussion of edgework, the two are brought together to consider the relationship between structure and agency (or, put differently, between determinism and voluntarism) in terms on how rule-breaking can be existentially rewarding. This then leads into a final discussion of the implications of this perspective for thinking about the purpose and logic of the penal system. This discussion concludes that if the penal system is to genuinely offer people the opportunity to honestly express themselves, and through this demonstrate the legitimacy and authenticity of the system and allow people to overcome their anxieties and fears, then it must give full vent to the range of emotions people experience as a consequence of victimisation: their own and that of others.

This book critiques communitarianism on the grounds that it is sociologically flawed. As a result of this flaw it carries with it certain dangers when applied as a strategy of crime control. The focus of the critique therefore operates at three quite distinct levels. The first is the internal validity of the communitarian argument. The second is its sociological basis and the third is the danger of applying this flawed perspective in the crime control arena. This combination offers a unique analysis of the communitarian school of thought. Unlike many other critiques of communitarianism which have often taken issue with the normative and ideological elements of Etzioni's (1995) work, this critique has attempted to avoid disagreements over values and to aim instead at a different level of analysis. Emerging from this analysis is an original synthesis of the ideas of Giddens (1991) and Lyng (1990) which is then used to push at the edges of cultural criminology to consider the impact of this perspective on the legitimacy and function of the penal system itself.

Of course it is the case that the ideas and theories used to develop this argument also have their weaknesses. Most of these limitations have been discussed within the relevant chapters but there are two overarching issues that are perhaps worthy of some concluding comments. The first is the general criticism that has been levelled against both late-modern and postmodern perspectives for over-stating their case. Both late-modern and postmodern perspectives are unfinished projects and it is surely the case that many aspects of traditional society persist. It is not, nor ever has been, the contention of this book that late-modern perspectives pervade all parts of the social world or social life. As already stated at the beginning of this conclusion, many forms of traditional community life continue unabated. Yet these types of community are not where the crime problem (as perceived politically) exists. Nor are they the focus of Etzioni's (1995) brand of communitarianism. In fact it would be fair to say that these types of community more closely reflect exactly what Etzioni (1995) and New Labour imagine must be rebuilt.

My argument is not with these communities, nor is it in any way a dispute over their existence and the existence of other similar traditional forms of social life. My argument is with the communitarian and political belief that where these traditional forms of social life appear to be in decline, this is because of rampant neo-liberalism rather than a myriad of social, economic and technological changes that bring with them new cultural conditions. It may be that neo-liberalism is part of this change, but it is not the entirety of it, nor does it follow that the end of tradition means the end of morality. Rather, it is the beginning of new values and social bonds that recalibrate the basis on which we generate our sense of who we are and what we are part of. Put differently, because the focus of this book is fixed, by communitarianism, on the decline of community and morality, the analysis inevitably draws on counter-explanations for these conditions. The development of the phrase late-modernity (or similar phrases) is in fact an explicit acknowledgement that we have yet to arrive at a fully postmodern era. Late-modernity is hence by its very nature transitionary, and people living within it will be influenced to a greater or lesser extent by its tensions. Yet, even if there are communities or individuals that have managed to preserve traditional ways of life, they are not immune to the 24/7 news cycle that pumps images of disaster and warfare into living rooms; the marketing and advertising that feeds and fuels the consumer society; or the dawn of the age of internet and social networking, with their associated new forms of interaction and expression. Even within the high crime urban environment, where notions of the neighbourhood or the ghetto resonate very strongly, this by no means immunises its residents from the contours of late-modernity. As Young (1999) argues in his discussion of hyper-masculinity in the Philadelphia ghetto, the young, black, socially and economically disadvantaged male is not less socialised but oversocialised into the consumer culture. Similarly, the discussion of Caldeira's (2000) São Paolo ethnography in Chapter 7 further illustrates this very point. Even in societies where it is much less easy to see the influence of late-modernity, the global spread of capitalism, advertising and information asserts its presence.

Stephen Lyng's (1990) edgework has also been criticised for its implicit focus on white male risk-taking behaviour (Miller 1991, Halsey and Young 2006). As Ferrell et al. (2008) argue, these criticisms are clearly important, but not insofar as they repudiate Lyng's (1990) concept, but in how they instead advance and deepen its use. The psycho-social model of rule-breaking offered in Chapter 7 is a combination of Giddens' (1991) notion of the pure relationship with Lyng's (1990) edgework. It is aimed at stepping back from traditional criminological explanations of offending that are usually located in either environment or social reaction to develop a perspective that fits within the wider discussion of the cultural conditions of late-modernity. They are both perspectives that explicitly fit within this framework and therefore both at risk of over-stating the case. Yet the purpose of developing this model was not to replace existing perspectives, but to reach beyond theories of criminality to the one thing that all criminal behaviour has in common, which is rule-breaking. It therefore neither replaces the existing sociological explanations of criminality nor puts itself above them. The model is designed to work at a different level: one which explores the existential and emotional appeals of rule-breaking, rather than the conditions that lead a particular individual or social group to commit particular types of crime in particular contexts. This in turn is intended to provide an explanation that sits within, rather than outside of, the conditions of late-modernity. Whilst it is certainly the case that there are problems and inconsistencies within discourses about late-modernity, the purpose of Chapter 6 was to both illustrate some of these differences and distil the core themes of late-modernity around which a broad sociological consensus exists. The psycho-social model of rule-breaking developed in the final chapter strives to build an explanation of transgressive behaviour that emerges out of this consensus, and which can then be usefully employed to think about the relationship between structural conditions and existential dilemmas in late-modernity.

The overarching aim of attempting this type of explanation is to try to move the debate about the causes of crime beyond community and morality. Because the late-modern critique levelled against communitarianism problematises both the concept of community and its relevance to understanding the causes of crime, it can also be equally levelled against other ideological or normative perspectives about community; or criminological perspectives that locate the causes of crime at the community level. Chapter 7 acknowledges this and seeks to move beyond community to consider a perspective that is at once more in tune with the conditions of late-modernity and less reliant on the concept of community.

Investigating how people experience rule-breaking is the next logical step on from this conceptual model. An important question for further research is to ask what the evidence is that people experience rule-breaking in this fashion. This can be applied either to particular types of criminality or to rule-breaking more generally. One of the unsaid assumptions of this model is that people choose to rule-break. This notion of choice is in itself contentious, as one obvious retort is that not everyone who rule-breaks does so deliberately or even knowingly. Clearly this type of rule-breaking is very different and beyond the model outlined here. Alternatively, another complaint might well be that our choices are constrained and directed by our environment and therefore choice can be understood only in terms of opportunities to rule-break. This is an entirely reasonable criticism of any model that was similarly based on the standard social science model of understanding behaviour, but it is also one that sits outside of the focus of the model presented here. The concern of this model is with the existential advantages of rule-breaking and it is thus unconcerned with the particulars of what rule is broken. As such, it neither contradicts nor replaces existing criminological theories of criminality. Yet, asking questions about a range of probable areas in which different types of people transgress the rules, what choices they faced and how it made them feel (both when they break the rules and when they don't) strikes me as a fascinating experiment that will, hopefully, help to develop and refine the psycho-social model of rule-breaking.

This book then considered the implications of this model for the logic and function of the penal process. If rule-breaking can be considered in existential terms – why not punishment? Drawing on the ideas of Garland (2000) and Karstedt (2002), the emotional content of social and political concerns about crime and of our penal system is mapped out. This is considered against a backdrop of social and cultural research into emotionalism in society. What becomes apparent is that people are becoming more overtly emotional in terms of how they respond and relate to both themselves and others. The penal system reflects this broad trend, and a greater range of expressive outlets have been introduced in recent years. Yet, following on from Karstedt's (2002) discussion of emotions and criminal justice, what also becomes apparent is that some emotions are afforded formal acknowledgement as both desirable and useful, whilst others are not. The final chapter of this book therefore concluded that this imbalance subordinates and inhibits the expression of certain feelings about crime. The consequence of which is problematic for the legitimacy and authenticity of the penal process, given that emotions are afforded such a high status in social interactions.

Whilst this is a sound logical position to take in terms of the arguments made within this book, it raises a number of ethical and practical questions about how a penal process that gives equal opportunity to express feelings of rage, retribution and disgust as well as shame, sorrow and forgiveness would look. The implications of letting the emotions loose in the penal system hark back to a time of brutal bodily punishments inflicted in front of a bloodthirsty and barbaric mob. It is a very real concern that giving full vent to emotions might lead to penal practices that are excessive and unfair. Yet it does not necessarily follow that punishment would necessarily take this path. The menacing spectre of the European 'bloody code' encapsulates only one particular strategy of punishment, and there are many others. Rather than conceive of emotions in justice as a retrograde and a potentially dangerous step, there are also potential advantages in affording society an opportunity to formally have its anger recognised, acknowledged and acted upon. Elsewhere I have argued that punishment serves functions beyond instrumental concerns with control and can provide educative, performative and expressive functions that recast how and why we become involved in penal decision making (Green 2011). As Christie (1977) argued, conflicts should be returned to individuals to resolve, though he never suggested that this resolution should always be conciliatory. In fact, despite the growth of restorative justice since the mid to late 1980s most common law countries do not appear to have become more tolerant and less punitive.

Perhaps one route to try to consider this tricky conundrum would be to look to those societies and points in history where punishment, justice and conflict resolution are driven more by emotional needs than by rational judgements. A personal rather than procedural justice that is premised on the feelings and needs of the wronged party does not by its very nature require either a more severe or a less humane response. The principles of honour, equivalence, accountability and atonement are all part of the drama surrounding conflict, and sometimes apology and forgiveness just doesn't cut the mustard. Exploring conceptions of punishment and justice alongside the sorts of cultures from where they emerged seems a sensible way forward when considering these themes. The work of Miller (2006) and Smith (2008) that provides a historical and cultural discussion of punishment begins to provide the basis on which this task might be conceived.

This book contributes to the discipline of criminology in three distinct ways. The first of these is to explore morality and political values in relation to debates about crime and crime control. I have stated that criminologists have given these themes less attention than they deserve, choosing instead to focus on the instrumental goals of justice, social control and penality, and have unconsciously reduced this moral dialogue about crime control to little more than sound-bite politics or self-justificatory rhetoric. This, I believe, is a mistake, as it is this moral dialogue between our leaders, our popular press and ourselves that shapes how crime is understood and responded to at both the political and practical levels. My contention is that this error explains the dissonance between criminological and public understandings of crime and punishment. Without a fuller, deeper and more considered critical engagement with these public debates the danger is that criminological research and ideas will struggle to connect with mainstream political and public concerns about crime and punishment.

Much of this book has tried to chart the prevailing political values and concerns that shape how crime is thought about and responded to. Rather than take issue with these values or subordinate them to ideological dogma or instrumental control strategies, this book goes further and seeks to examine how they provide a framework for understanding and responding to the crime problem. Thus, the argument outlined in this book is not simply that neo-conservative values inform political and public thought, but that they provide the basis for a paradigmatic shift that has led to a new explanation for the causes of crime that simultaneously legitimates and co-opts a range of community crime control strategies within it.

The second contribution is a critique of communitarian ideology and its ongoing political influence on governments on both sides of the Atlantic. This critique is not based on a normative or ideological disagreement but on its sociological shortcomings. This, I contend, is a more powerful and damning critique which exposes both the sociological nostalgia and naivety of communitarianism as well as the implausible and unacknowledged utopianism of its vision for community revival. As a consequence of this weakness, communitarianism provides a dangerous ideological base from which to progress crime control strategies. Rather than reducing crime or building communities, communitarianism will have the exact opposite consequence and create the conditions in which crime and the fear of crime will flourish.

The third contribution to criminology returns to a more personal point that I alluded to in the Preface to this book. Criminology often seems to be caught between two broad hegemonic traditions: administrative and critical. On the one hand, administrative criminology is focused on governmental questions about how to reduce crime or improve punishment, and on the other hand, critical criminology is focused on an oppressive state leading to a critique of its criminal justice and penal strategies. Both come with their own internal normative assumptions and both are reliant on state definitions, ideology and policy to fuel their discourses. Not wishing to get caught in this debate by arguing about the relative merits of each, it is sometimes difficult to see from which direction fresh perspectives on crime and punishment will emerge. Cultural criminology has begun to provide an alternative, weaving a new path with its interest in the media, transgression, consumerism and so forth. Yet cultural criminology has bought into these two criminological projects by at least partly defining itself in opposition to the administrative.

This book, whilst drawing on some of the ideas of cultural criminology, has endeavoured to step away from either of the two mainstream criminological positions and present a vision of both crime and the penal system which aims to offer something genuinely different for criminological thought. Thus, this book ends with a new psycho-social theory of rule-breaking and its associated implications for our way of 'doing' justice that I don't think relies on either of these criminological stances. The hope is that, in so doing, this book tentatively begins to offer an alternative perspective to those so firmly enshrined within current criminological debates.

References

Bauman, Z. (2000) *Liquid Modernity*, Cambridge: Polity Press.

Beck, U. (1992) *Risk Society: Towards a New Modernity*, London: Sage.

Caldeira, T.P.R. (2000) *City of Walls: Crime, Segregation and Citizenship in São Paulo*, London: University of California Press.

Christie, N. (1977) Conflicts as Property, *British Journal of Criminology*, 17 (1): 1–15.

Etzioni, A. (1995) *The Spirit of Community: Rights, Responsibilities and the Communitarian Agenda*, Hammersmith: Fontana Press.

Ferrell, J., Hayward, K. and Young, J. (2008) *Cultural Criminology*, London: Sage.

Garland, D. (2000) The Culture of High Crime Societies: Some Preconditions of Recent 'Law and Order' Policies, *British Journal of Criminology*, 40 (3): 347–75.

Giddens, A. (1991) *Modernity and Self Identity: Self and Society in the Late Modern Age*, Cambridge: Polity Press.

Green, S. (2011) Vengeance and Furies: Existential Dilemmas in Penal Decision-making, in J. Hardie-Bick and R. Lippens (eds) *Crime, Governance and Existential Predicaments*, Basingstoke: Palgrave Macmillan.

Halsey, M. and Young, A. (2006) 'Our Desires Are Ungovernable': Writing Grafitti in Urban Space, *Theoretical Criminology*, 10 (3): 275–306.

Hughes, G. (1996) Communitarianism and Law and Order, *Critical Social Policy* 16 (4): 17–42.

Karstedt, S. (2002) Emotions and Criminal Justice, *Theoretical Criminology*, 6 (3): 299–317.

Levitas, R. (1998) *The Inclusive Society? Social Exclusion and New Labour*, Basingstoke: Macmillan.

Little, A. (2002) Community and Radical Democracy, *Journal of Political Ideologies*, 7 (3): 369–82.

Lyng, S. (1990) Edgework: A Social Psychological Analysis of Voluntary Risk Taking, *The American Journal of Sociology*, 95 (4): 851–86.

Miller, E.M. (1991) Assessing the Risk of Inattention to Class, Race/Ethnicity and Gender: Comment on Lyng, *American Journal of Sociology*, 96: 1530–1534.

Miller, W.I. (2006) *Eye for an Eye*, Cambridge: Cambridge University Press.

Smith, P. (2008) *Punishment and Culture*, London: University of Chicago Press.

Young, J. (1999) *The Exclusive Society*, London: Sage.

Index

advanced liberalism 81–5
Advisory Council on the Penal System (1970) 49
Altschuler, D.M. 75
Anderson, B. 131–2, 134
anomie 14
anthropological theory 131–4
anti-social behaviour 60, 103, 111, 116
anti-social behaviour orders 145, 146
Ashworth, A. 53, 67
Aslama, M. 195
attendance centres 47
Audit Commission 59, 60
authenticity 194–201, 205
Averill, J.R. 195

Baker, N. 63, 144
Baldwin, J. 13
Baudrillard, J. 196
Bauman, Z. 36, 88–9, 93–4, 155, 156, 169–73, 174, 175, 186–7
Beck, U. 155, 159, 166–9, 173–4, 175–6
Bell, C. 127
Bennett, C. 205
Benyon, J. 31–2, 35
Bevir, M. 111
bifurcation strategy 42, 51
Big Society 3, 86, 104, 117–20
Blair, T. 29–30, 102, 103, 106, 110, 111, 112, 114; see also New Labour
Blanchot, M. 137
Blears, H. 115
Borstal 47, 50
Bottoms, A. 42, 51, 52, 56–7, 139, 141, 144
Bottoms, A.E. 13, 28
boundaries 133, 134, 140, 182, 186
Bourdieu, P. 100, 152
Boyson, R. 48
Braithwaite, J. 65–6, 75, 142–3, 145
Brake, M. 102
Brave New World 181–2, 209

Brixton Riots 18, 33
broken Britain 104, 105–6, 117, 119
'broken windows' thesis 13
Brown, G. 35, 103–4; see also New Labour
Brownlee, I. 54, 78
Buerger, M.E. 20
Burgess, A. 206
Burgess, E.W. 11
Burnside, J. 63, 144
Butler, R. 100
Butskellism 100–1

Caldeira, T.P.R. 184–6, 188–9
Calhoun, C. 135, 136
Cameron, D. 104, 105, 106, 107, 108, 119–20; see also Coalition government
Caney, S. 76, 91
capital punishment 43, 45, 206
care orders 50–1
Casey, L. 104
Casey Report (2008) 2, 35
Castells, M. 135, 186
Cavadino, M. 23, 47
Centre for Social Justice 105
Chicago Area Project (CAP) 16
Chicago School 3, 11, 12, 14, 16, 139
child regulations 59
Christie, N. 208–9
civil society 2, 67, 77, 83, 102
Clear, T.R. 66
Clegg, N. 106, 107, 108; see also Coalition government
Clinton, B. 36
Cloward, R.A. 14, 15
Coalition government 104–5, 117–20
Cochran, C.E. 93, 94
Cohen, A. 14, 15
Cohen, A.P. 86–7, 128, 131, 132–4, 140
Cohen, S. 69
combination orders 56
communion 127, 130, 132, 183

communitarianism 2, 4–6, 146;
    assumptions and tensions 86–9, 182–3;
    concepts 75–8; Etzioni's ideas 76,
    77–8, 86–7; and late-modernity 164,
    175–8; moral philosophy and moral
    authoritarianism 78, 89–94, 189–90;
    and New Labour 2, 29–30, 61, 76, 109–
    11, 114; vicious cycle 189–90
community 1–2, 9–10; as agent 16,
    17–22; as beneficiary 16, 25–8;
    and crime control 16–17; as crime
    control 147–8; as culture 137; decline
    of and rise of crime 2–4, 10–17, 35–6,
    109, 183, 190–4; and education 67;
    efficacy 66; empowerment 66–7;
    and freedom 88–9; government
    through 81–5; interdependency 65–6;
    as locus 16, 22–5; neighbourhood and
    crime control 138–47; and restorative
    justice 62–7; solidarity 45; utopian or
    dystopian? 94–5; *see also* community,
    definitions of; community, theories of
community courts 16
community, definitions of 5, 9, 36–7,
    127–8, 142
community governance of crime 30–5,
    32*t*, 33*t*, 78–9
community justice 75, 79, 141
community justice centres 17
community orders 23
community payback 23, 24
community policing 17–21, 28, 34
community prisons 16–17
community safety 4, 5–6, 25, 26, 27, 28,
    31–2, 34, 67
community sentences 23–5, 55, 56, 58
community service *see* community payback
community service orders 49, 53, 54
community, theories of 126–38;
    anthropological theory 131–4;
    boundaries 133, 134, 140, 182,
    186; collapse of stability 135–8;
    emotional community 137;
    imagined community 131–2;
    reflexive community 137;
    sociological theory 134, 135;
    symbolic community 132–4; virtual
    communities 135
compensation orders 49–50
concentric zone theory 11
Conservative Party *see* Coalition government;
    Major government; New Right
consumerism 171–3, 175, 186–7, 196, 200
corporal punishment 43, 45, 47
Crawford, A. 10, 12, 13, 14, 24, 25–6, 27,
    30–1, 32, 66, 69, 81, 85, 86–7, 111, 114,
    139, 140, 141, 143, 146

crime: attractions of 197–8, 199;
    causes of 2–4, 10–17; and decline of
    community 2–4, 10–17, 35–6, 109,
    183, 190–4; fear of crime 59, 85,
    140, 183–90; and morality 191–2;
    as offence against people 63; and
    segregation 183–90
Crime and Disorder Act (1998) 29, 34–5,
    37, 59–61, 111, 145
crime control: and community 16–17;
    community as crime control 147–8;
    and morality 190; neighbourhood and
    community 138–47; responsibility
    for 59–61
crime prevention 4, 25–8, 31–5, 33*t*, 60;
    juvenile offenders 59–61; situational
    crime prevention 26–7; social crime
    prevention 26–7
Criminal Justice Act (1925) 47
Criminal Justice Act (1948) 47
Criminal Justice Act (1967) 49
Criminal Justice Act (1972) 49–50
Criminal Justice Act (1982) 50–1
Criminal Justice Act (1988) 50, 51
Criminal Justice Act (1991) 55–6, 57
Criminal Justice Act (1993) 56
Criminal Justice Act (2003) 23
Criminal Justice and Public Order Act
    (1994) 57–8
criminal subcultures 15
criminality, theories of 3–4; authenticity
    and risk-taking 194–201; community
    and immorality 190–4
criminogenic situation 80
criminogenic values 12, 13
cultural criminology 147, 193–4
culture 137, 157–8
curfew orders 50, 53, 56
custodial sentences 47–8; diversions
    from 48–52, 55

Daly, K. 205
Davidson, R.N. 139
Davies, C. 144
Davis, M. 184–5, 187
day training centres 49
De Haan, W. 202
defensible space 13
Delanty, G. 131, 135
democratisation of social life and
    culture 159–60
demonstrators 57
deprivation and inequality 3
Detention Centres 47, 50, 51
deterrence 44, 47, 49
devolution 30, 35, 74, 79, 108, 115, 116–17
differential association 13, 15

Dignan, J. 23, 47
disadvantaged communities 14, 15
disembedding social relations 160–4, 165, 170, 200
diversity 12
Downes, D. 12–13
Driver, S. 59, 75, 81, 111, 112, 114–15, 116
dual cities 186
Duncan Smith, I. 105
Durkheim, E. 130, 146, 154
Dworkin, R. 75, 91
dystopia 172–3
Dzur, A.W. 66–7

early release scheme 55
economic conditions 156–7
edgework 198–200
education 15, 20, 67, 105, 107–8
Edwards, A. 31–2, 35
electronic tagging 53, 56
Elias, N. 100
emotional community 137
emotions 46; and authenticity 195–200, 205; and justice 202–9
Engels, F. 109, 129
environment 60–1
environmental criminology 10, 11–14, 139, 190–1
ethnic minorities 33
Etzioni, A. 2, 6, 24, 28–9, 61, 76, 77–8, 81, 86–9, 91, 109, 112–14, 116, 131, 135, 138, 164, 176–8
expert systems 161

family 3, 78, 87, 103, 105, 107–8, 109, 111
family group conferencing 60
family structure 157–8
Farrall, S. 102, 192
fear of crime 59, 85, 140, 183–90
Ferrell, J. et al. 194, 199
Field, F. 111
fines 47, 50, 55, 56
Foster, J. 139
Foucault, M. 21, 43, 44, 45, 46, 78, 81, 82–3, 85
Freiberg, A. 203
Friedman, M. 101
Fry, E. 45, 46
Furedi, F. 195

Gaitskell, H. 100
Garland, D. 74, 79–80, 83, 85, 153, 156–60, 183–4, 189, 201–2
Gatrell, V.A.C. 206
gender 87
Giddens, A. 2, 5, 29, 102, 110, 111, 115,

154, 155–6, 160–4, 165–6, 168, 169, 173–4, 194, 195, 196, 198, 200
Gill, O. 139
Gilling, D. 81, 147
Gladstone Report (1895) 47
Glasman, M. 118
governance 78, 79, 83–5; *see also* community governance of crime
governmentality 21, 78–9, 81, 82–5
Green Papers: *Policing Our Communities Together* (2008) 35, 104; *Punishment, Custody and the Community* (1988) 53–4, 58; *Strengthening Punishment in the Community* (1995) 58; *Supervision and Punishment in the Community: A Framework for Action* (1990) 54–5
Greer, C. 195
Grinc, R.M. 19–20

Hale, C. 102
Hay, C. 102
Hayward, K.J. 184, 185, 187, 193, 196–7, 200
Hillery, G.A. 127, 130
Hoggart, R. 130–1
Hope, T. 11, 14, 26–7, 139
Hough, M. 139, 208
Howard, J. 45, 46
Howard, M. 56, 57–8
Hoyle, C. et al. 142
Hudson, B.A. 51
Hughes, G. 32, 34, 69, 75, 76–7, 80–1, 87, 147
Huxley, A. 181–2, 209
hyperreality 196

identity 86–7, 174; authenticity 194–201, 205; and ontological insecurity 164–6, 194–7; quest for identity 170–1, 194–8; self and other 136–7; self-reflexivity 162–3, 165–6, 169; and social identity 165
ideology 109; communitarianism 75–8, 86–9; devolving justice 78–81; governing through communities 81–5; moral philosophy and moral authoritarianism 89–94
Ignatieff, M. 43, 44–5
imagined community 131–2
inclusion and exclusion 86–7, 112–14, 191
individualisation 167–9, 175–6
individualism 75–6, 78, 100, 101
industrialisation 2, 129–30
interdependency 65–6
internet 135–6
intimacy 163–4, 195, 200

James, A. 59, 61
Jenkins, R. 165
Johnston, L. 21, 80
Johnstone, G. 66
Jordan, B. 111, 118
justice: community justice 75, 79,
    141; devolving justice 78–81; and
    emotion 202–9; social justice 104–5;
    see also punishment; restorative justice
Juvenile Courts 55
juvenile offenders 15, 55, 56; crime
    prevention 59–61; parental responsibility
    for 111; punishment 47, 48, 50–1, 54;
    restorative justice 60, 64, 145

Karstedt, S. 192, 203, 204, 208
Katz, J. 194, 196, 197–8, 199–200, 208
Kelling, G. 13–14, 20, 139
Kennedy, J.F. 120
Kornhauser, R. 12
Kumar, K. 154
Kymlicka, W. 86

Labour Party 102, 105, 107; *see also* New
    Labour
Lacey, N. 21–2
Lasch, C. 171–2
Lash, S. 137, 155, 173–4
Laster, K. 203
late-modernity 153–6; characteristics
    of 174–5; and communitarianism 164,
    175–8; conditions of 156–60; the
    consumer society 171–3; disembedding
    social relations 160–4, 165, 170,
    200; divergence and convergence in
    discourses 173–4; dystopia 172–3;
    identity and ontological insecurity 164–
    6, 194–7; liquid modernity 169–72; the
    risk society and individualisation 166–
    9; urban geography 183–90
Lee, D. 127, 130
Levitas, R. 87–8, 111, 112–13
Liberal Democrats 104, 107; *see also*
    Coalition government
lifestyle theory 26
liquid modernity 169–72
Loader, I. 202
local governance of crime *see* community
    governance of crime
local government 31–2, 32*t*
London Riots 18, 33, 105–7
Los Angeles 184–5, 188
Lyng, S. 5, 194, 198–200

McGowen, R. 206
MacIntyre, A. 90–1, 92
McKay, H. 11, 12, 13, 139

Maffesoli, M. 137
Maguire, M. 118
Mair, G. 50
Major government 34, 52, 53, 56–9
*Manifesto for Community Safety and
    Crime Prevention* (1997) 60–1
Marshall, T.F. 63–4
Martell, L. 59, 75, 81, 111, 112, 114–15, 116
Martinson, R. 50
Marx, K. 109, 131, 154
mass media 158–9, 203
Matthews, R. 112, 113
Matza D. 12
May, T. 172
Mays, J.B. 13
mediation 62, 63–4
Merton, R.K. 14–15
Mika, H. 64–5
Miliband, E. 106, 107, 108
Miller, P. 81, 84, 85
Misztal, B.A. 162–3
Mobilisation for Youth (MFY) 16
modernism 153–4
modernity 153–6, 191
moral authoritarianism 24, 189–91; and
    moral philosophy 89–94
moral commonwealth 90, 94
moral communitarianism 90
moral conservatism 4, 29; *see also* New
    Labour
moral degeneration: Butskellism 100–1;
    Coalition government 104–5, 117–20;
    and communitarianism 176–7; and
    crime 191–2; New Labour 102–4, 109–
    17; New Right 100, 101–2; political
    consensus 105–9; and politics 99–100,
    120–1;
moral philosophy 89–94
moral relativism 160
morality 1, 2–3, 4, 78, 106–7, 190
Morgan, C. 195
Morgan, R. 118
Morgan Report (1991) 34
Morison Report (1962) 49
Morris, A. 132
Morris, T. 13, 139
Morton, G. 132
multi-agency partnerships 19, 27, 145

Nancy, J.-L. 137
National Association for the Care and
    Resettlement of Offenders (NACRO) 60
National Association of Probation Officers
    (NAPO) 47
neighbourhood, community and crime
    control 138–47
neighbourhood watch 17, 19, 21

Nelken, D. 9, 10, 16, 17, 20, 21, 22, 25, 28
Nellis, M. 29, 59, 111
neo-conservatism 68–9, 76
neo-liberalism 68, 84
networks of sociability 135
new capitalism 157
New Labour 68, 119; communitarianism 2, 29–30, 61, 76, 109–11, 114; Crime and Disorder Act 59–61; moral conservatism and the third way 29, 36, 102, 110, 114–17; rights and responsibilities 81, 89, 102–4, 109–14; social exclusion 112–14
New Right: causes of crime 4; crime control 3, 21; Criminal Justice Acts 50–2, 56; individualism 76, 78, 100, 101–2; origins of 48
New Statesman 30, 77
Newburn, T. 57
Newby, H. 127, 130
Newman, K. 18
Newman, O. 13, 139
Nozick, R. 75, 91

offenders in the community 22–5
Ohlin, L.E. 14, 15
Olson, S.M. 66–7
O'Malley, P. 84, 203
opportunity theory 15

Pahl, R. 138
Pantti, M. 195
parenting 78, 87, 111; *see also* family
parenting orders 145, 146
parole system 55
Payment by Results (PBR) 118, 119
penal policy *see* punishment
pillory 43, 44–5
Pitts, J. 51
Police and Crime Commissioners (PCCs) 104, 118–19
Police and Criminal Evidence Act (PACE; 1984) 34
Police Reform and Social Responsibility Act (2011) 118–19
policing 18, 35, 104; community policing 17–21, 28, 34
political values *see* moral degeneration
postmodernism 90, 153–4, 160
postmodernity 135, 136–7, 153–6
Pre-Sentence reports (PSRs) 55
preventative turn 80–1
prison 47, 48, 49, 56; community prisons 16–17; intermittent/weekend imprisonment 53
'prison works' 57–9
probation 23, 46, 47, 49, 50, 51, 54–5, 56, 58

Probation of Offenders Act (1907) 47
problem-oriented policing *see* community policing
public space 184–6
punishment 41–2, 67–9, 74–5; cultural and emotional framing of 201–7; diversions from custody 48–52; populist punitiveness 52–9; public spectacle 42–6, 205–6; the rehabilitative ideal 46–8; responsibility for crime control 59–61; restorative justice 62–7;
Putnam, R. 152

Raine, J. 59, 61
rational choice theory 26
raves 57
Rawls, J. 75, 91
Reagan, R. 4, 36, 76
referral orders 64
reflexive biographies 168–9
reflexive community 137
reflexive modernity 155, 166–7
reflexivity 155–6, 162–3, 173–4; self-reflexivity 162–3, 165–6, 169; structural reflexivity 159, 169
rehabilitation 46–8, 50, 60, 62
reintegration 60, 62, 63, 64–6
reintegrative shaming 65–6, 142–3, 145, 146
Reiss, A.J. 18
relational justice 143–4, 146
reparation 50
reparation orders 145, 146
Respect Task Force (2006) 2, 29
responsibilisation 79, 80
responsibility 2, 3, 29, 48, 68, 102, 106–7, 120; for crime control 59–61; *see also* rights and responsibilities
restorative cautioning 142, 145
restorative justice 6, 79, 143, 146, 204, 205; and community 62–7; and juvenile offenders 60, 64, 145
retreatist subcultures 15
Rheingold, H. 135
rights and responsibilities 2, 29, 61, 81, 101; New Labour view 81, 89, 102–4, 109–14
risk society 156, 159, 161–2, 166–9
risk-taking 198–201
Roberts, J.V. 208
Rock, P. 12–13
Rose, N. 81, 82, 83, 84, 85
Rosenbaum, D.P. 19
routine activity theory 26
rule-breaking 1, 193–4, 198, 200–1
rural–urban divide 130–1

Sampson, A. et al. 20
Sandel, M. 90–1

Sanders, A. 55
São Paulo 184–6, 188
Scarman Report (1981) 18, 33–4
Schluter, M. 144
security and insecurity 88–9, 164–6, 169, 174, 183–6, 194–7; *see also* community safety
segregation 183–90
self-reflexivity 162–3, 165–6, 169
Selznick, P. 90–1, 183
Senior, P. 55
Sennett, R. 157, 186, 188
sexual offences 54, 55
shame 204; *see also* reintegrative shaming
Shaw, C. 11, 12, 13, 139
Shaw, M. 11, 14, 26–7
Shearing, C. 21, 80
short, sharp shock 50
Siegel, L.J. 11–12
Simmel, G. 129
Simon, J. 69, 84–5, 147
situational crime prevention 26–7
Skogan, W.G. 19, 139
social capital 152–3
social crime prevention 26–7
social democracy 2
social disorganisation 11–13
social ecology 158
social exclusion *see* inclusion and exclusion
social identity 165
Social Impact Bonds (SIBs) 118, 119
Social Inquiry Reports (SIRs) 55
social justice 104–5
Social Justice Policy Group (2006) 105
society 101
sociological theory 134, 135
space 161
Spencer, L. 138
squatters 57
Stacey, M. 128
standardisation 168
Statement of National Objectcives and Priorities (SNOP; 1984) 51
Stenson, K. 82, 84
stigmatisation 65
Straw, J. 59, 103, 104, 111
structural reflexivity 159, 169
subcultural theory 11, 13, 14–15, 190–1, 200
suspended sentences 49
Sutherland, E. H. et al. 13, 15
symbolic community 132–4
symbolic tokens 161

Tackling Offenders: An Action Plan (1988) 54

Taylor, C. 90–1
Tebbit, N. 101–2
Thames Valley Police 142–3
Thatcher, M. 3, 50, 101; *see also* New Right
the third way 29, 102, 110, 114–17
time 160–1
Toby, J. 24
Tonnies, F. 129, 146
trust 161–2, 163, 195, 196

uncertainty 174
urban geography 183–90

victimisation 84–5, 140–1, 183–4, 188
victim–offender mediation 62, 64, 145
victims 25, 201; rights of the victim 50, 63; symbolic power of 202–3; *see also* restorative cautioning; restorative justice
violent offences 54, 55
violent subcultures 15
virtual communities 135

Wacquant, L. 152
Walgrave, L. 66
Walklate, S. 27, 140, 146
war on crime 84–5
Weber, M. 154, 155
welfare 48, 83, 105, 115
White Papers: *Crime, Justice and Protecting the Public* (1990) 54, 55; *Protecting the Public* (1996) 58
Whitman, J.Q. 152
Wiles, P. 28
Willmott, P. 128, 130–1, 143
Wilson, J.Q. 13–14, 20, 139
Wirth, L. 36, 127, 129–30
Wittgenstein, L. 128
Woolf Report (1991) 16–17
Worrall, A. 49, 55, 56
Worsley, P. 130

Yar, M. 208
Young, J. 3, 36, 42, 112, 113, 140–1, 186, 187, 191, 193, 196, 197
Young, M. 130–1
Young, P. 201–2
Youth Courts 55
youth custody orders 50
Youth Justice and Criminal Justice Act (1999) 64
youth offender institutions 51

Zedner, L. 21–2
Zehr, H. 63, 64–5
zone in transition 11, 12, 50